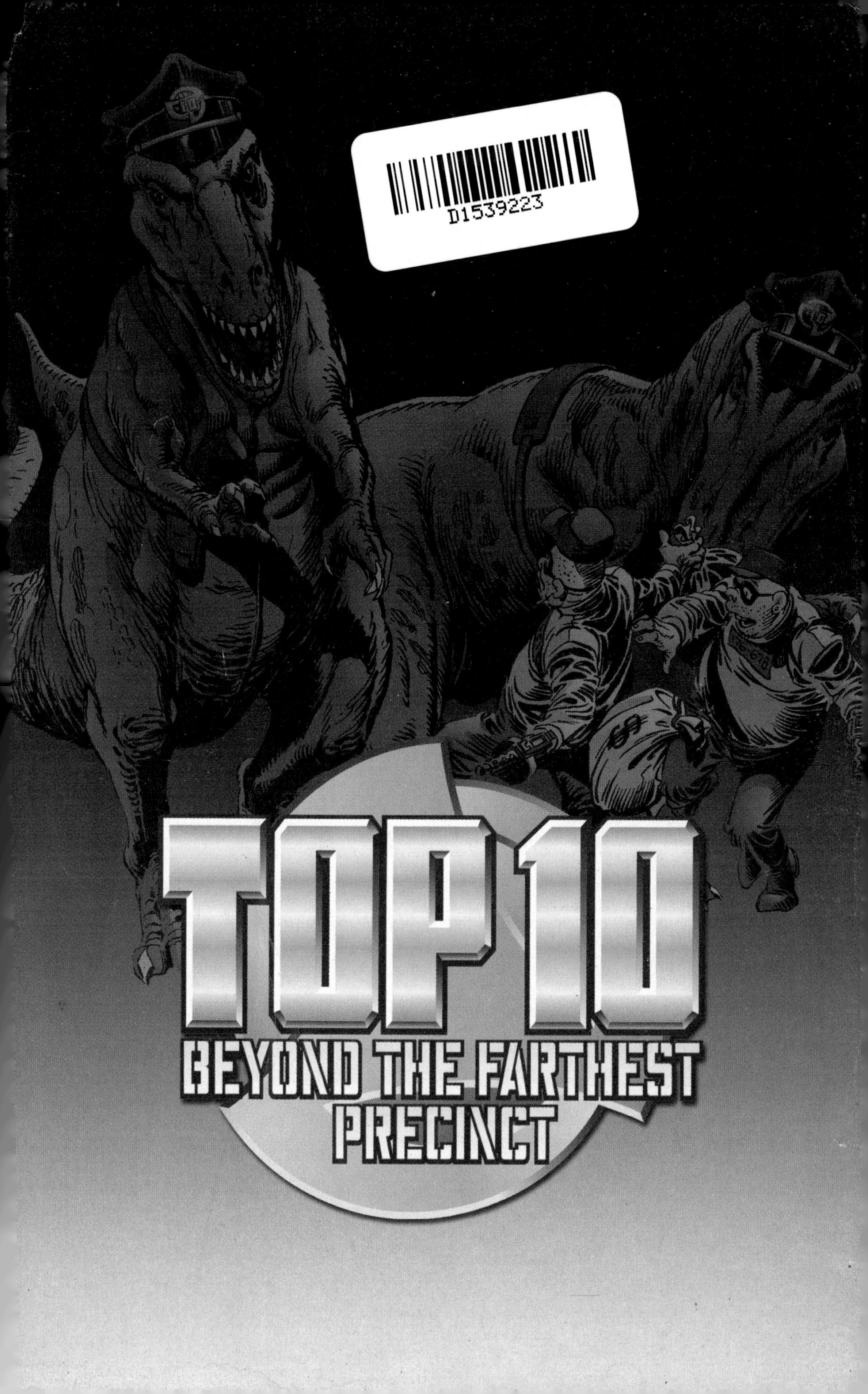
TOP 10
BEYOND THE FARTHEST PRECINCT

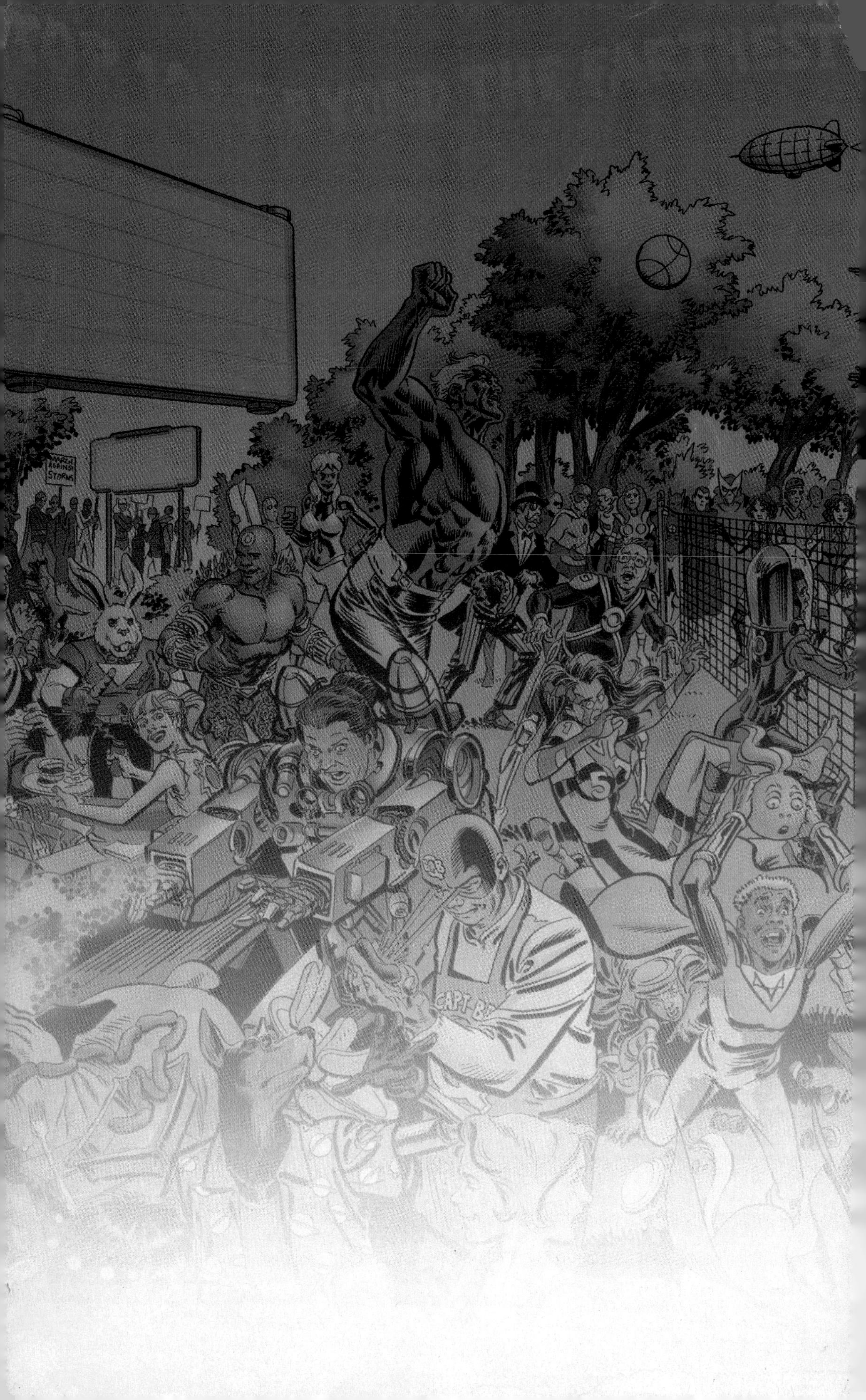
MARCH AGAINST STORMS

CHAPTER #1

Paul Di Filippo: Writer   Jerry Ordway: Artist

Wendy Broome: Colors (#1, 2)
Jeromy Cox: Colors (#3-4)
Jonny Rench with
Randy Mayor: Colors (#5)

Todd Klein: Letters

TOP10 created by Alan Moore & Gene Ha
Original series covers by Jerry Ordway
Collected Edition design by Ed Roeder

Jim Lee, Editorial Director · John Nee, VP–Business Development
Scott Dunbier, Executive Editor & Editor, Original Series · Kristy Quinn: Assistant Editor

TOP 10: BEYOND THE FARTHEST PRECINCT. Published by America's Best Comics, LLC. Editorial offices: 888 Prospect St, Suite 240, La Jolla, CA 92037. Compilation and sketchbook © 2006 America's Best Comics, LLC. TOP10 and all related characters and elements are trademarks of America's Best Comics. All Rights Reserved. Originally published in single magazine form as TOP 10: Beyond the Farthest Precinct #1-5, © 2005, 2006 America's Best Comics. Any similarities to persons living or dead are purely coincidental. America's Best Comics does not read or accept unsolicited submissions of ideas, stories, or artwork. PRINTED IN CANADA.
ISBN: 1-4012-0991-2   ISBN-13: 978-1-4012-0991-9

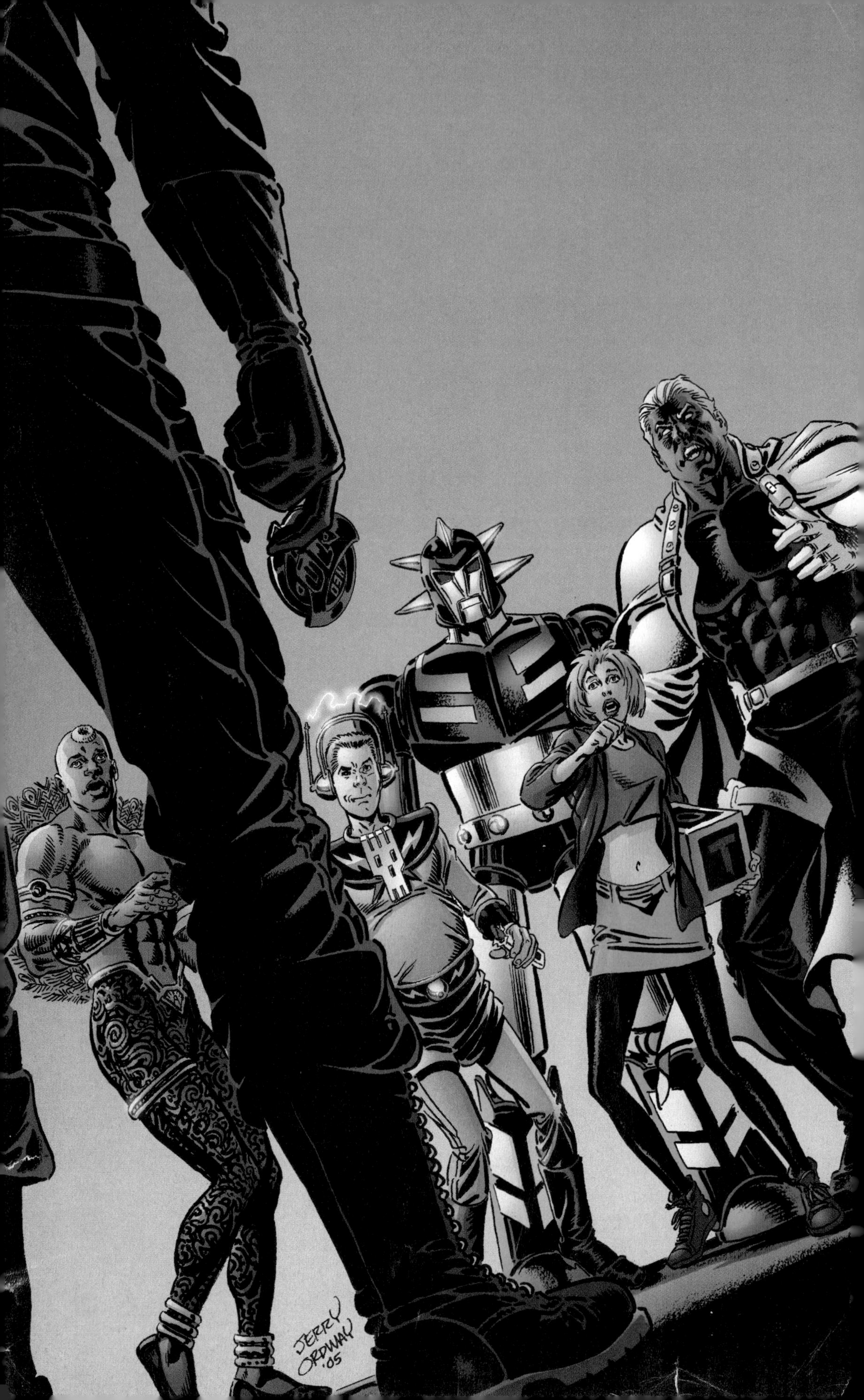
JERRY ORDWAY '05

IRMA GEDDON "DON'T LET HIM GET *AWAY.*"

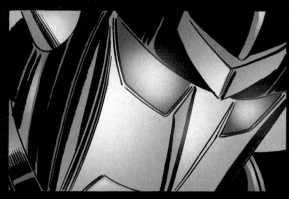

JOE PI "Yet another dead soldier."

SMAX "STAND *ASIDE!*"

GIRL FIFTY-FOUR "I'M *DOWN.*"

KEMLO "THIS DOG IS *SCORCHED!*"

TOYBOX "I'VE GOT WHAT WE NEED RIGHT *HERE.*"

SHOCK-HEADED PETER "GET BACK! I'LL *JUMPSTART* IT!"

KING PEACOCK "SOMEONE FIND THE *CHILDREN!*"

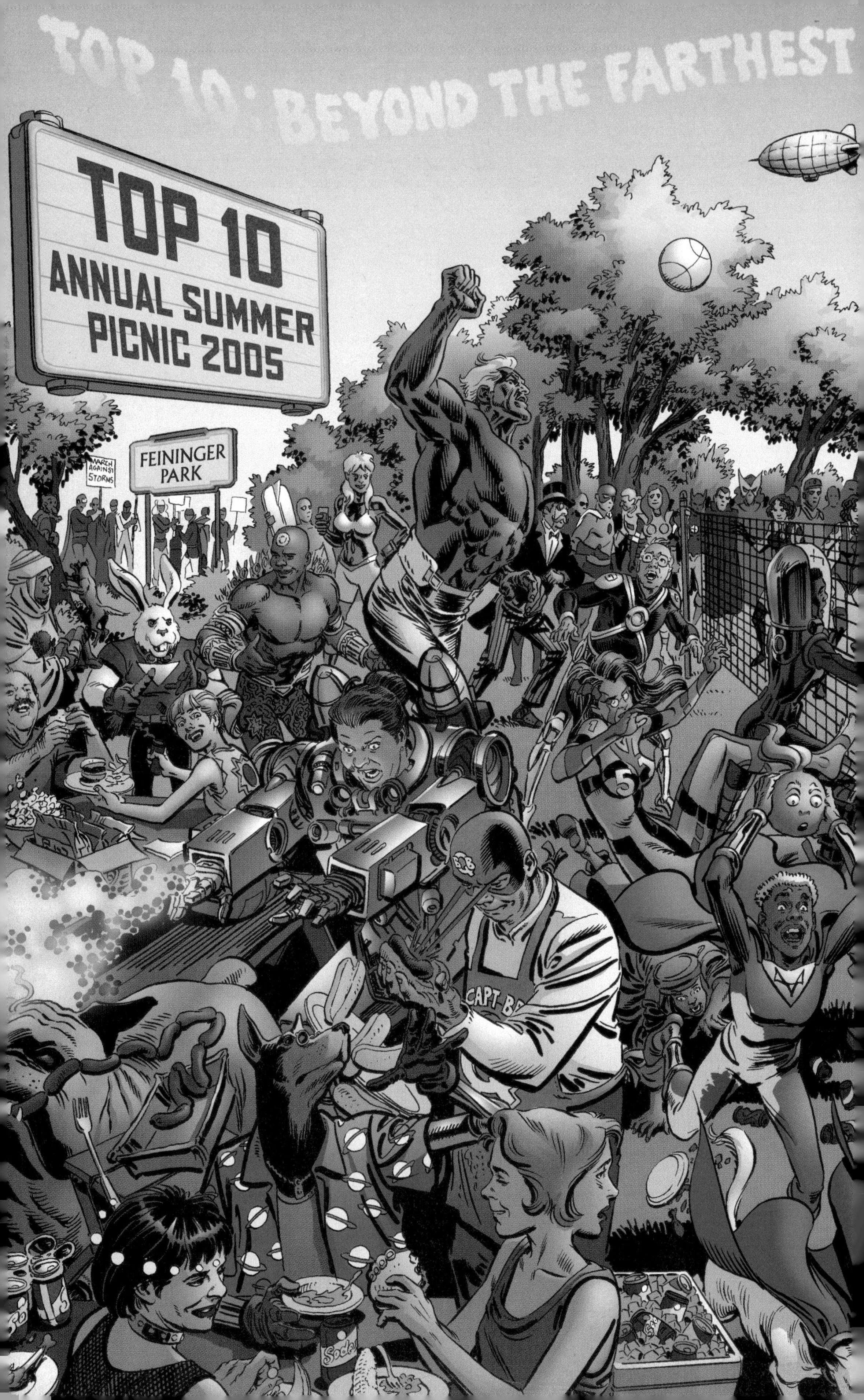
TOP 10: BEYOND THE FARTHEST
TOP 10
ANNUAL SUMMER
PICNIC 2005
FEININGER
PARK
MARCH
AGAINST
STORMS
Soda

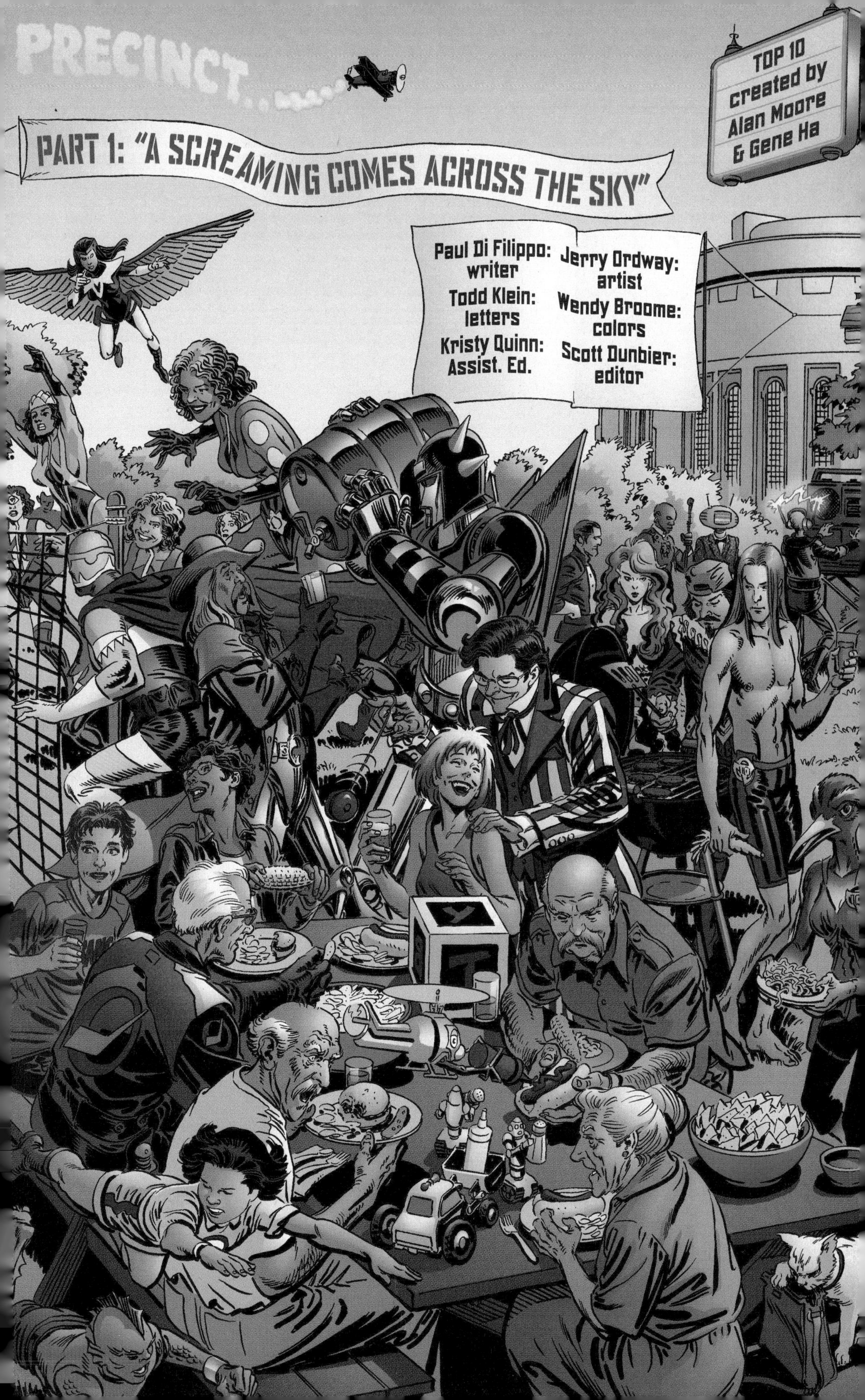
PRECINCT...
PART 1: "A SCREAMING COMES ACROSS THE SKY"
TOP 10 created by Alan Moore & Gene Ha
Paul Di Filippo: writer
Jerry Ordway: artist
Todd Klein: letters
Wendy Broome: colors
Kristy Quinn: Assist. Ed.
Scott Dunbier: editor

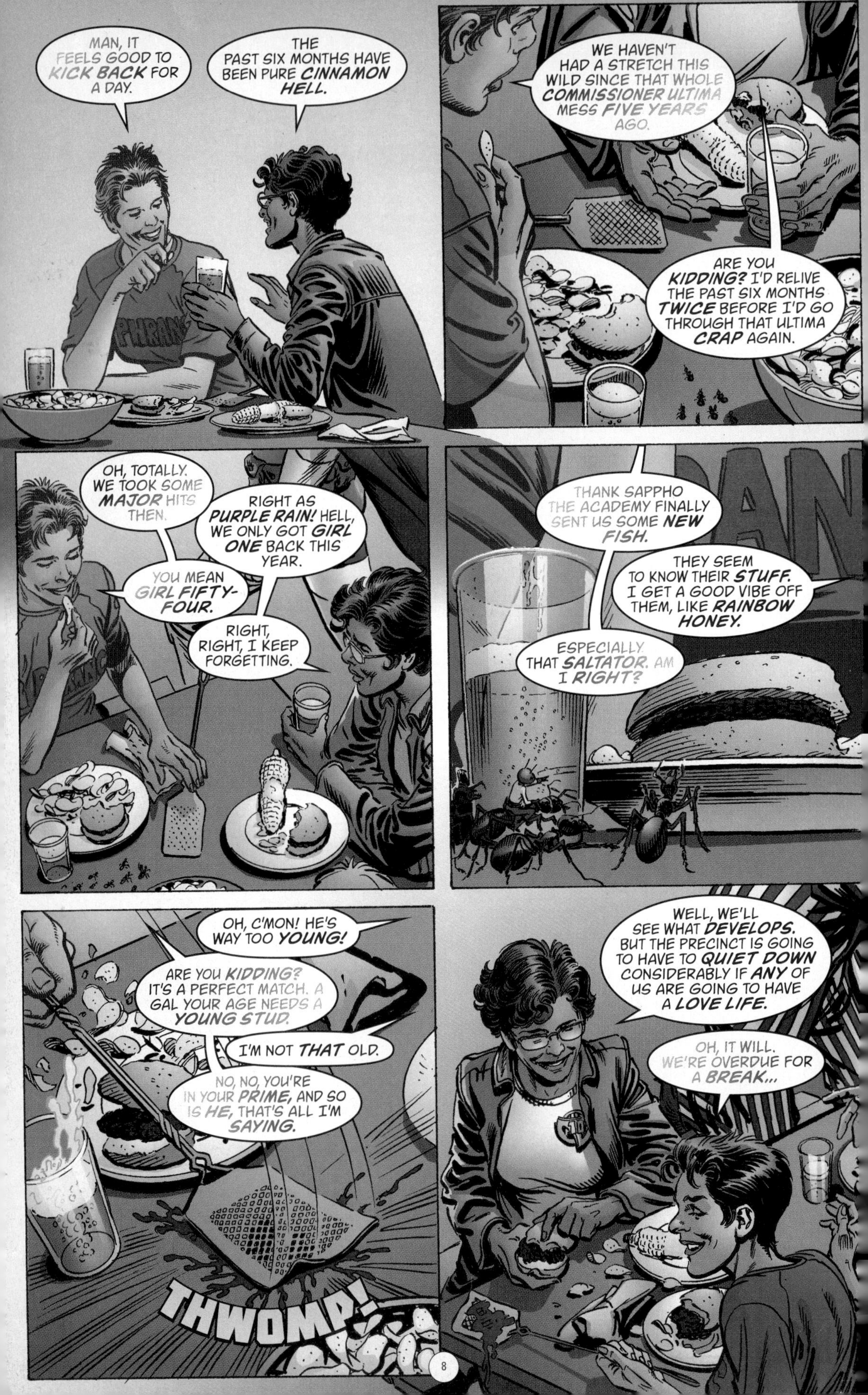
MAN, IT FEELS GOOD TO KICK BACK FOR A DAY.
THE PAST SIX MONTHS HAVE BEEN PURE CINNAMON HELL.
WE HAVEN'T HAD A STRETCH THIS WILD SINCE THAT WHOLE COMMISSIONER ULTIMA MESS FIVE YEARS AGO.
ARE YOU KIDDING? I'D RELIVE THE PAST SIX MONTHS TWICE BEFORE I'D GO THROUGH THAT ULTIMA CRAP AGAIN.
OH, TOTALLY. WE TOOK SOME MAJOR HITS THEN.
RIGHT AS PURPLE RAIN! HELL, WE ONLY GOT GIRL ONE BACK THIS YEAR.
YOU MEAN GIRL FIFTY-FOUR.
RIGHT, RIGHT, I KEEP FORGETTING.
THANK SAPPHO THE ACADEMY FINALLY SENT US SOME NEW FISH.
THEY SEEM TO KNOW THEIR STUFF. I GET A GOOD VIBE OFF THEM, LIKE RAINBOW HONEY.
ESPECIALLY THAT SALTATOR. AM I RIGHT?
OH, C'MON! HE'S WAY TOO YOUNG!
ARE YOU KIDDING? IT'S A PERFECT MATCH. A GAL YOUR AGE NEEDS A YOUNG STUD.
I'M NOT THAT OLD.
NO, NO, YOU'RE IN YOUR PRIME, AND SO IS HE, THAT'S ALL I'M SAYING.
THWOMP!
WELL, WE'LL SEE WHAT DEVELOPS. BUT THE PRECINCT IS GOING TO HAVE TO QUIET DOWN CONSIDERABLY IF ANY OF US ARE GOING TO HAVE A LOVE LIFE.
OH, IT WILL. WE'RE OVERDUE FOR A BREAK...

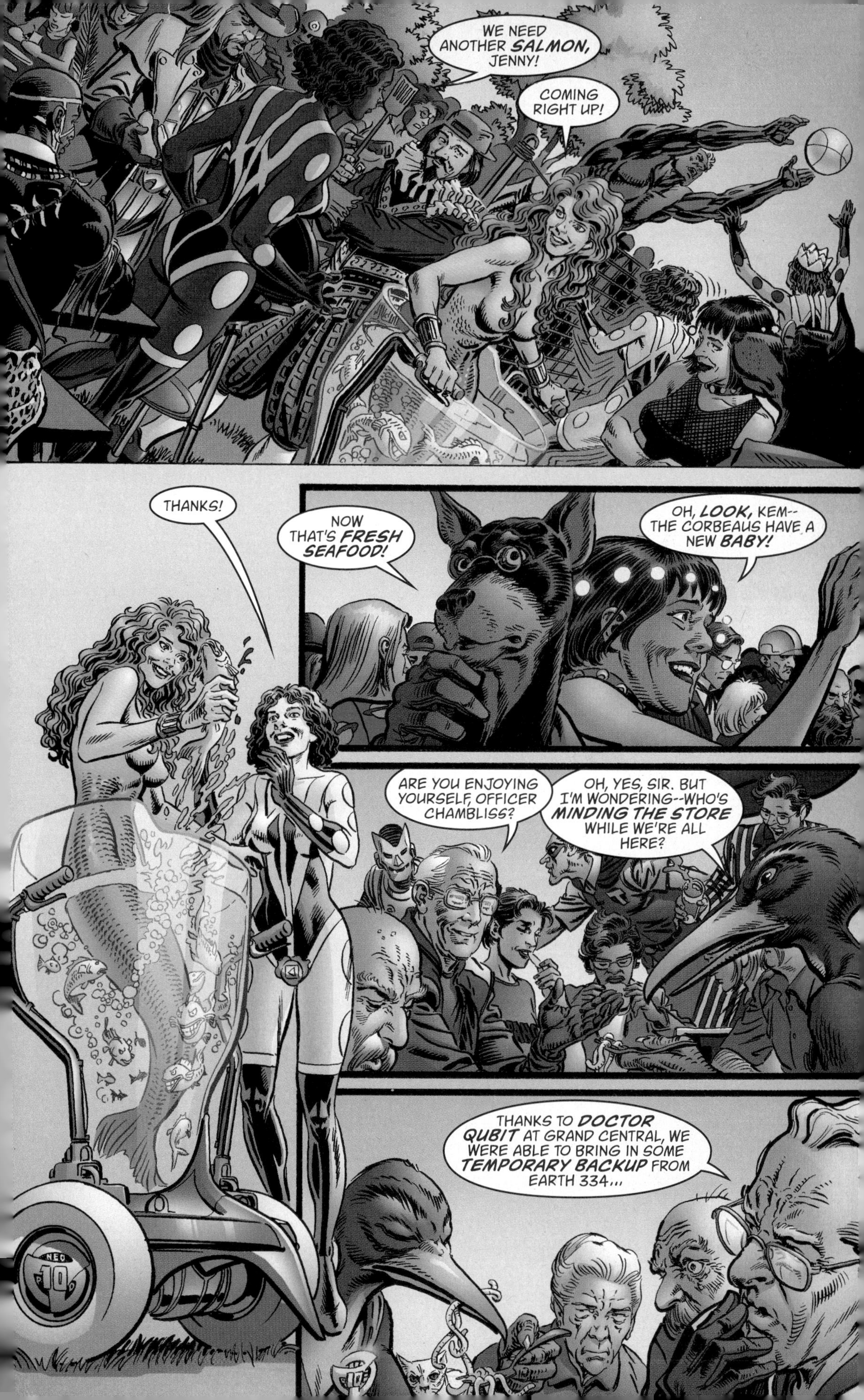

WE NEED ANOTHER SALMON, JENNY!
COMING RIGHT UP!
THANKS!
NOW THAT'S FRESH SEAFOOD!
OH, LOOK, KEM-- THE CORBEAUS HAVE A NEW BABY!
ARE YOU ENJOYING YOURSELF, OFFICER CHAMBLISS?
OH, YES, SIR. BUT I'M WONDERING--WHO'S MINDING THE STORE WHILE WE'RE ALL HERE?
THANKS TO DOCTOR QUBIT AT GRAND CENTRAL, WE WERE ABLE TO BRING IN SOME TEMPORARY BACKUP FROM EARTH 334...
NEO 10

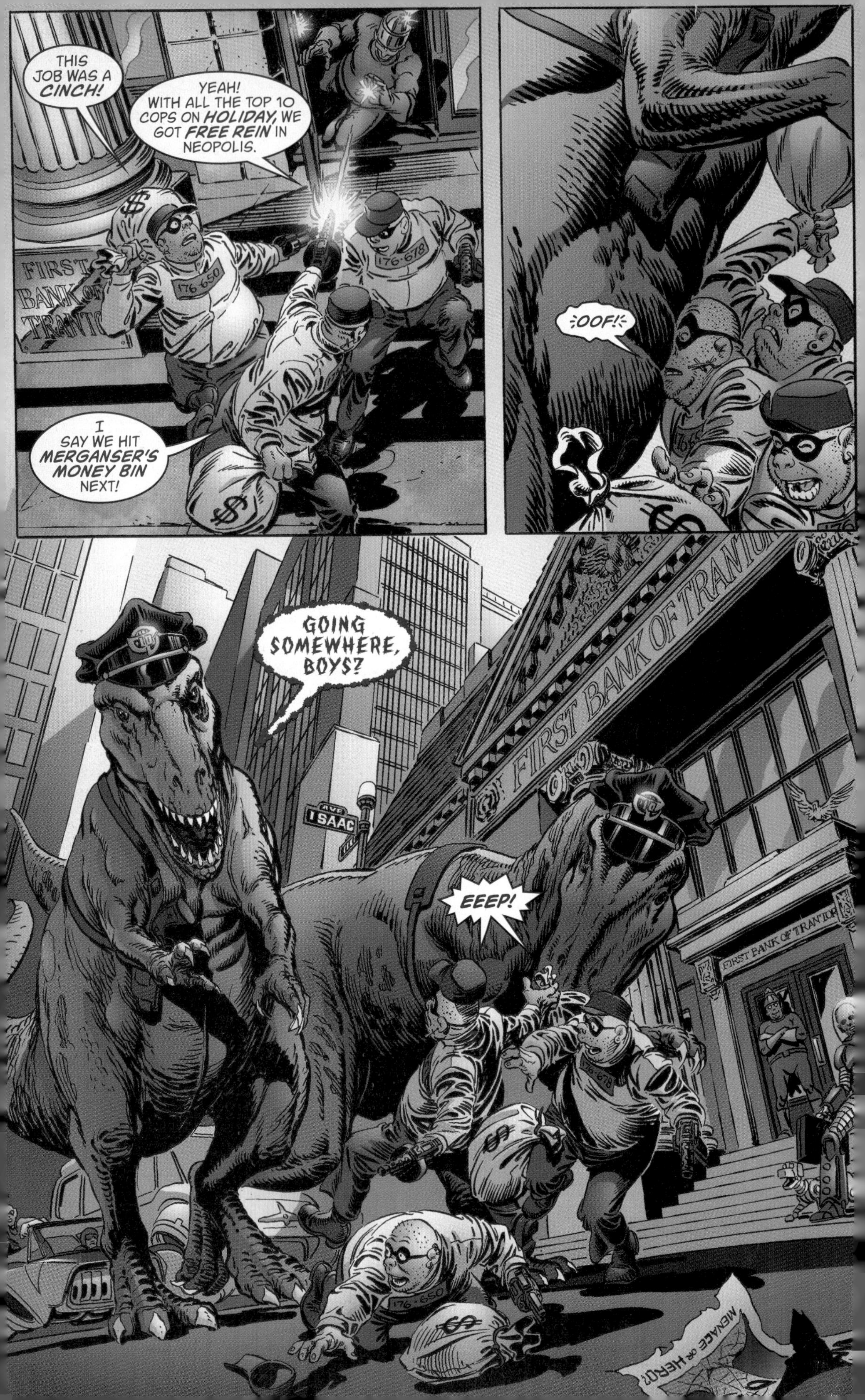
THIS JOB WAS A CINCH!
YEAH! WITH ALL THE TOP 10 COPS ON HOLIDAY, WE GOT FREE REIN IN NEOPOLIS.
FIRST BANK OF TRANTOR
176-650
176-678
I SAY WE HIT MERGANSER'S MONEY BIN NEXT!
OOF!
GOING SOMEWHERE, BOYS?
FIRST BANK OF TRANTOR
AVE
ISAAC
EEEP!
FIRST BANK OF TRANTOR
176-678
176-650
MENACE OR HERO?

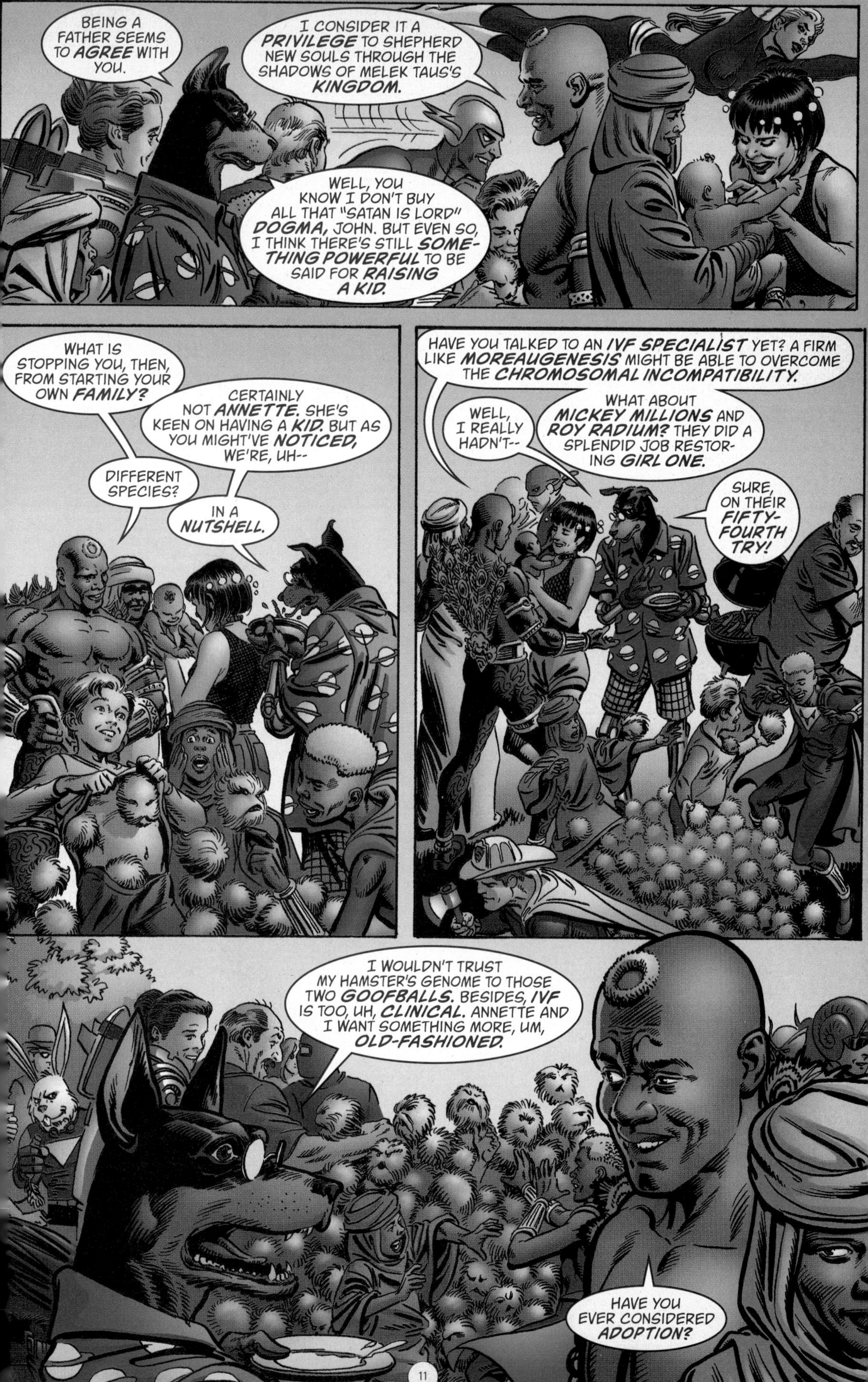
BEING A FATHER SEEMS TO AGREE WITH YOU.
I CONSIDER IT A PRIVILEGE TO SHEPHERD NEW SOULS THROUGH THE SHADOWS OF MELEK TAUS'S KINGDOM.
WELL, YOU KNOW I DON'T BUY ALL THAT "SATAN IS LORD" DOGMA, JOHN. BUT EVEN SO, I THINK THERE'S STILL SOME-THING POWERFUL TO BE SAID FOR RAISING A KID.
WHAT IS STOPPING YOU, THEN, FROM STARTING YOUR OWN FAMILY?
CERTAINLY NOT ANNETTE. SHE'S KEEN ON HAVING A KID. BUT AS YOU MIGHT'VE NOTICED, WE'RE, UH--
DIFFERENT SPECIES?
IN A NUTSHELL.
HAVE YOU TALKED TO AN IVF SPECIALIST YET? A FIRM LIKE MOREAUGENESIS MIGHT BE ABLE TO OVERCOME THE CHROMOSOMAL INCOMPATIBILITY.
WELL, I REALLY HADN'T--
WHAT ABOUT MICKEY MILLIONS AND ROY RADIUM? THEY DID A SPLENDID JOB RESTOR-ING GIRL ONE.
SURE, ON THEIR FIFTY-FOURTH TRY!
I WOULDN'T TRUST MY HAMSTER'S GENOME TO THOSE TWO GOOFBALLS. BESIDES, IVF IS TOO, UH, CLINICAL. ANNETTE AND I WANT SOMETHING MORE, UM, OLD-FASHIONED.
HAVE YOU EVER CONSIDERED ADOPTION?

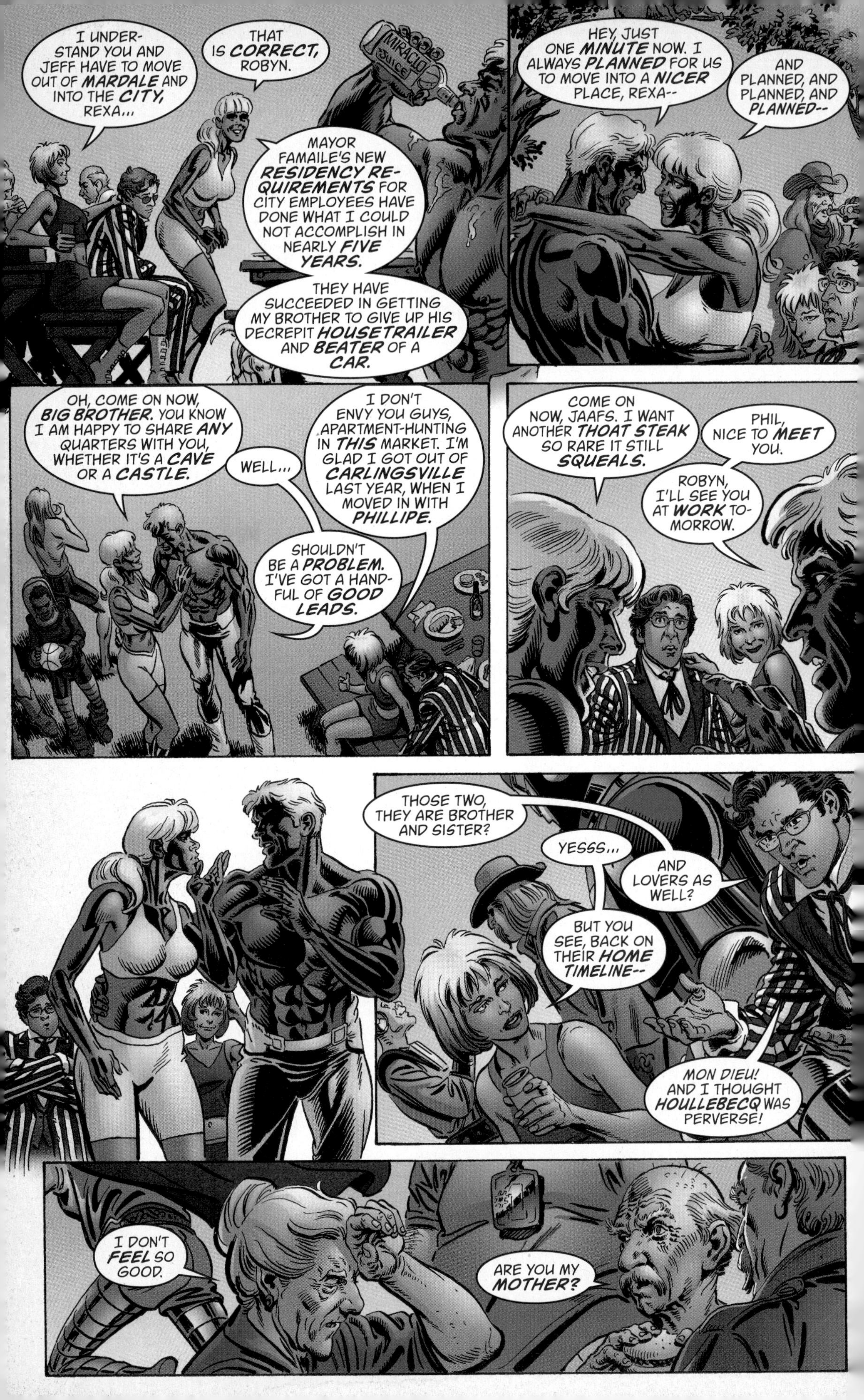
I UNDER-STAND YOU AND JEFF HAVE TO MOVE OUT OF MARDALE AND INTO THE CITY, REXA...
THAT IS CORRECT, ROBYN.
MIRACLO JUICE
MAYOR FAMAILE'S NEW RESIDENCY RE-QUIREMENTS FOR CITY EMPLOYEES HAVE DONE WHAT I COULD NOT ACCOMPLISH IN NEARLY FIVE YEARS.
THEY HAVE SUCCEEDED IN GETTING MY BROTHER TO GIVE UP HIS DECREPIT HOUSETRAILER AND BEATER OF A CAR.
HEY, JUST ONE MINUTE NOW. I ALWAYS PLANNED FOR US TO MOVE INTO A NICER PLACE, REXA--
AND PLANNED, AND PLANNED, AND PLANNED--
OH, COME ON NOW, BIG BROTHER. YOU KNOW I AM HAPPY TO SHARE ANY QUARTERS WITH YOU, WHETHER IT'S A CAVE OR A CASTLE.
WELL...
I DON'T ENVY YOU GUYS, APARTMENT-HUNTING IN THIS MARKET. I'M GLAD I GOT OUT OF CARLINGSVILLE LAST YEAR, WHEN I MOVED IN WITH PHILLIPE.
SHOULDN'T BE A PROBLEM. I'VE GOT A HAND-FUL OF GOOD LEADS.
COME ON NOW, JAAFS. I WANT ANOTHER THOAT STEAK SO RARE IT STILL SQUEALS.
PHIL, NICE TO MEET YOU.
ROBYN, I'LL SEE YOU AT WORK TO-MORROW.
THOSE TWO, THEY ARE BROTHER AND SISTER?
YESSS...
AND LOVERS AS WELL?
BUT YOU SEE, BACK ON THEIR HOME TIMELINE--
MON DIEU! AND I THOUGHT HOULLEBECQ WAS PERVERSE!
I DON'T FEEL SO GOOD.
ARE YOU MY MOTHER?

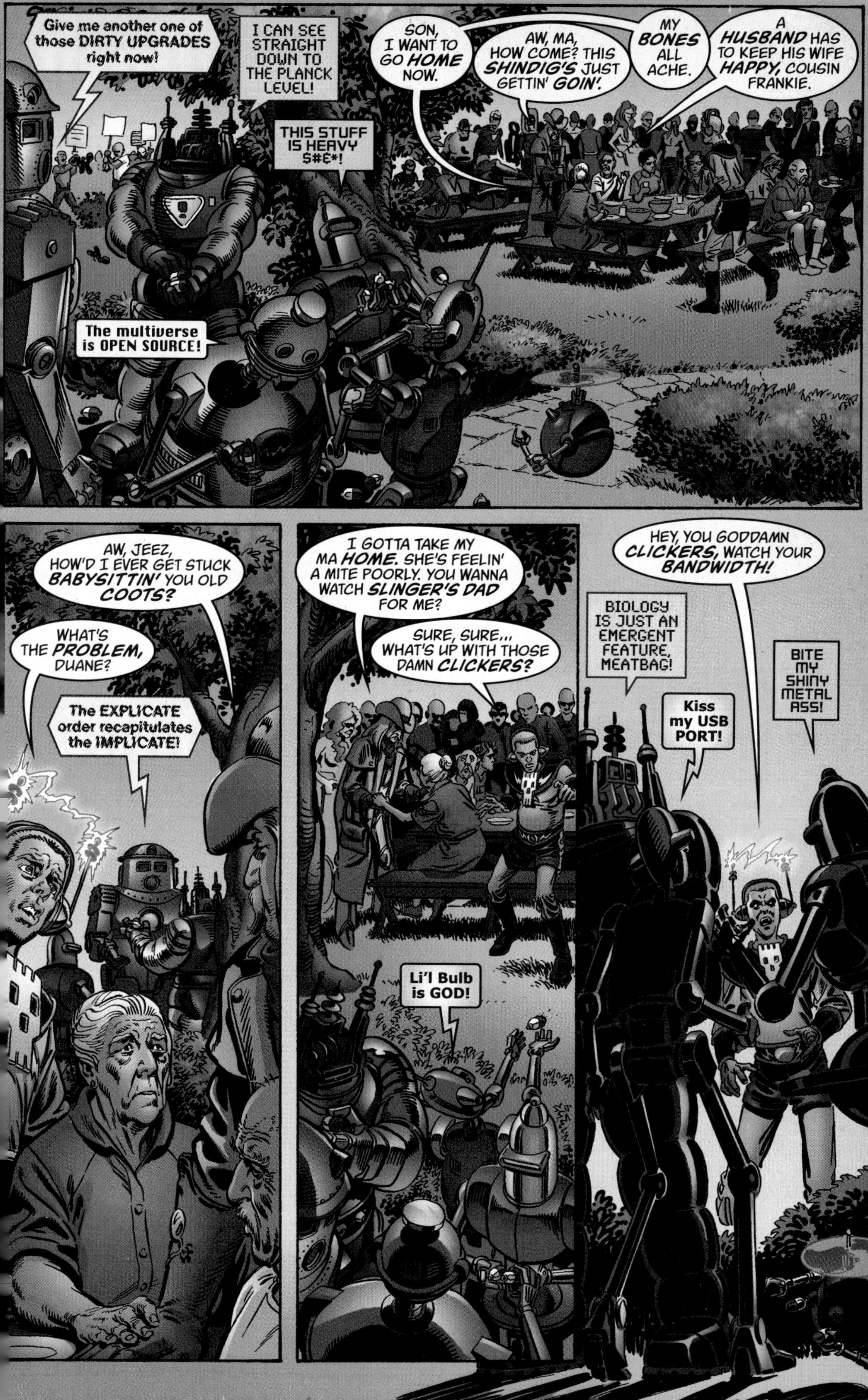
Give me another one of those DIRTY UPGRADES right now!
I CAN SEE STRAIGHT DOWN TO THE PLANCK LEVEL!
THIS STUFF IS HEAVY $#£*!
The multiverse is OPEN SOURCE!
SON, I WANT TO GO HOME NOW.
AW, MA, HOW COME? THIS SHINDIG'S JUST GETTIN' GOIN'.
MY BONES ALL ACHE.
A HUSBAND HAS TO KEEP HIS WIFE HAPPY, COUSIN FRANKIE.
AW, JEEZ, HOW'D I EVER GET STUCK BABYSITTIN' YOU OLD COOTS?
WHAT'S THE PROBLEM, DUANE?
The EXPLICATE order recapitulates the IMPLICATE!
I GOTTA TAKE MY MA HOME. SHE'S FEELIN' A MITE POORLY. YOU WANNA WATCH SLINGER'S DAD FOR ME?
SURE, SURE... WHAT'S UP WITH THOSE DAMN CLICKERS?
Li'l Bulb is GOD!
HEY, YOU GODDAMN CLICKERS, WATCH YOUR BANDWIDTH!
BIOLOGY IS JUST AN EMERGENT FEATURE, MEATBAG!
Kiss my USB PORT!
BITE MY SHINY METAL ASS!

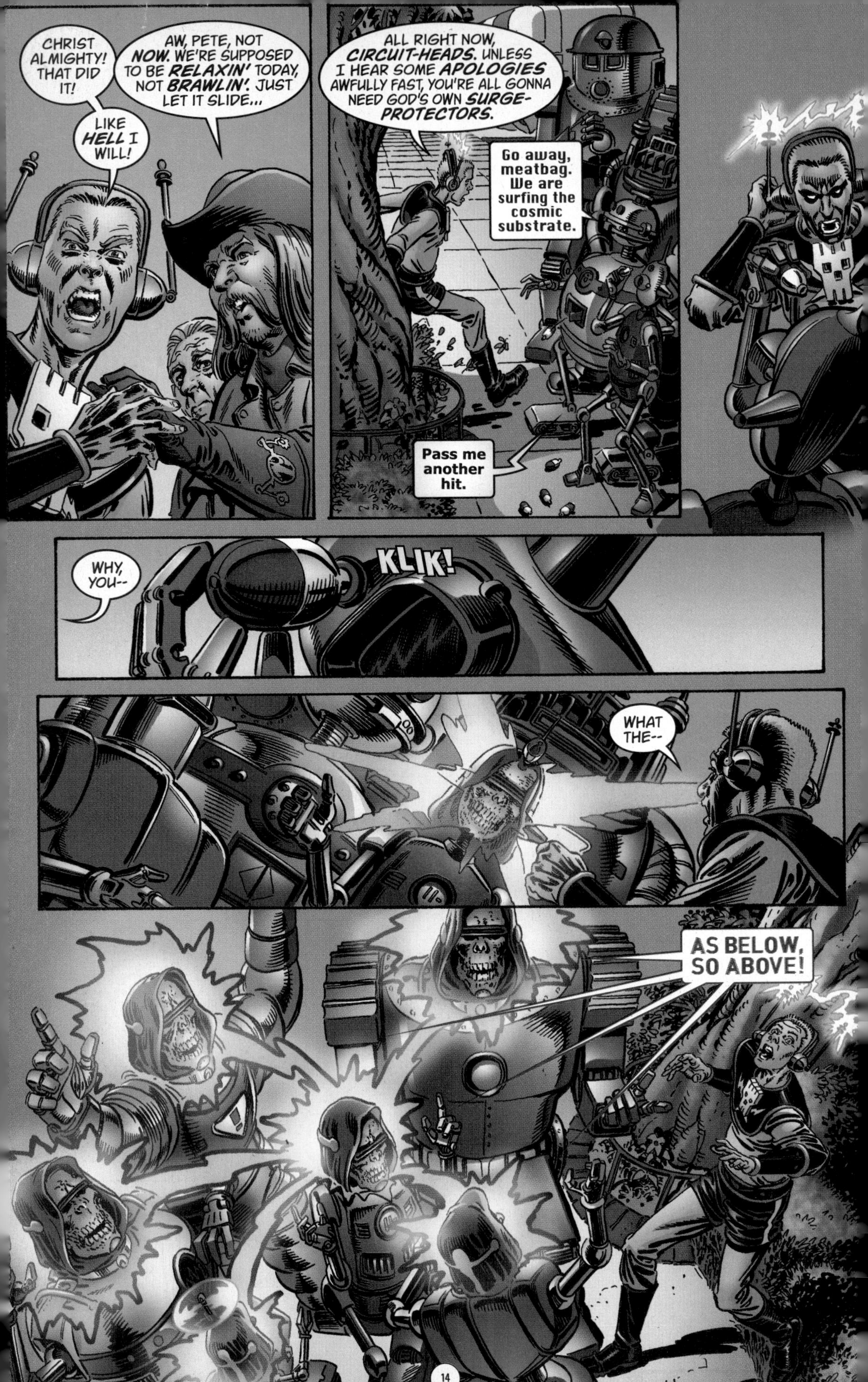
CHRIST ALMIGHTY! THAT DID IT!
AW, PETE, NOT NOW. WE'RE SUPPOSED TO BE RELAXIN' TODAY, NOT BRAWLIN'. JUST LET IT SLIDE...
LIKE HELL I WILL!
ALL RIGHT NOW, CIRCUIT-HEADS. UNLESS I HEAR SOME APOLOGIES AWFULLY FAST, YOU'RE ALL GONNA NEED GOD'S OWN SURGE-PROTECTORS.
Go away, meatbag. We are surfing the cosmic substrate.
Pass me another hit.
WHY, YOU--
KLIK!
WHAT THE--
AS BELOW, SO ABOVE!

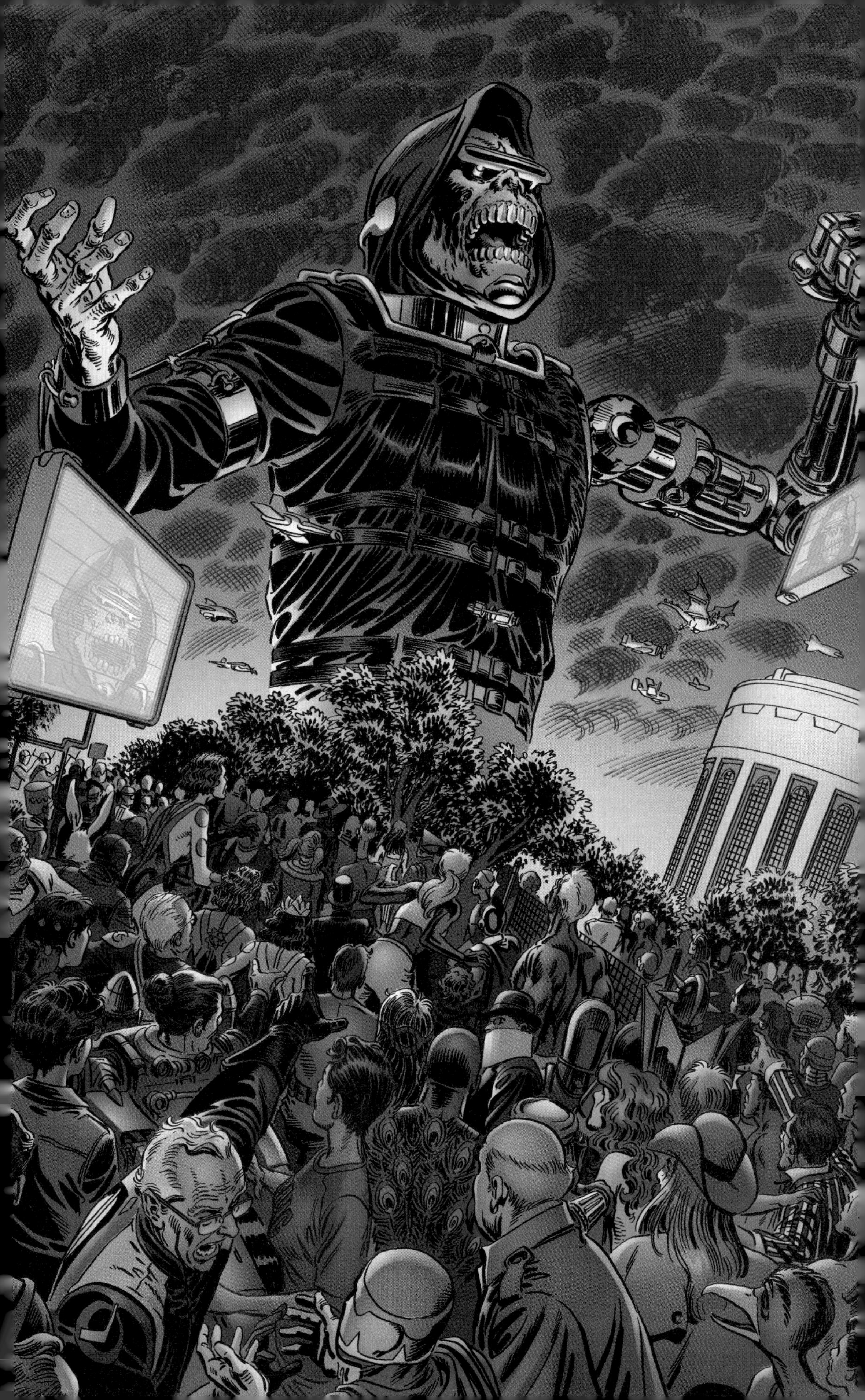

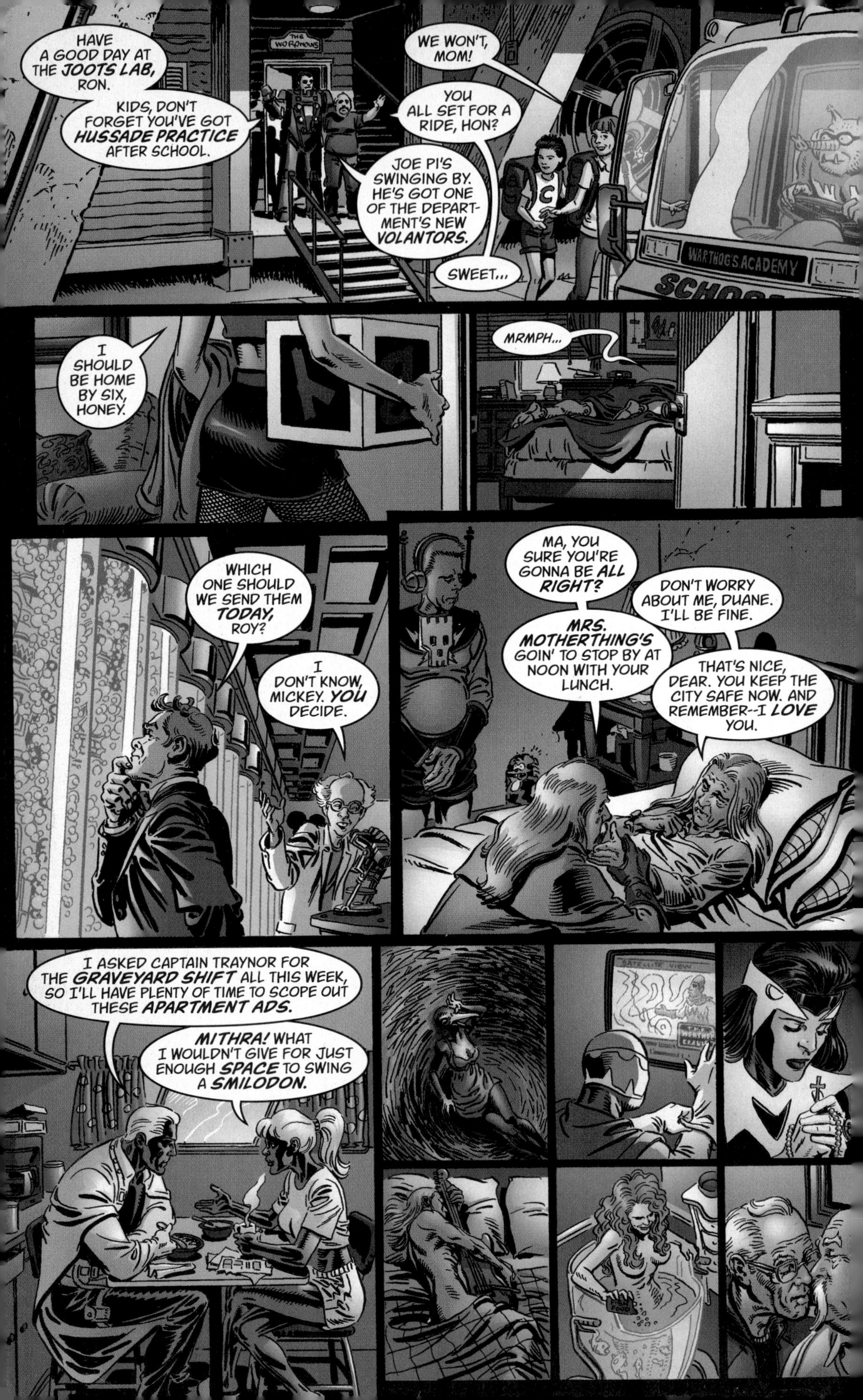
HAVE A GOOD DAY AT THE JOOTS LAB, RON.
KIDS, DON'T FORGET YOU'VE GOT HUSSADE PRACTICE AFTER SCHOOL.
WE WON'T, MOM!
YOU ALL SET FOR A RIDE, HON?
JOE PI'S SWINGING BY. HE'S GOT ONE OF THE DEPART-MENT'S NEW VOLANTORS.
SWEET...
WARTHOG'S ACADEMY
I SHOULD BE HOME BY SIX, HONEY.
MRMPH...
WHICH ONE SHOULD WE SEND THEM TODAY, ROY?
I DON'T KNOW, MICKEY. YOU DECIDE.
MA, YOU SURE YOU'RE GONNA BE ALL RIGHT?
MRS. MOTHERTHING'S GOIN' TO STOP BY AT NOON WITH YOUR LUNCH.
DON'T WORRY ABOUT ME, DUANE. I'LL BE FINE.
THAT'S NICE, DEAR. YOU KEEP THE CITY SAFE NOW. AND REMEMBER--I LOVE YOU.
I ASKED CAPTAIN TRAYNOR FOR THE GRAVEYARD SHIFT ALL THIS WEEK, SO I'LL HAVE PLENTY OF TIME TO SCOPE OUT THESE APARTMENT ADS.
MITHRA! WHAT I WOULDN'T GIVE FOR JUST ENOUGH SPACE TO SWING A SMILODON.

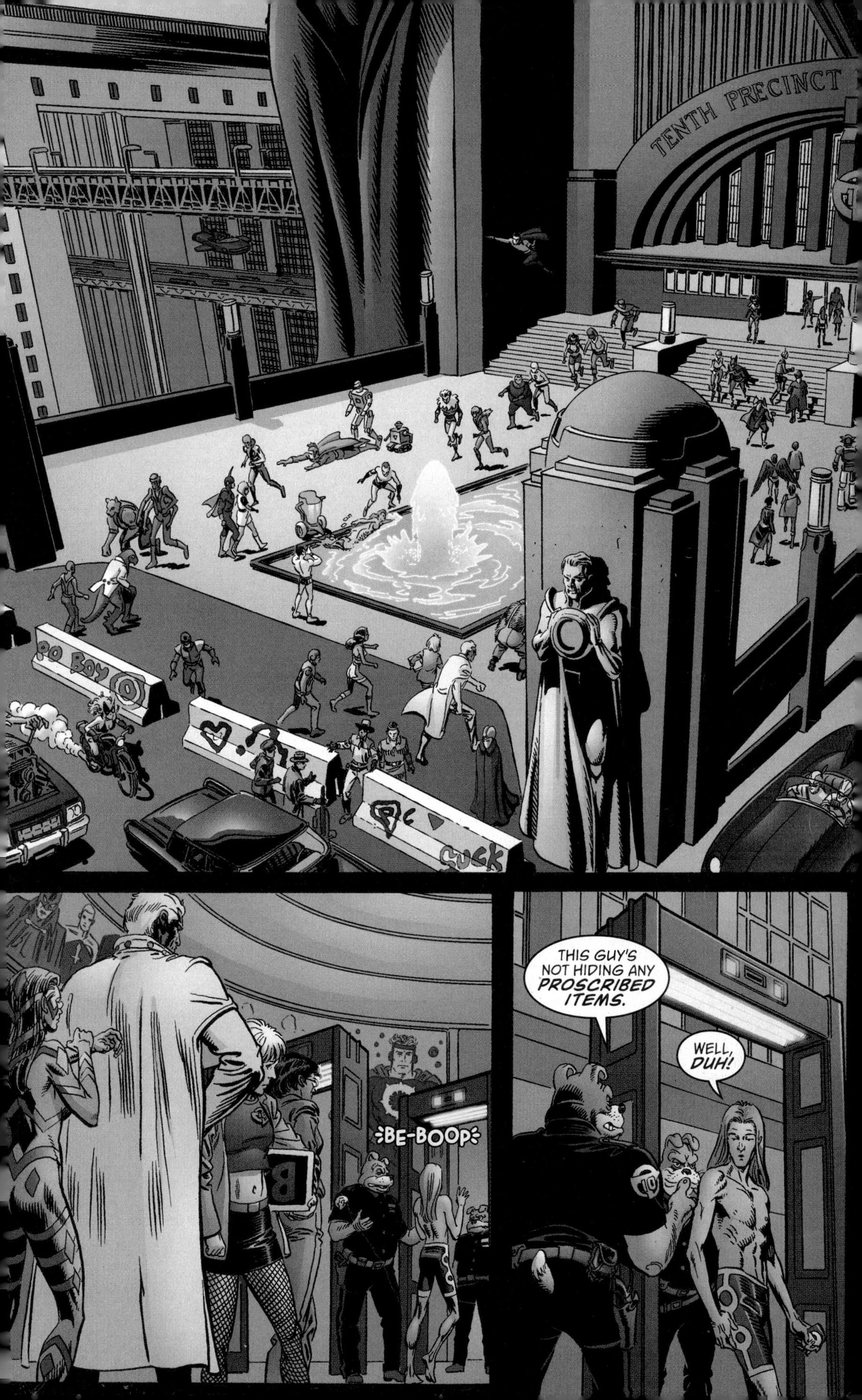
TENTH PRECINCT
BE-BOOP
THIS GUY'S NOT HIDING ANY *PROSCRIBED* ITEMS.
WELL, *DUH!*

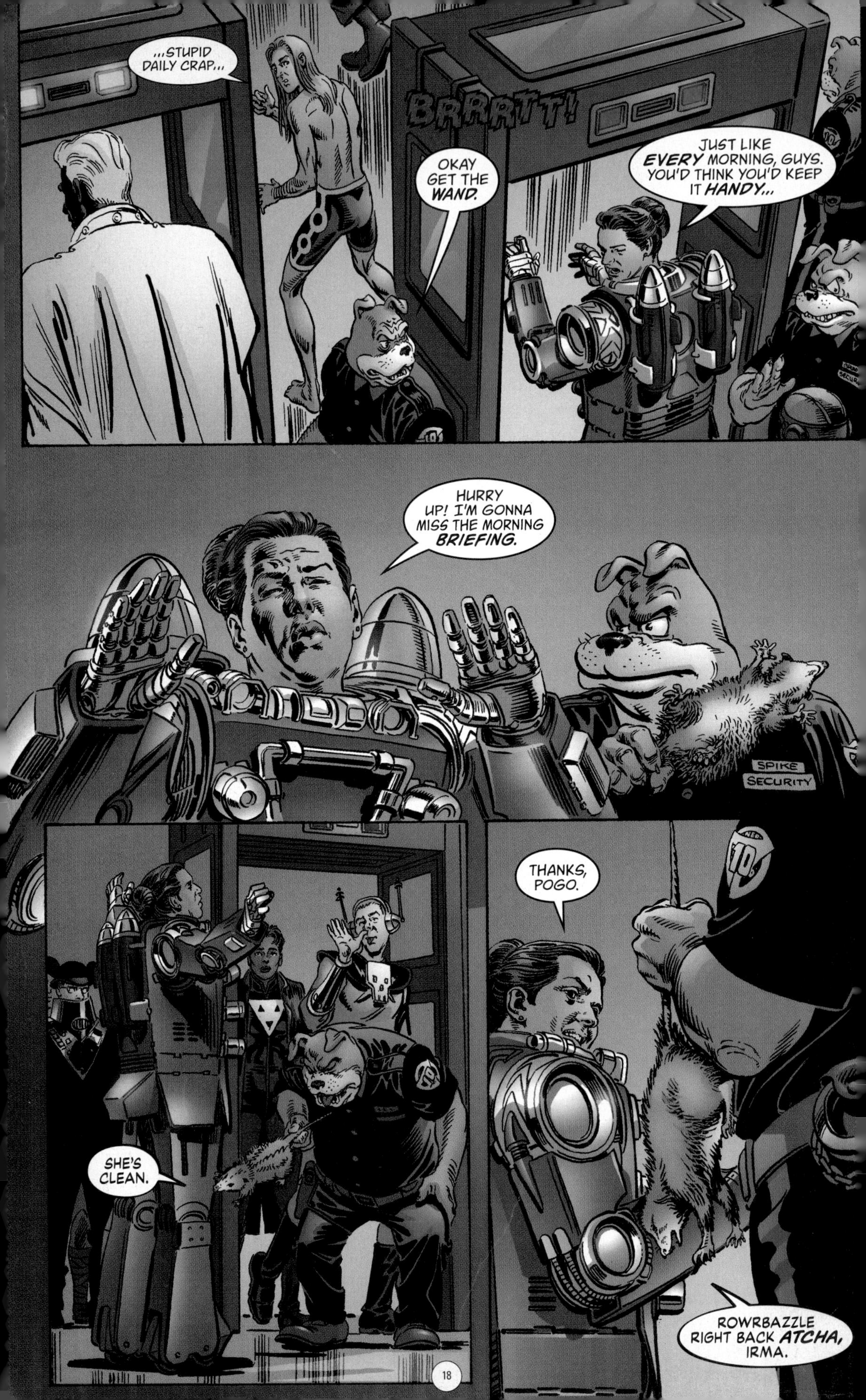
...STUPID DAILY CRAP...
BRRRRTT!
OKAY GET THE WAND.
JUST LIKE EVERY MORNING, GUYS. YOU'D THINK YOU'D KEEP IT HANDY...
HURRY UP! I'M GONNA MISS THE MORNING BRIEFING.
SPIKE
SECURITY
SHE'S CLEAN.
THANKS, POGO.
ROWRBAZZLE RIGHT BACK ATCHA, IRMA.

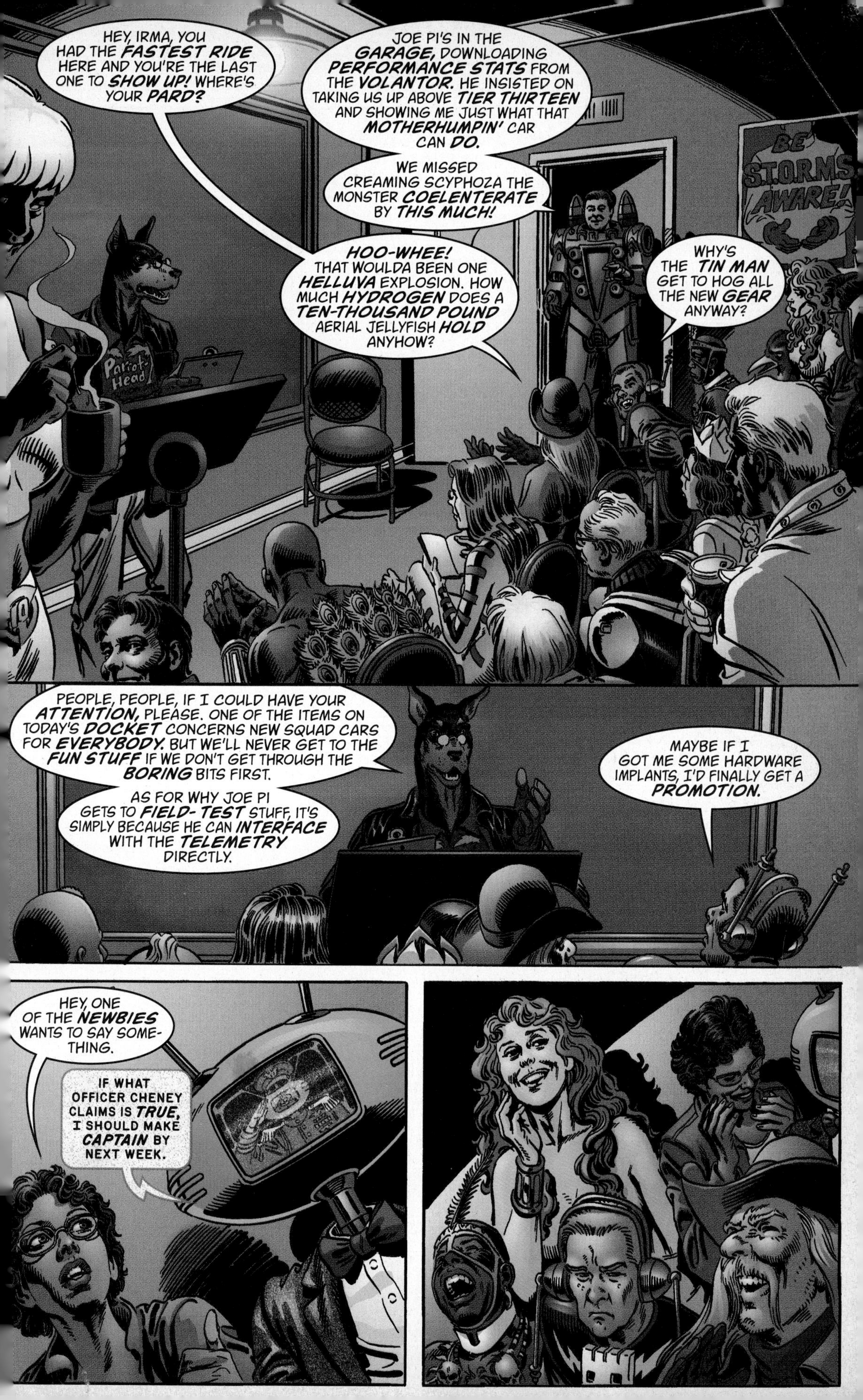
HEY, IRMA, YOU HAD THE FASTEST RIDE HERE AND YOU'RE THE LAST ONE TO SHOW UP! WHERE'S YOUR PARD?
JOE PI'S IN THE GARAGE, DOWNLOADING PERFORMANCE STATS FROM THE VOLANTOR. HE INSISTED ON TAKING US UP ABOVE TIER THIRTEEN AND SHOWING ME JUST WHAT THAT MOTHERHUMPIN' CAR CAN DO.
WE MISSED CREAMING SCYPHOZA THE MONSTER COELENTERATE BY THIS MUCH!
HOO-WHEE! THAT WOULDA BEEN ONE HELLUVA EXPLOSION. HOW MUCH HYDROGEN DOES A TEN-THOUSAND POUND AERIAL JELLYFISH HOLD ANYHOW?
WHY'S THE TIN MAN GET TO HOG ALL THE NEW GEAR ANYWAY?
BE S.T.O.R.M.S. AWARE!
Parrot-Head
PEOPLE, PEOPLE, IF I COULD HAVE YOUR ATTENTION, PLEASE. ONE OF THE ITEMS ON TODAY'S DOCKET CONCERNS NEW SQUAD CARS FOR EVERYBODY. BUT WE'LL NEVER GET TO THE FUN STUFF IF WE DON'T GET THROUGH THE BORING BITS FIRST.
AS FOR WHY JOE PI GETS TO FIELD-TEST STUFF, IT'S SIMPLY BECAUSE HE CAN INTERFACE WITH THE TELEMETRY DIRECTLY.
MAYBE IF I GOT ME SOME HARDWARE IMPLANTS, I'D FINALLY GET A PROMOTION.
HEY, ONE OF THE NEWBIES WANTS TO SAY SOME-THING.
IF WHAT OFFICER CHENEY CLAIMS IS TRUE, I SHOULD MAKE CAPTAIN BY NEXT WEEK.

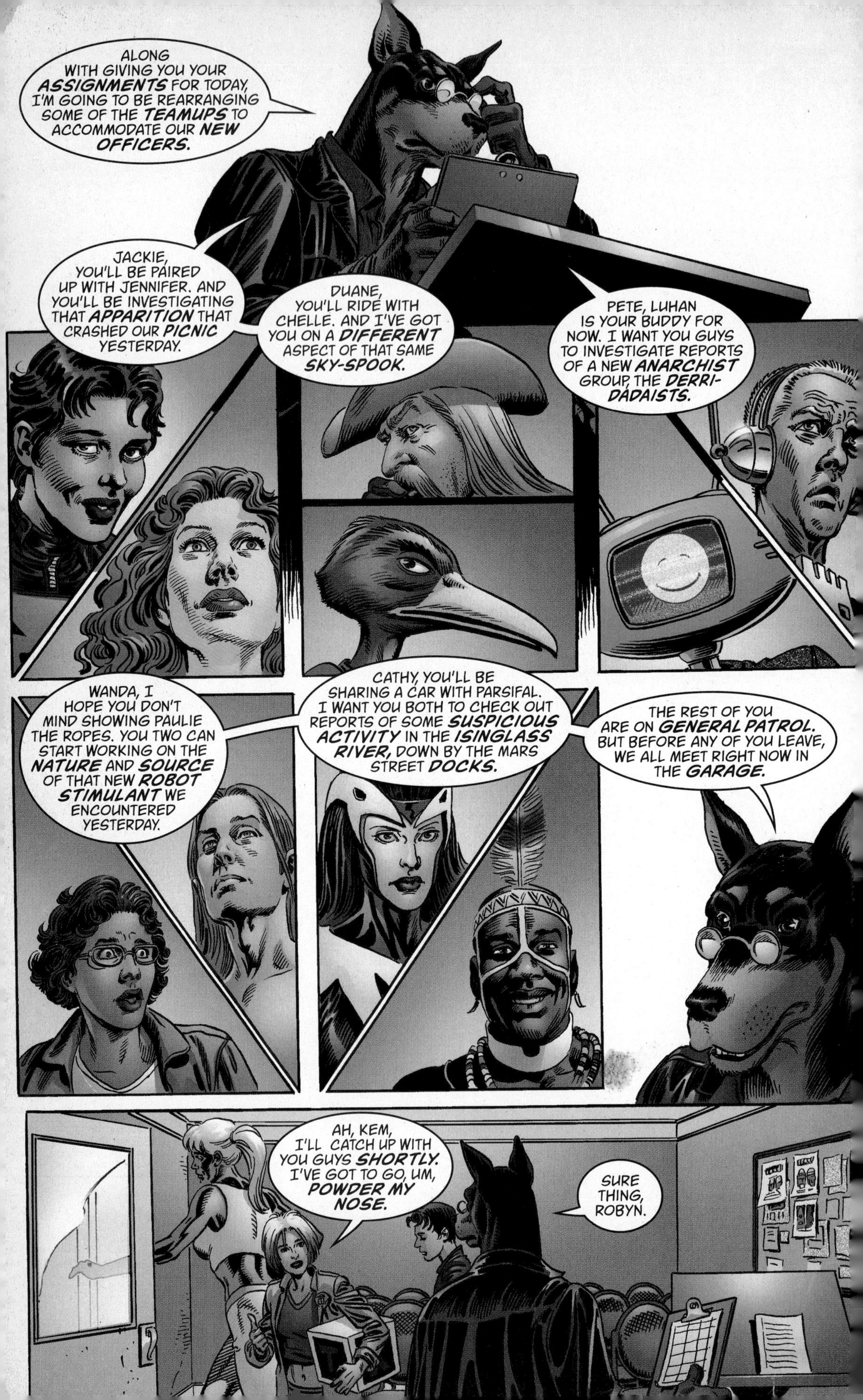
ALONG WITH GIVING YOU YOUR ASSIGNMENTS FOR TODAY, I'M GOING TO BE REARRANGING SOME OF THE TEAMUPS TO ACCOMMODATE OUR NEW OFFICERS.
JACKIE, YOU'LL BE PAIRED UP WITH JENNIFER. AND YOU'LL BE INVESTIGATING THAT APPARITION THAT CRASHED OUR PICNIC YESTERDAY.
DUANE, YOU'LL RIDE WITH CHELLE. AND I'VE GOT YOU ON A DIFFERENT ASPECT OF THAT SAME SKY-SPOOK.
PETE, LUHAN IS YOUR BUDDY FOR NOW. I WANT YOU GUYS TO INVESTIGATE REPORTS OF A NEW ANARCHIST GROUP, THE DERRI-DADAISTS.
WANDA, I HOPE YOU DON'T MIND SHOWING PAULIE THE ROPES. YOU TWO CAN START WORKING ON THE NATURE AND SOURCE OF THAT NEW ROBOT STIMULANT WE ENCOUNTERED YESTERDAY.
CATHY, YOU'LL BE SHARING A CAR WITH PARSIFAL. I WANT YOU BOTH TO CHECK OUT REPORTS OF SOME SUSPICIOUS ACTIVITY IN THE ISINGLASS RIVER, DOWN BY THE MARS STREET DOCKS.
THE REST OF YOU ARE ON GENERAL PATROL. BUT BEFORE ANY OF YOU LEAVE, WE ALL MEET RIGHT NOW IN THE GARAGE.
AH, KEM, I'LL CATCH UP WITH YOU GUYS SHORTLY. I'VE GOT TO GO, UM, POWDER MY NOSE.
SURE THING, ROBYN.

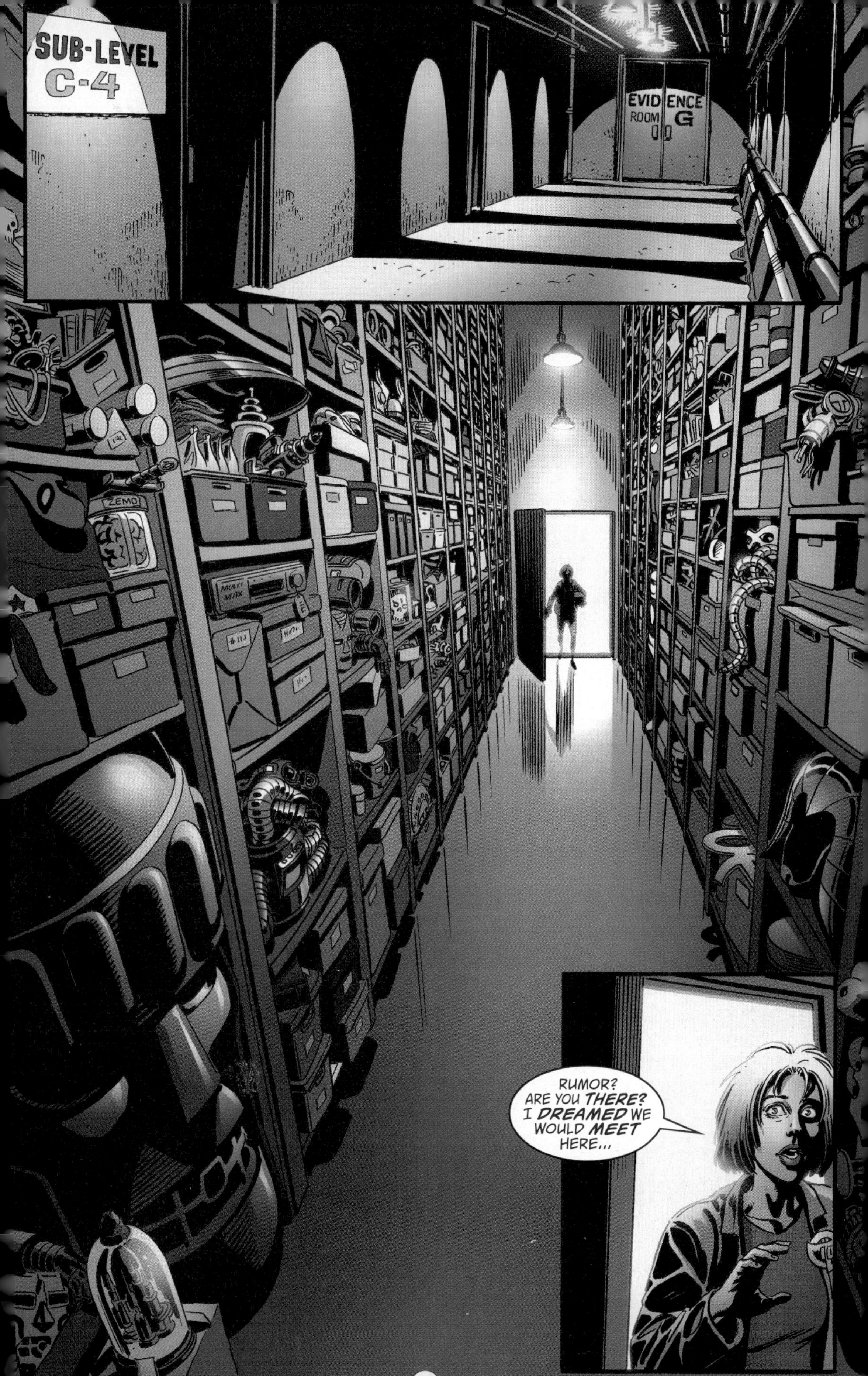
SUB-LEVEL C-4
EVIDENCE ROOM G
ZEMO
RUMOR? ARE YOU *THERE?* I *DREAMED* WE WOULD *MEET* HERE...

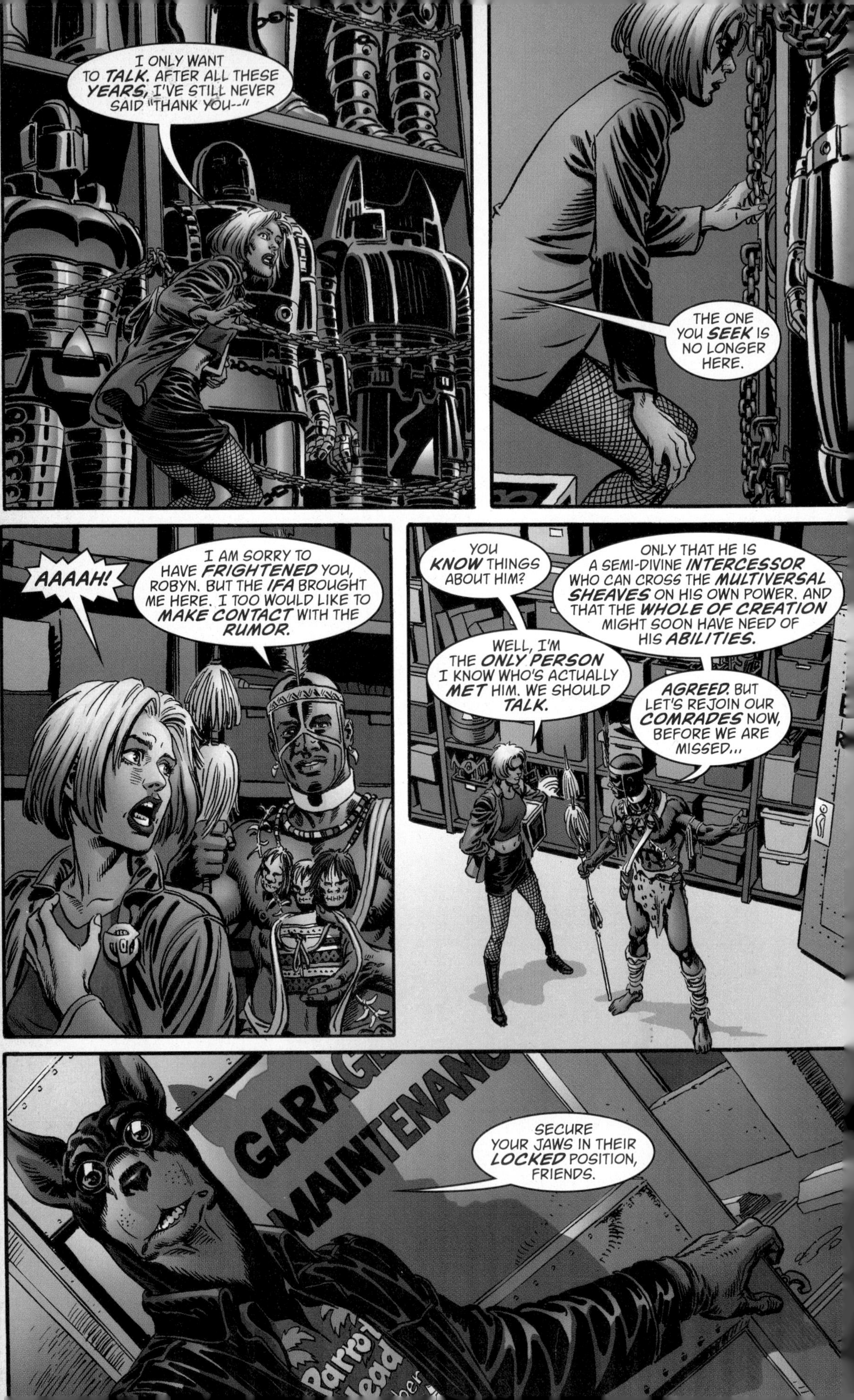
I ONLY WANT TO TALK. AFTER ALL THESE YEARS, I'VE STILL NEVER SAID "THANK YOU--"
THE ONE YOU SEEK IS NO LONGER HERE.
AAAAH!
I AM SORRY TO HAVE FRIGHTENED YOU, ROBYN. BUT THE IFA BROUGHT ME HERE. I TOO WOULD LIKE TO MAKE CONTACT WITH THE RUMOR.
YOU KNOW THINGS ABOUT HIM?
ONLY THAT HE IS A SEMI-DIVINE INTERCESSOR WHO CAN CROSS THE MULTIVERSAL SHEAVES ON HIS OWN POWER. AND THAT THE WHOLE OF CREATION MIGHT SOON HAVE NEED OF HIS ABILITIES.
WELL, I'M THE ONLY PERSON I KNOW WHO'S ACTUALLY MET HIM. WE SHOULD TALK.
AGREED. BUT LET'S REJOIN OUR COMRADES NOW, BEFORE WE ARE MISSED...
GARAGE
MAINTENANC
SECURE YOUR JAWS IN THEIR LOCKED POSITION, FRIENDS.

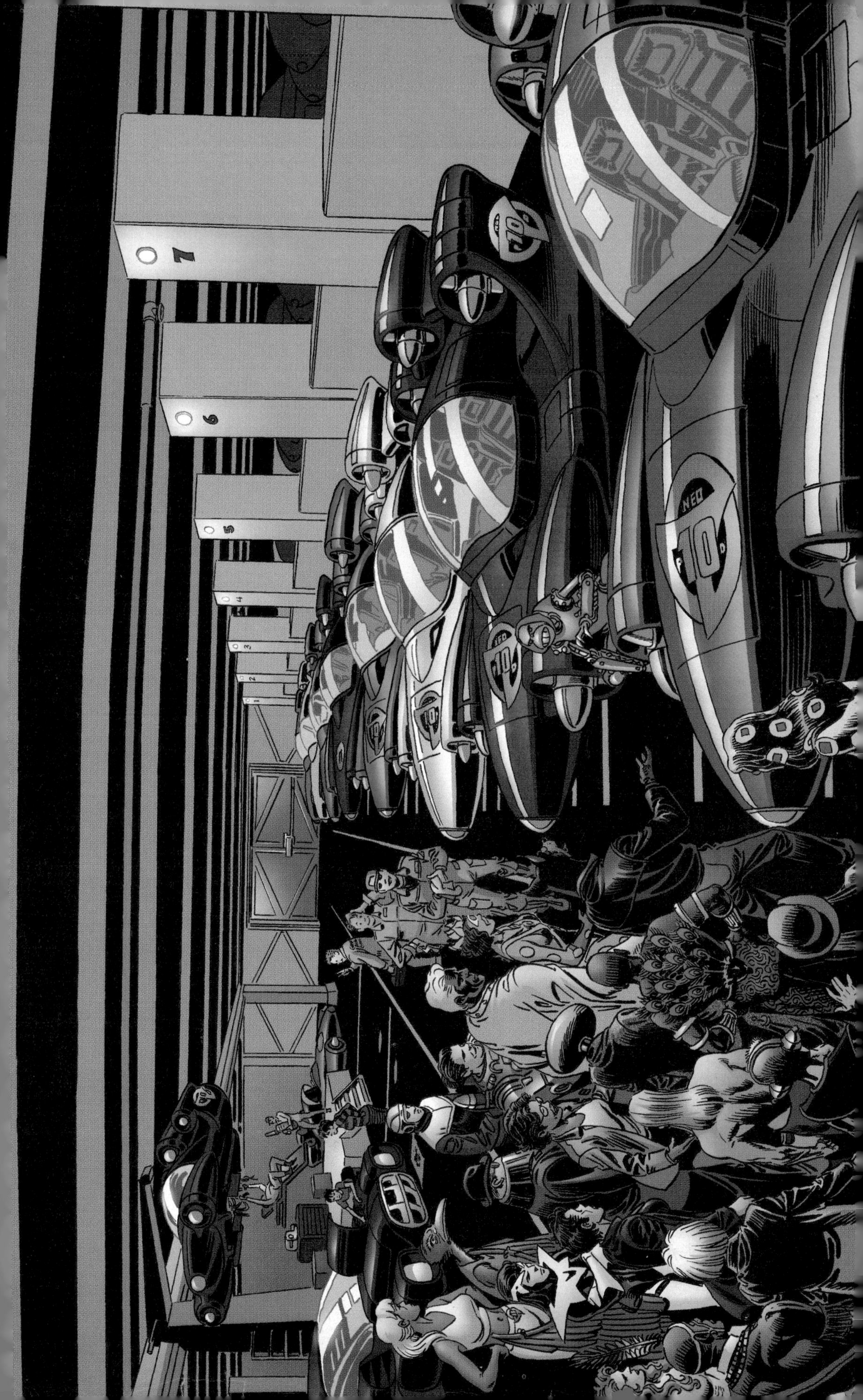

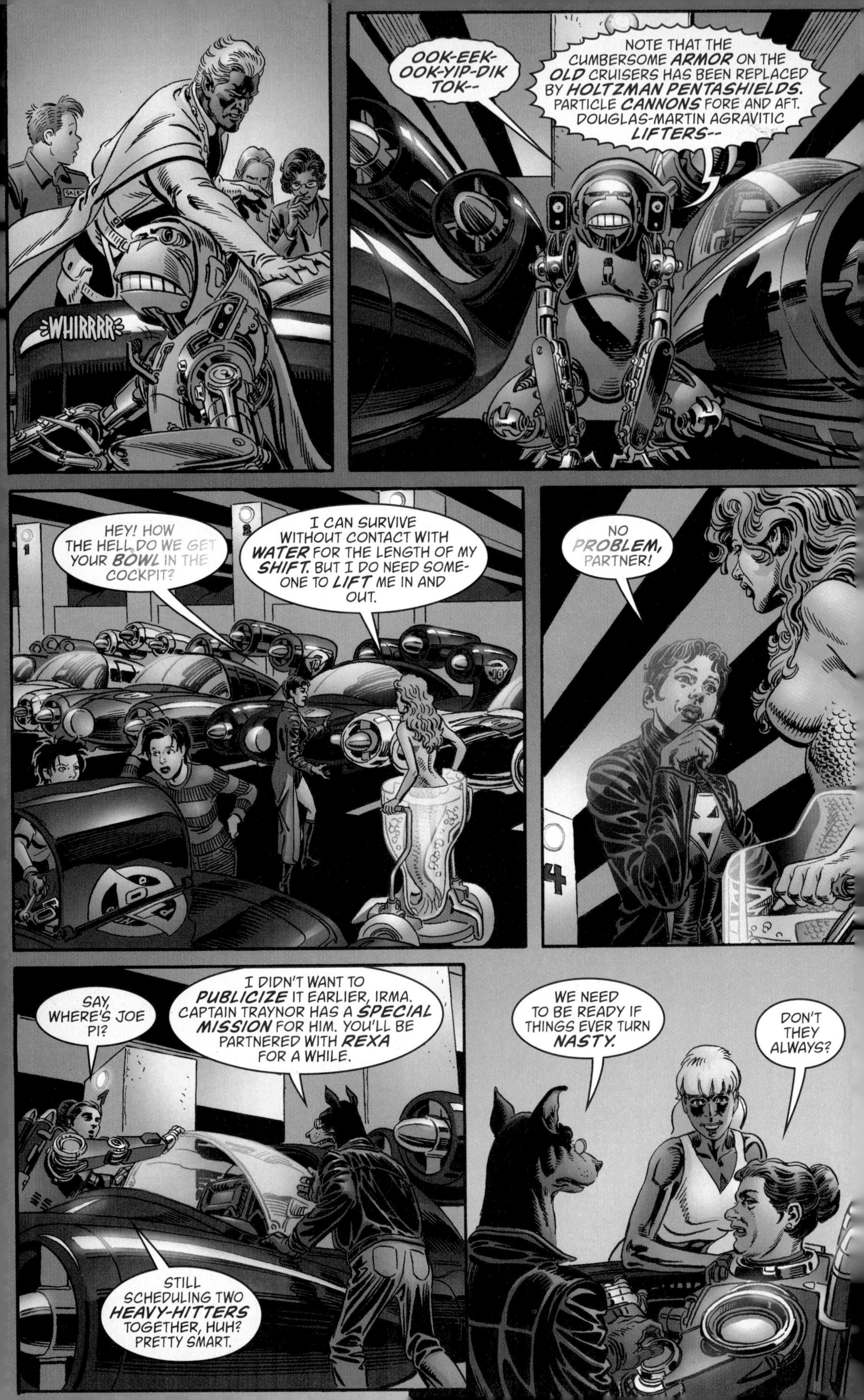
WHIRRRR
OOK-EEK-OOK-YIP-DIK TOK--
NOTE THAT THE CUMBERSOME ARMOR ON THE OLD CRUISERS HAS BEEN REPLACED BY HOLTZMAN PENTASHIELDS. PARTICLE CANNONS FORE AND AFT. DOUGLAS-MARTIN AGRAVITIC LIFTERS--
HEY! HOW THE HELL DO WE GET YOUR BOWL IN THE COCKPIT?
I CAN SURVIVE WITHOUT CONTACT WITH WATER FOR THE LENGTH OF MY SHIFT. BUT I DO NEED SOME-ONE TO LIFT ME IN AND OUT.
NO PROBLEM, PARTNER!
SAY, WHERE'S JOE PI?
I DIDN'T WANT TO PUBLICIZE IT EARLIER, IRMA. CAPTAIN TRAYNOR HAS A SPECIAL MISSION FOR HIM. YOU'LL BE PARTNERED WITH REXA FOR A WHILE.
STILL SCHEDULING TWO HEAVY-HITTERS TOGETHER, HUH? PRETTY SMART.
WE NEED TO BE READY IF THINGS EVER TURN NASTY.
DON'T THEY ALWAYS?

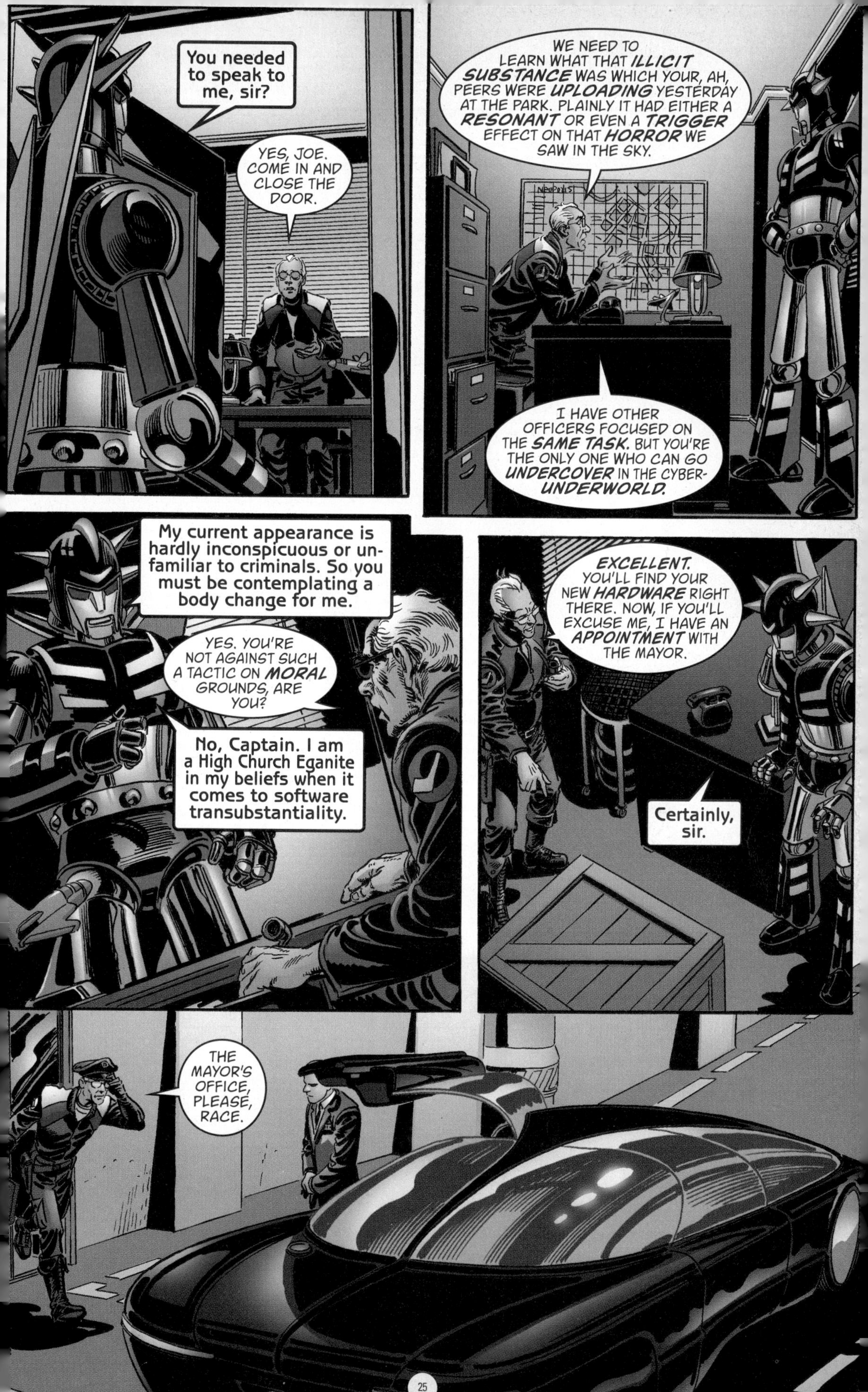
You needed to speak to me, sir?
YES, JOE. COME IN AND CLOSE THE DOOR.
WE NEED TO LEARN WHAT THAT ILLICIT SUBSTANCE WAS WHICH YOUR, AH, PEERS WERE UPLOADING YESTERDAY AT THE PARK. PLAINLY IT HAD EITHER A RESONANT OR EVEN A TRIGGER EFFECT ON THAT HORROR WE SAW IN THE SKY.
I HAVE OTHER OFFICERS FOCUSED ON THE SAME TASK. BUT YOU'RE THE ONLY ONE WHO CAN GO UNDERCOVER IN THE CYBER-UNDERWORLD.
My current appearance is hardly inconspicuous or unfamiliar to criminals. So you must be contemplating a body change for me.
YES. YOU'RE NOT AGAINST SUCH A TACTIC ON MORAL GROUNDS, ARE YOU?
No, Captain. I am a High Church Eganite in my beliefs when it comes to software transubstantiality.
EXCELLENT. YOU'LL FIND YOUR NEW HARDWARE RIGHT THERE. NOW, IF YOU'LL EXCUSE ME, I HAVE AN APPOINTMENT WITH THE MAYOR.
Certainly, sir.
THE MAYOR'S OFFICE, PLEASE, RACE.

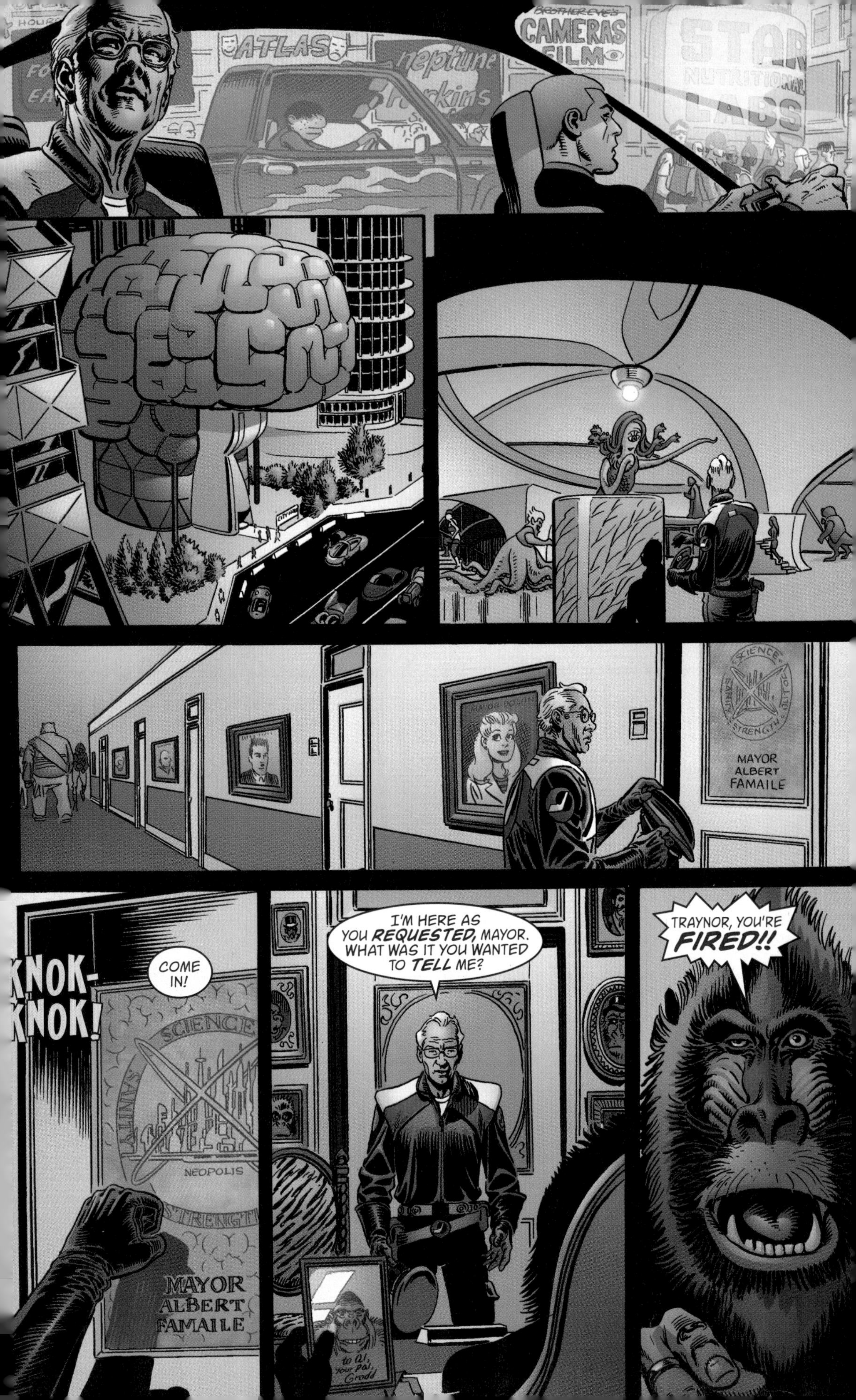

ATLAS
neptune perkins
BROTHER EYE'S
CAMERAS
FILM
STAR
NUTRITIONAL
LABS
SCIENCE
SANITY
STRENGTH
MAYOR
ALBERT
FAMAILE
KNOK-
KNOK!
COME IN!
NEOPOLIS
MAYOR
ALBERT
FAMAILE
I'M HERE AS YOU REQUESTED, MAYOR. WHAT WAS IT YOU WANTED TO TELL ME?
to Al, Your Pal, Grodd
TRAYNOR, YOU'RE FIRED!!

CHAPTER #2

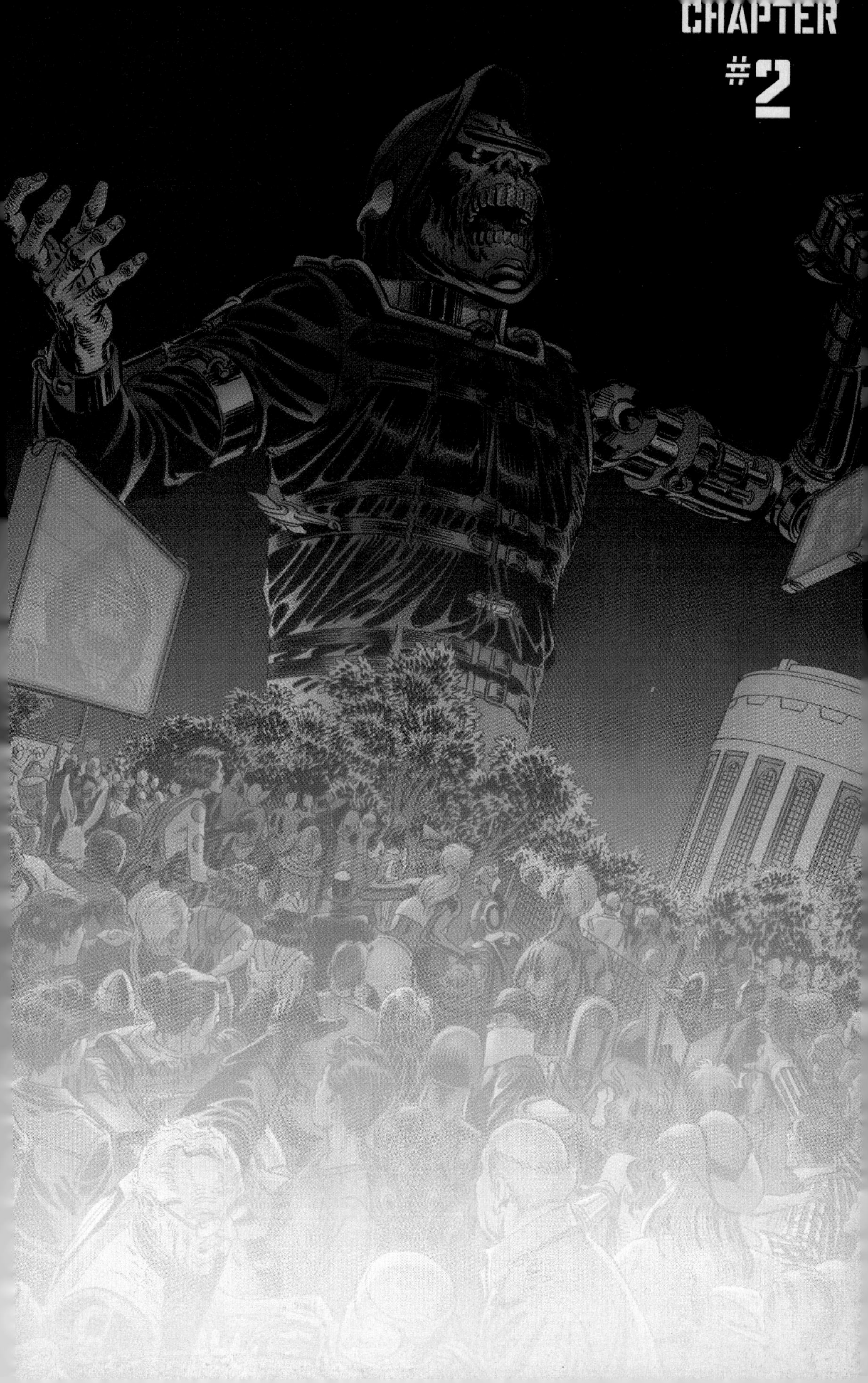

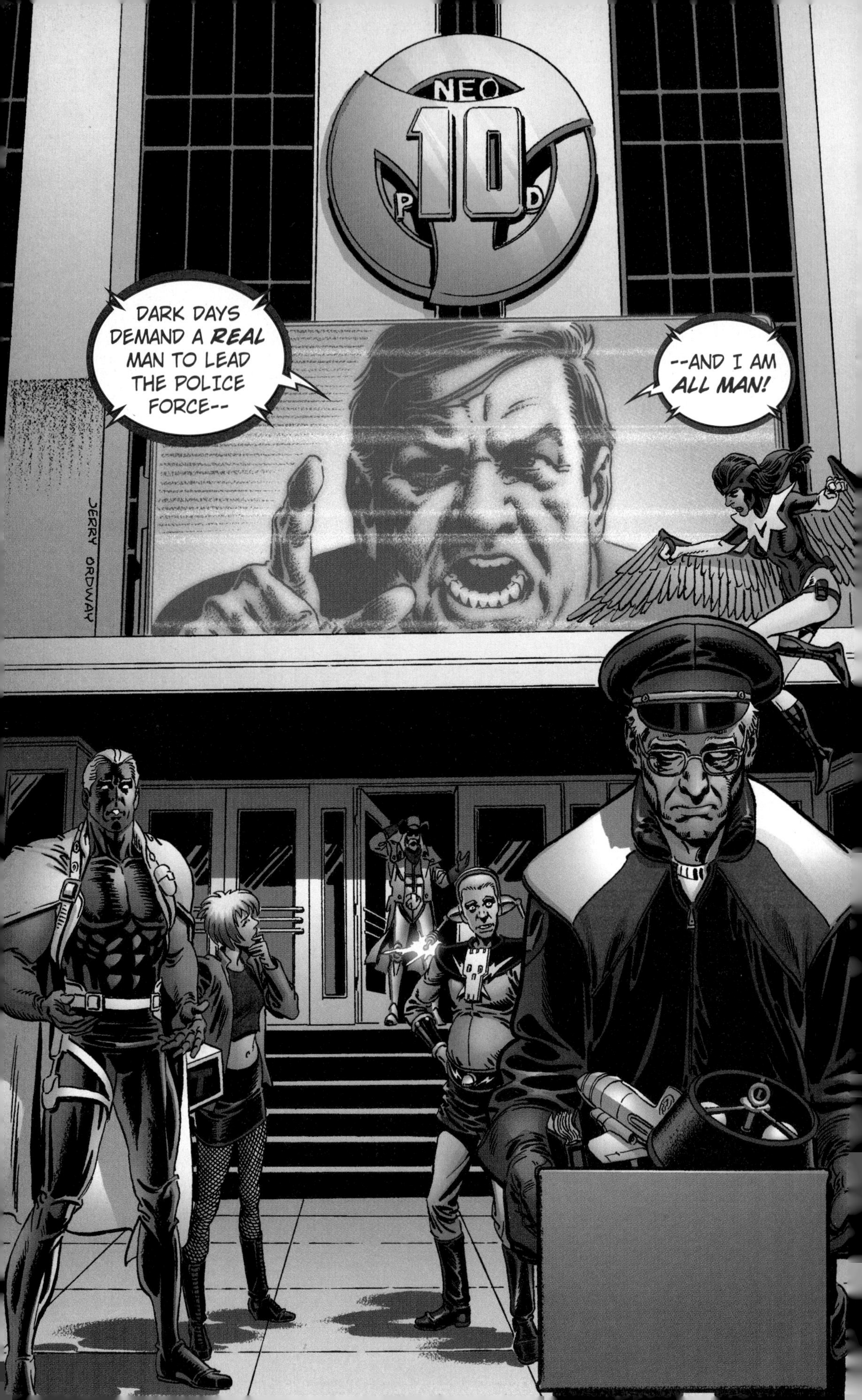
NEO 10 PD
DARK DAYS DEMAND A *REAL* MAN TO LEAD THE POLICE FORCE--
--AND I AM *ALL MAN!*
JERRY ORDWAY

TRAYNOR, YOU'RE **FIRED!!**

BUT--BUT **WHY?**

BECAUSE YOU'RE NOT **TOUGH ENOUGH** FOR THESE TIMES, CAPTAIN. BECAUSE YOUR **TENURE** HAS PRODUCED HEADLINES LIKE **THIS**--

PAGE SIX:
ALIEN ENCOUNTER
WITH **KENT CLARKSON**

DIURNAL ✖ WANDERER
★ ★ ★ ★ ★

LOSE WEIGHT!
BEFORE ... AFTER
S.TAR LABS
NOW WITH FAST ACTING KRYPTONIAN

SPECTRAL SKY SCREAMER SHOCKS NEOPOLIS

POLICE PARTY HEARTY WHILE CITY REELS

TOP 10: BEYOND THE FARTHEST PRECINCT

PART 2: A New Broom Sweeps Mean

PAUL DI FILIPPO writer
JERRY ORDWAY artist

KRISTY QUINN assistant editor

WENDY BROOME cover colors

TODD KLEIN letters
JEROMY COX colors

SCOTT DUNBIER editor

TOP 10 created by Alan Moore and Gene Ha

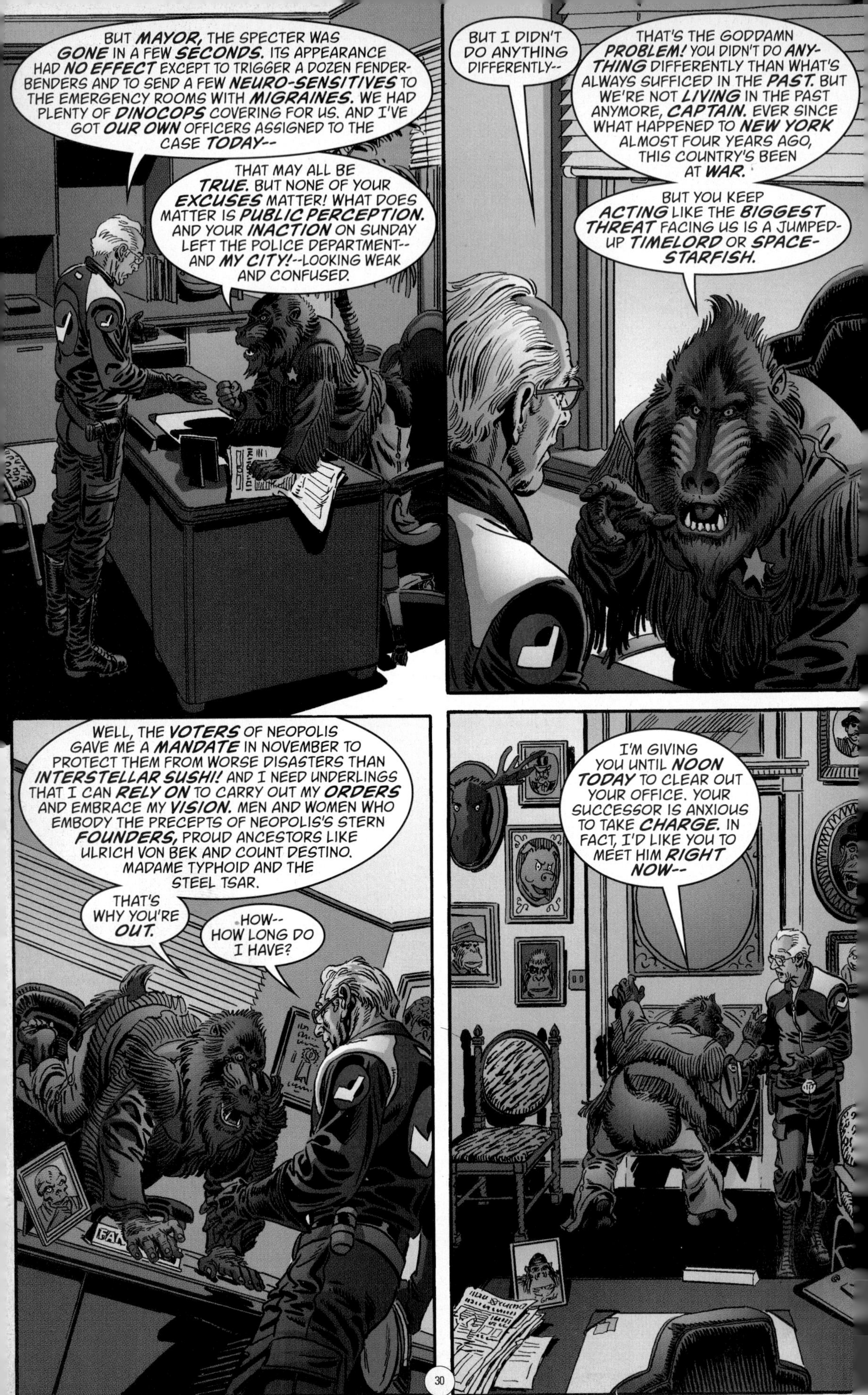
BUT MAYOR, THE SPECTER WAS GONE IN A FEW SECONDS. ITS APPEARANCE HAD NO EFFECT EXCEPT TO TRIGGER A DOZEN FENDER-BENDERS AND TO SEND A FEW NEURO-SENSITIVES TO THE EMERGENCY ROOMS WITH MIGRAINES. WE HAD PLENTY OF DINOCOPS COVERING FOR US. AND I'VE GOT OUR OWN OFFICERS ASSIGNED TO THE CASE TODAY--
THAT MAY ALL BE TRUE. BUT NONE OF YOUR EXCUSES MATTER! WHAT DOES MATTER IS PUBLIC PERCEPTION. AND YOUR INACTION ON SUNDAY LEFT THE POLICE DEPARTMENT--AND MY CITY!--LOOKING WEAK AND CONFUSED.
BUT I DIDN'T DO ANYTHING DIFFERENTLY--
THAT'S THE GODDAMN PROBLEM! YOU DIDN'T DO ANYTHING DIFFERENTLY THAN WHAT'S ALWAYS SUFFICED IN THE PAST. BUT WE'RE NOT LIVING IN THE PAST ANYMORE, CAPTAIN. EVER SINCE WHAT HAPPENED TO NEW YORK ALMOST FOUR YEARS AGO, THIS COUNTRY'S BEEN AT WAR.
BUT YOU KEEP ACTING LIKE THE BIGGEST THREAT FACING US IS A JUMPED-UP TIMELORD OR SPACE-STARFISH.
WELL, THE VOTERS OF NEOPOLIS GAVE ME A MANDATE IN NOVEMBER TO PROTECT THEM FROM WORSE DISASTERS THAN INTERSTELLAR SUSHI! AND I NEED UNDERLINGS THAT I CAN RELY ON TO CARRY OUT MY ORDERS AND EMBRACE MY VISION. MEN AND WOMEN WHO EMBODY THE PRECEPTS OF NEOPOLIS'S STERN FOUNDERS, PROUD ANCESTORS LIKE ULRICH VON BEK AND COUNT DESTINO. MADAME TYPHOID AND THE STEEL TSAR.
THAT'S WHY YOU'RE OUT.
HOW--HOW LONG DO I HAVE?
I'M GIVING YOU UNTIL NOON TODAY TO CLEAR OUT YOUR OFFICE. YOUR SUCCESSOR IS ANXIOUS TO TAKE CHARGE. IN FACT, I'D LIKE YOU TO MEET HIM RIGHT NOW--

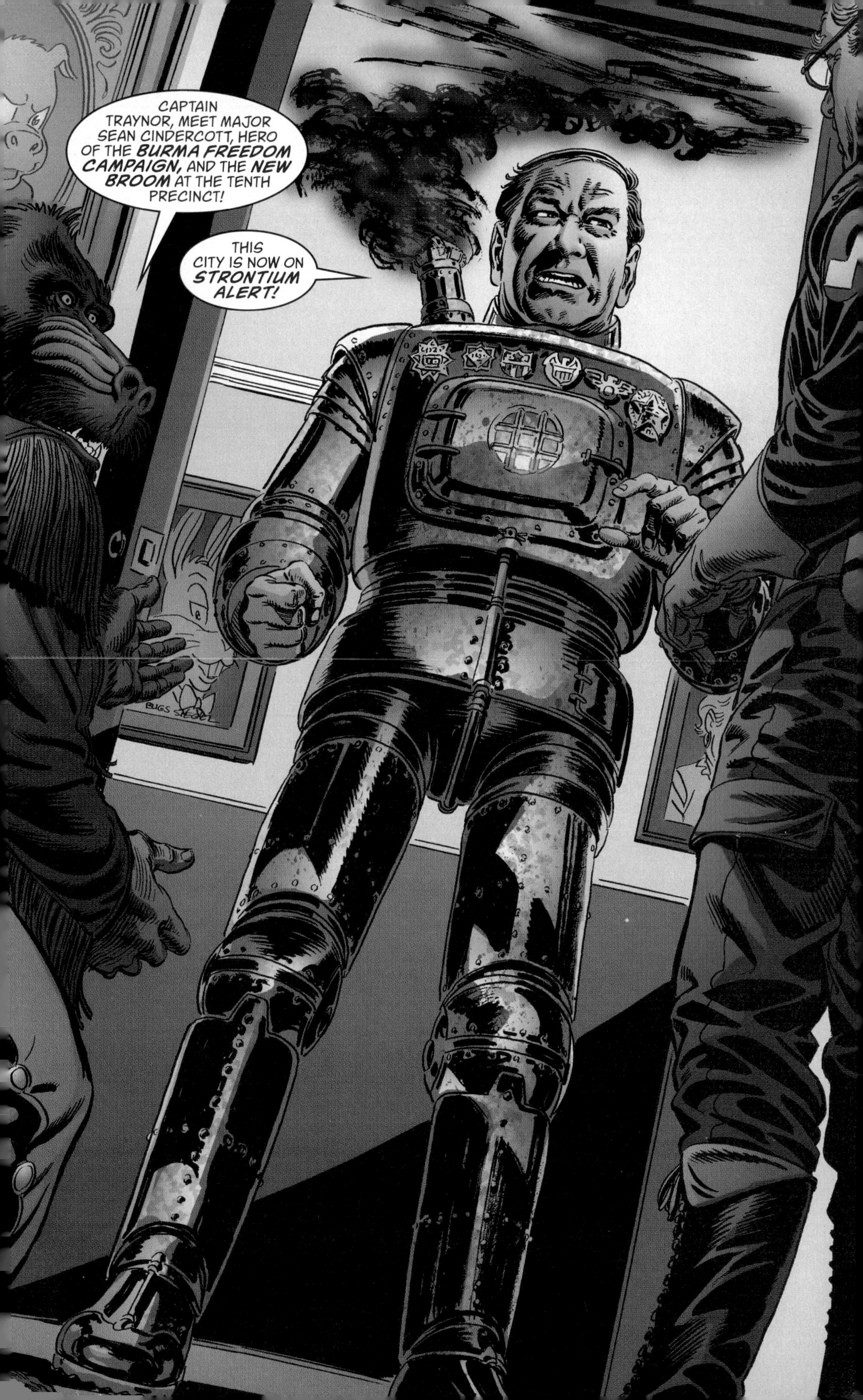
CAPTAIN TRAYNOR, MEET MAJOR SEAN CINDERCOTT, HERO OF THE ***BURMA FREEDOM CAMPAIGN,*** AND THE ***NEW BROOM*** AT THE TENTH PRECINCT!
THIS CITY IS NOW ON ***STRONTIUM ALERT!***

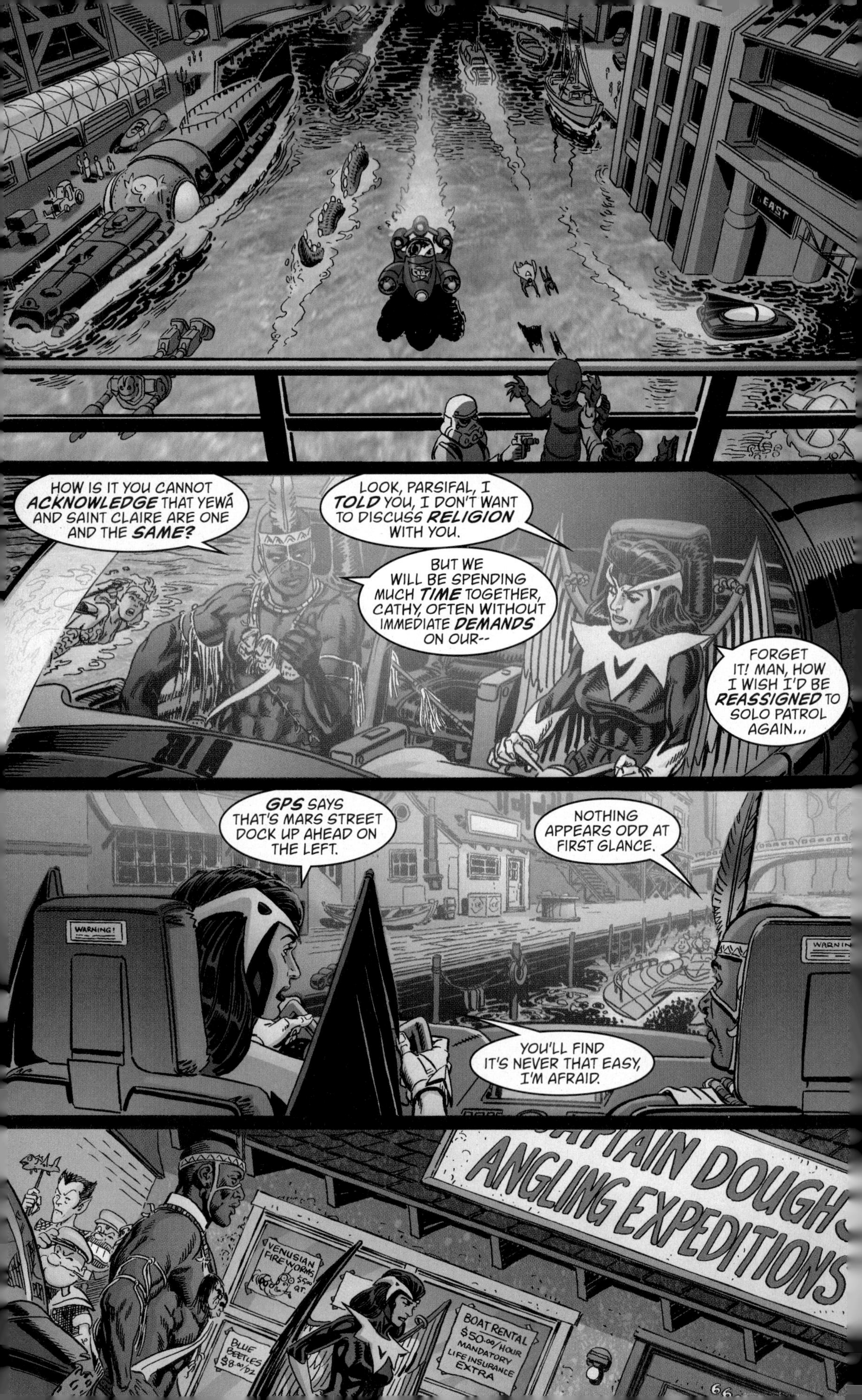
EAST
HOW IS IT YOU CANNOT ACKNOWLEDGE THAT YEWÁ AND SAINT CLAIRE ARE ONE AND THE SAME?
LOOK, PARSIFAL, I TOLD YOU, I DON'T WANT TO DISCUSS RELIGION WITH YOU.
BUT WE WILL BE SPENDING MUCH TIME TOGETHER, CATHY, OFTEN WITHOUT IMMEDIATE DEMANDS ON OUR--
FORGET IT! MAN, HOW I WISH I'D BE REASSIGNED TO SOLO PATROL AGAIN...
GPS SAYS THAT'S MARS STREET DOCK UP AHEAD ON THE LEFT.
NOTHING APPEARS ODD AT FIRST GLANCE.
WARNING!
YOU'LL FIND IT'S NEVER THAT EASY, I'M AFRAID.
ANGLING EXPEDITIONS
VENUSIAN FIREWORMS $5.50 QT.
BOAT RENTAL $50.00/HOUR MANDATORY LIFE INSURANCE EXTRA
BLUE BEETLES $8.00/DZ

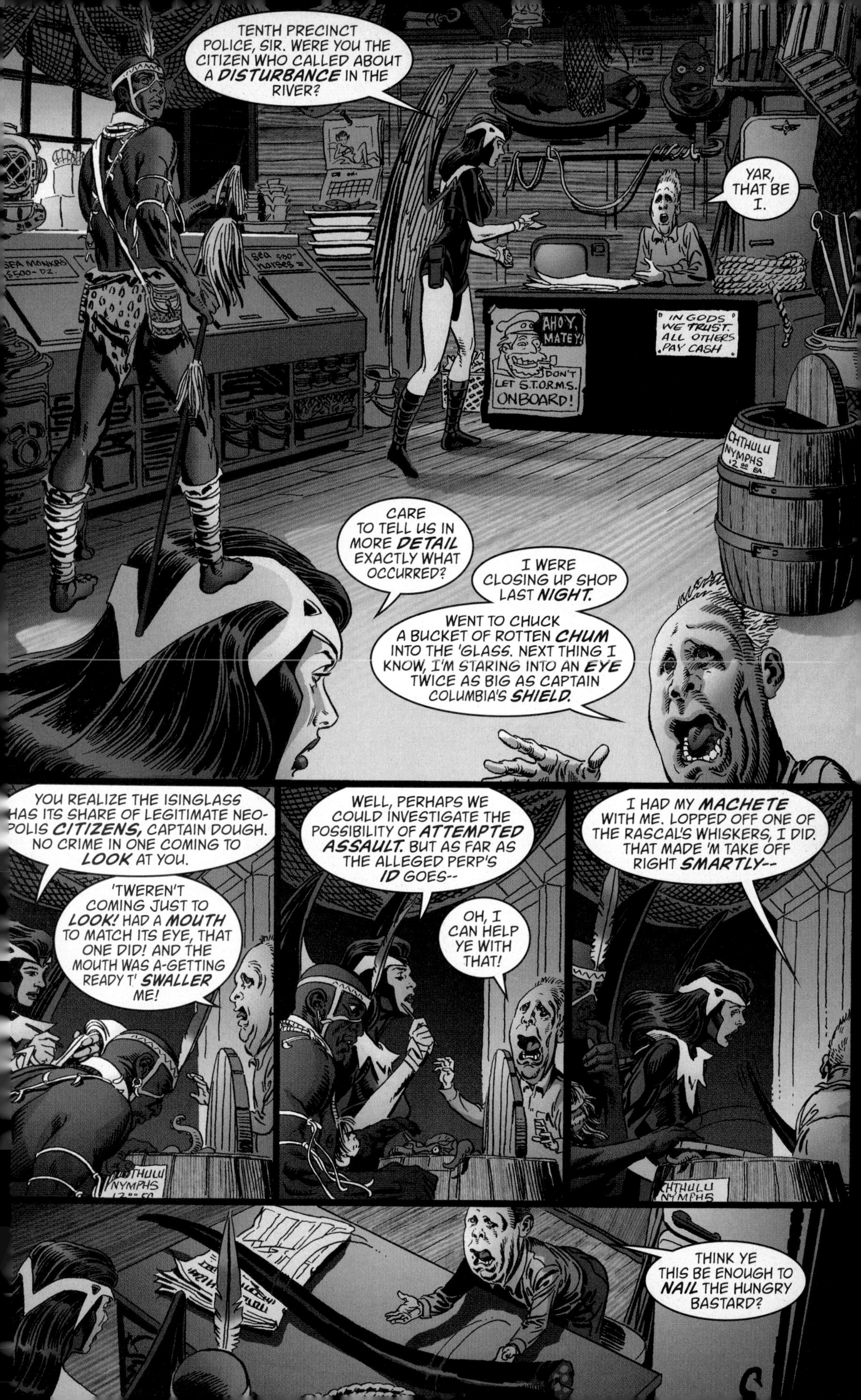
TENTH PRECINCT POLICE, SIR. WERE YOU THE CITIZEN WHO CALLED ABOUT A DISTURBANCE IN THE RIVER?
YAR, THAT BE I.
SEA MONKEYS $500~ DZ.
SEA HORSES
AHOY, MATEY! DON'T LET S.T.O.R.M.S. ONBOARD!
IN GODS WE TRUST. ALL OTHERS PAY CASH
CHTHULU NYMPHS 12.00 EA.
CARE TO TELL US IN MORE DETAIL EXACTLY WHAT OCCURRED?
I WERE CLOSING UP SHOP LAST NIGHT.
WENT TO CHUCK A BUCKET OF ROTTEN CHUM INTO THE 'GLASS. NEXT THING I KNOW, I'M STARING INTO AN EYE TWICE AS BIG AS CAPTAIN COLUMBIA'S SHIELD.
YOU REALIZE THE ISINGLASS HAS ITS SHARE OF LEGITIMATE NEOPOLIS CITIZENS, CAPTAIN DOUGH. NO CRIME IN ONE COMING TO LOOK AT YOU.
'TWEREN'T COMING JUST TO LOOK! HAD A MOUTH TO MATCH ITS EYE, THAT ONE DID! AND THE MOUTH WAS A-GETTING READY T' SWALLER ME!
WELL, PERHAPS WE COULD INVESTIGATE THE POSSIBILITY OF ATTEMPTED ASSAULT. BUT AS FAR AS THE ALLEGED PERP'S ID GOES--
OH, I CAN HELP YE WITH THAT!
I HAD MY MACHETE WITH ME. LOPPED OFF ONE OF THE RASCAL'S WHISKERS, I DID. THAT MADE 'M TAKE OFF RIGHT SMARTLY--
THINK YE THIS BE ENOUGH TO NAIL THE HUNGRY BASTARD?

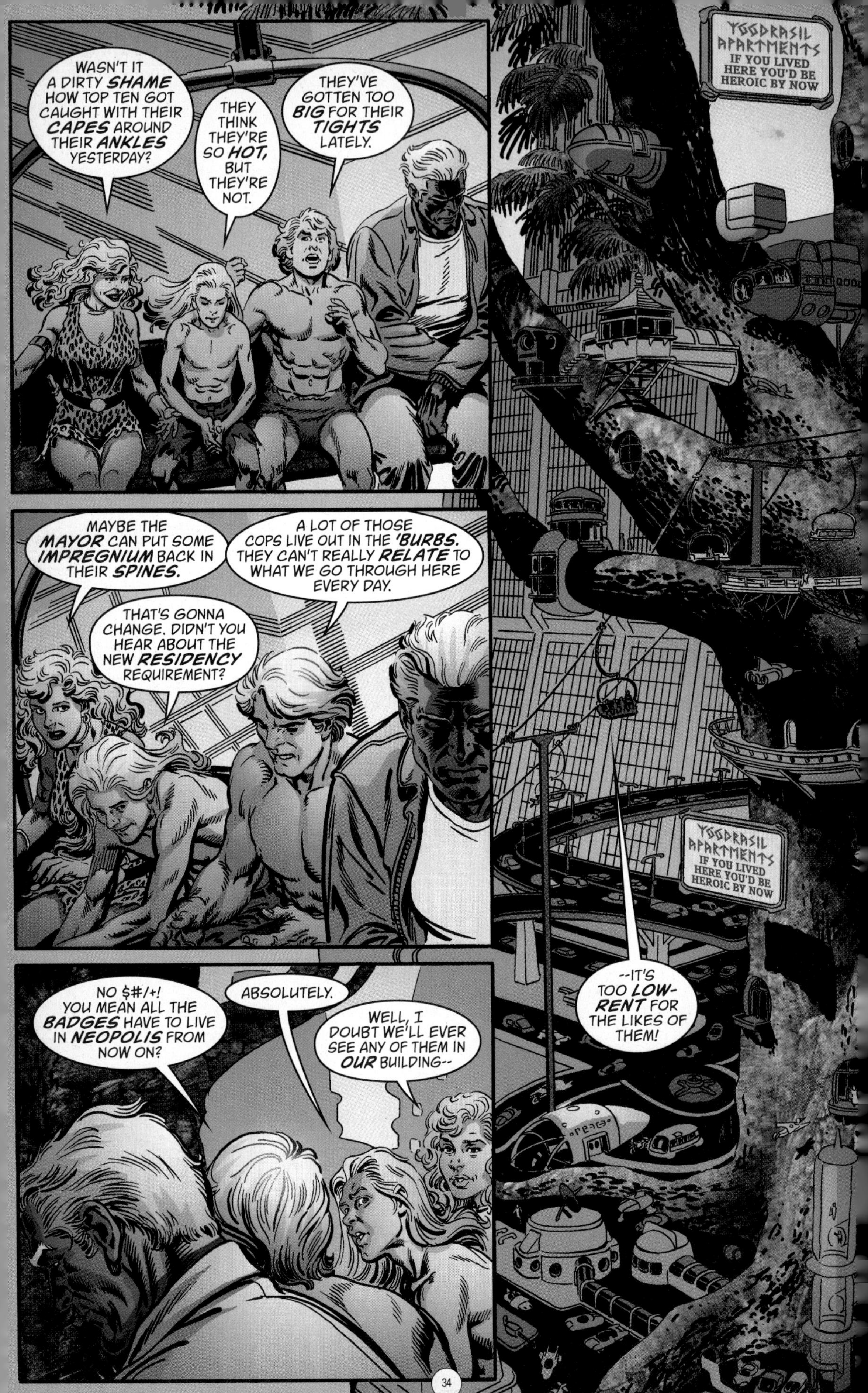

WASN'T IT A DIRTY SHAME HOW TOP TEN GOT CAUGHT WITH THEIR CAPES AROUND THEIR ANKLES YESTERDAY?
THEY THINK THEY'RE SO HOT, BUT THEY'RE NOT.
THEY'VE GOTTEN TOO BIG FOR THEIR TIGHTS LATELY.
YGGDRASIL APARTMENTS
IF YOU LIVED HERE YOU'D BE HEROIC BY NOW
MAYBE THE MAYOR CAN PUT SOME IMPREGNIUM BACK IN THEIR SPINES.
A LOT OF THOSE COPS LIVE OUT IN THE 'BURBS. THEY CAN'T REALLY RELATE TO WHAT WE GO THROUGH HERE EVERY DAY.
THAT'S GONNA CHANGE. DIDN'T YOU HEAR ABOUT THE NEW RESIDENCY REQUIREMENT?
YGGDRASIL APARTMENTS
IF YOU LIVED HERE YOU'D BE HEROIC BY NOW
NO $#/+! YOU MEAN ALL THE BADGES HAVE TO LIVE IN NEOPOLIS FROM NOW ON?
ABSOLUTELY.
WELL, I DOUBT WE'LL EVER SEE ANY OF THEM IN OUR BUILDING--
--IT'S TOO LOW-RENT FOR THE LIKES OF THEM!

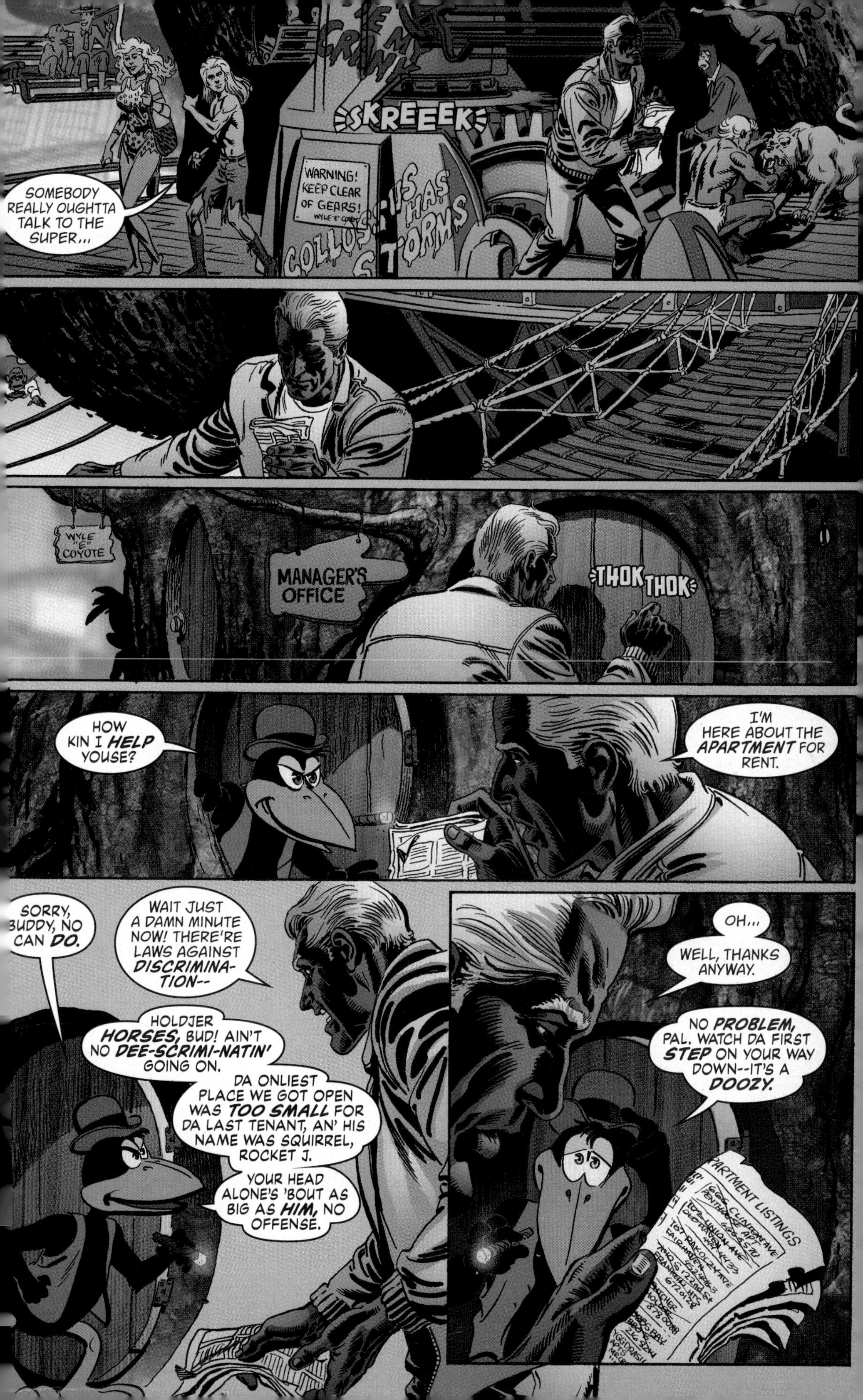
SOMEBODY REALLY OUGHTTA TALK TO THE SUPER...
SKREEEK
WARNING! KEEP CLEAR OF GEARS!
COLLOSSUS HAS STORMS
WYLE "E" COYOTE
MANAGER'S OFFICE
THOK THOK
HOW KIN I HELP YOUSE?
I'M HERE ABOUT THE APARTMENT FOR RENT.
SORRY, BUDDY, NO CAN DO.
WAIT JUST A DAMN MINUTE NOW! THERE'RE LAWS AGAINST DISCRIMINA-TION--
HOLDJER HORSES, BUD! AIN'T NO DEE-SCRIMI-NATIN' GOING ON.
DA ONLIEST PLACE WE GOT OPEN WAS TOO SMALL FOR DA LAST TENANT, AN' HIS NAME WAS SQUIRREL, ROCKET J.
YOUR HEAD ALONE'S 'BOUT AS BIG AS HIM, NO OFFENSE.
OH...
WELL, THANKS ANYWAY.
NO PROBLEM, PAL. WATCH DA FIRST STEP ON YOUR WAY DOWN--IT'S A DOOZY.
APARTMENT LISTINGS

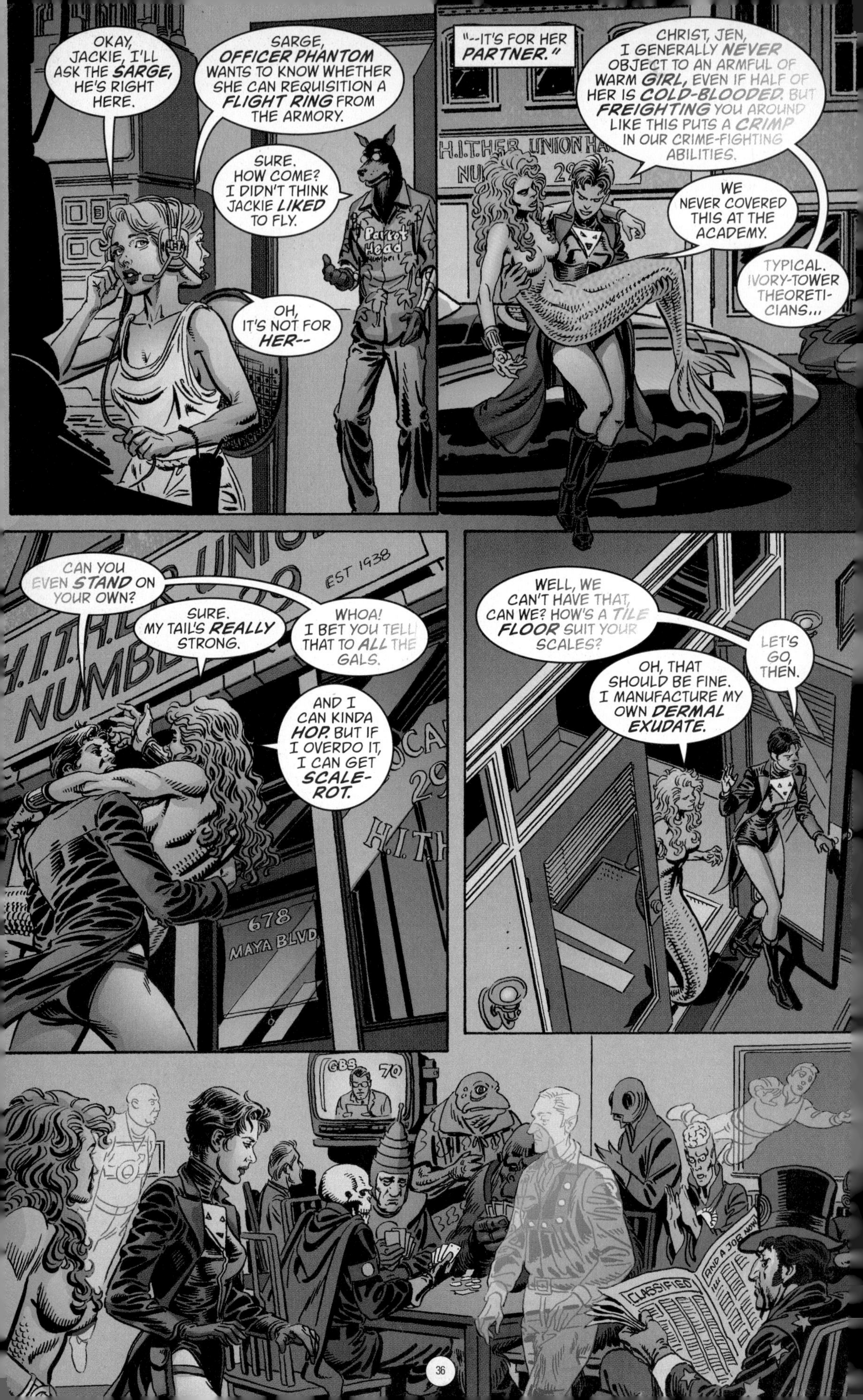
OKAY, JACKIE, I'LL ASK THE SARGE, HE'S RIGHT HERE.
SARGE, OFFICER PHANTOM WANTS TO KNOW WHETHER SHE CAN REQUISITION A FLIGHT RING FROM THE ARMORY.
SURE. HOW COME? I DIDN'T THINK JACKIE LIKED TO FLY.
OH, IT'S NOT FOR HER--
Parrot Head
"--IT'S FOR HER PARTNER."
CHRIST, JEN, I GENERALLY NEVER OBJECT TO AN ARMFUL OF WARM GIRL, EVEN IF HALF OF HER IS COLD-BLOODED. BUT FREIGHTING YOU AROUND LIKE THIS PUTS A CRIMP IN OUR CRIME-FIGHTING ABILITIES.
WE NEVER COVERED THIS AT THE ACADEMY.
TYPICAL. IVORY-TOWER THEORETICIANS...
EST 1938
CAN YOU EVEN STAND ON YOUR OWN?
SURE. MY TAIL'S REALLY STRONG.
WHOA! I BET YOU TELL THAT TO ALL THE GALS.
AND I CAN KINDA HOP. BUT IF I OVERDO IT, I CAN GET SCALE-ROT.
678 MAYA BLVD.
WELL, WE CAN'T HAVE THAT, CAN WE? HOW'S A TILE FLOOR SUIT YOUR SCALES?
LET'S GO, THEN.
OH, THAT SHOULD BE FINE. I MANUFACTURE MY OWN DERMAL EXUDATE.
GBS 70
CLASSIFIED
AND A JOB NOW

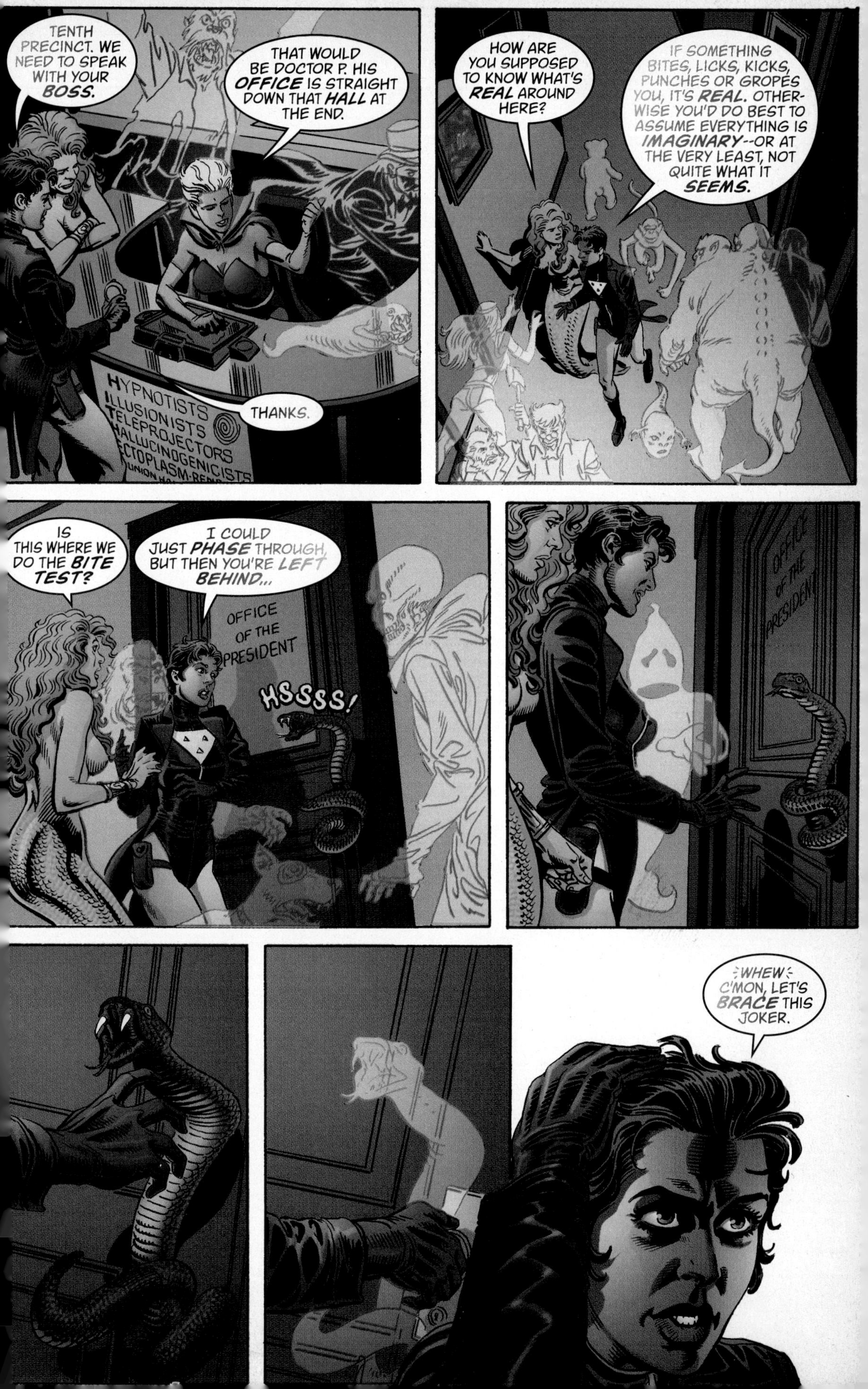
TENTH PRECINCT. WE NEED TO SPEAK WITH YOUR BOSS.
THAT WOULD BE DOCTOR P. HIS OFFICE IS STRAIGHT DOWN THAT HALL AT THE END.
HYPNOTISTS
ILLUSIONISTS
TELEPROJECTORS
HALLUCINOGENICISTS
ECTOPLASM-REND...
UNION HA...
THANKS.
HOW ARE YOU SUPPOSED TO KNOW WHAT'S REAL AROUND HERE?
IF SOMETHING BITES, LICKS, KICKS, PUNCHES OR GROPES YOU, IT'S REAL. OTHERWISE YOU'D DO BEST TO ASSUME EVERYTHING IS IMAGINARY--OR AT THE VERY LEAST, NOT QUITE WHAT IT SEEMS.
IS THIS WHERE WE DO THE BITE TEST?
I COULD JUST PHASE THROUGH, BUT THEN YOU'RE LEFT BEHIND...
OFFICE OF THE PRESIDENT
HSSSS!
OFFICE OF THE PRESIDENT
WHEW
C'MON, LET'S BRACE THIS JOKER.

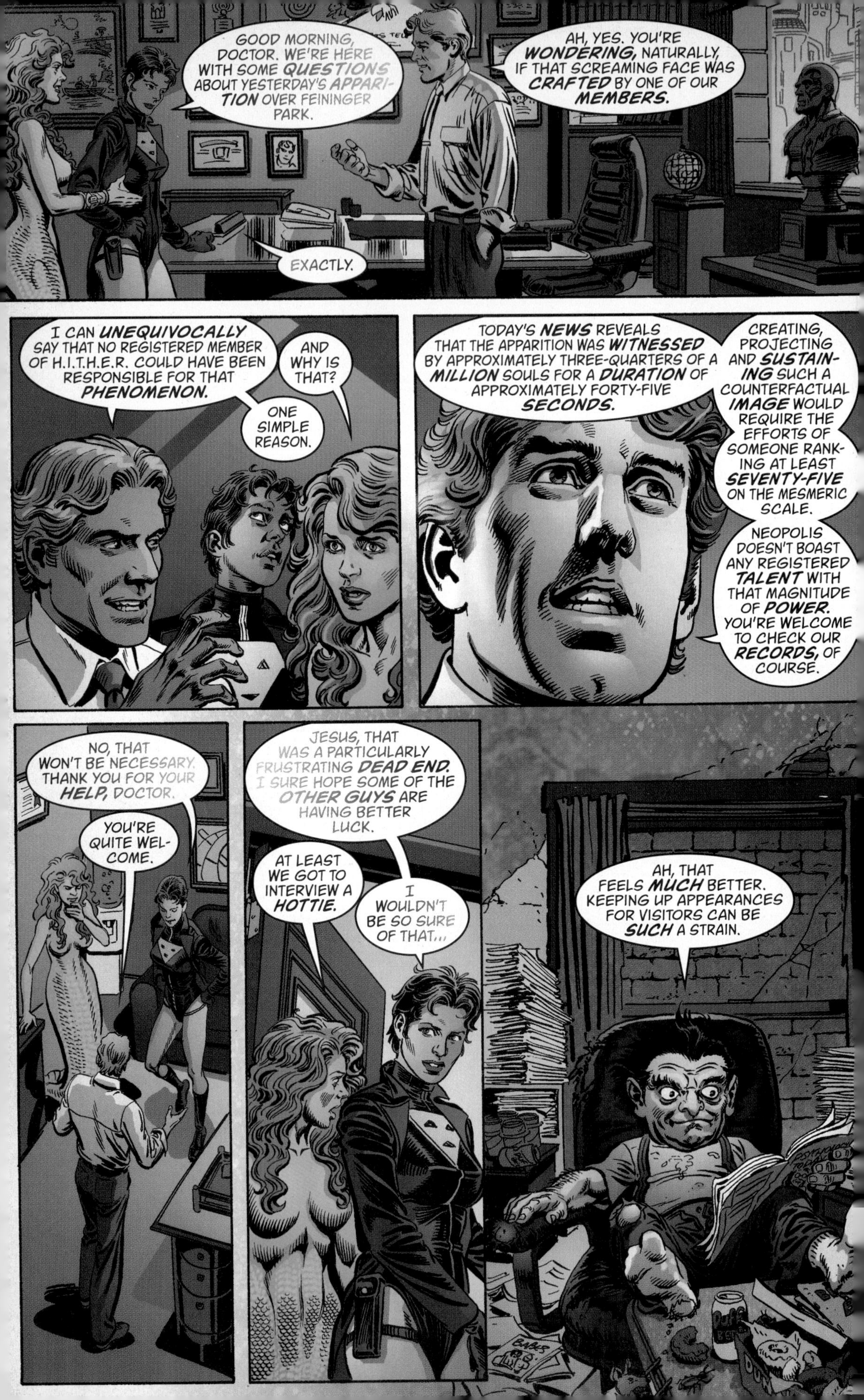
GOOD MORNING, DOCTOR. WE'RE HERE WITH SOME QUESTIONS ABOUT YESTERDAY'S APPARITION OVER FEININGER PARK.
AH, YES. YOU'RE WONDERING, NATURALLY, IF THAT SCREAMING FACE WAS CRAFTED BY ONE OF OUR MEMBERS.
EXACTLY.
I CAN UNEQUIVOCALLY SAY THAT NO REGISTERED MEMBER OF H.I.T.H.E.R. COULD HAVE BEEN RESPONSIBLE FOR THAT PHENOMENON.
AND WHY IS THAT?
ONE SIMPLE REASON.
TODAY'S NEWS REVEALS THAT THE APPARITION WAS WITNESSED BY APPROXIMATELY THREE-QUARTERS OF A MILLION SOULS FOR A DURATION OF APPROXIMATELY FORTY-FIVE SECONDS.
CREATING, PROJECTING AND SUSTAINING SUCH A COUNTERFACTUAL IMAGE WOULD REQUIRE THE EFFORTS OF SOMEONE RANKING AT LEAST SEVENTY-FIVE ON THE MESMERIC SCALE.
NEOPOLIS DOESN'T BOAST ANY REGISTERED TALENT WITH THAT MAGNITUDE OF POWER. YOU'RE WELCOME TO CHECK OUR RECORDS, OF COURSE.
NO, THAT WON'T BE NECESSARY. THANK YOU FOR YOUR HELP, DOCTOR.
YOU'RE QUITE WELCOME.
JESUS, THAT WAS A PARTICULARLY FRUSTRATING DEAD END. I SURE HOPE SOME OF THE OTHER GUYS ARE HAVING BETTER LUCK.
AT LEAST WE GOT TO INTERVIEW A HOTTIE.
I WOULDN'T BE SO SURE OF THAT...
AH, THAT FEELS MUCH BETTER. KEEPING UP APPEARANCES FOR VISITORS CAN BE SUCH A STRAIN.
BABES

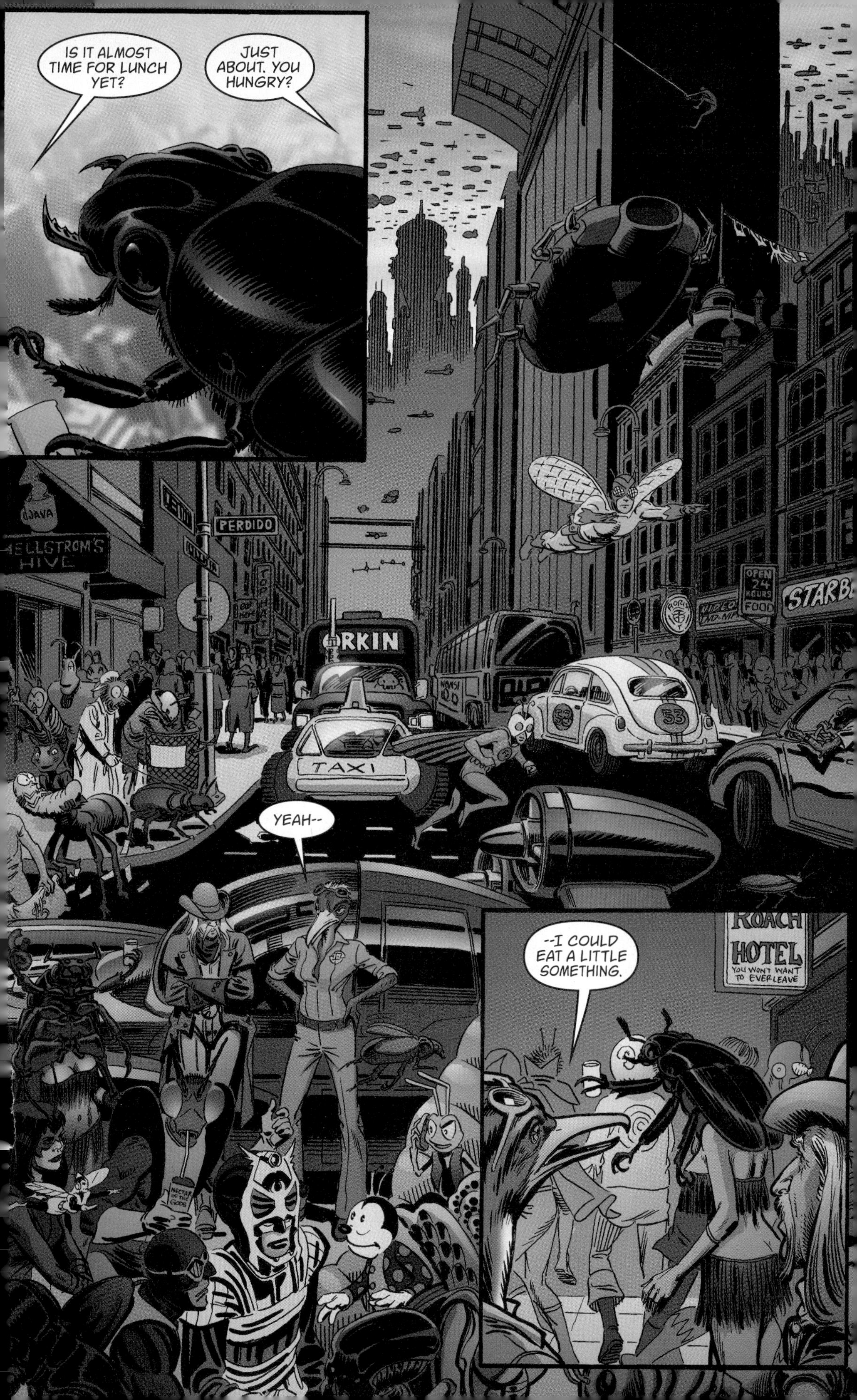
IS IT ALMOST TIME FOR LUNCH YET?
JUST ABOUT. YOU HUNGRY?
JAVA
HELLSTROM'S HIVE
PERDIDO
TOP HAT
ORKIN
TAXI
OPEN 24 HOURS FOOD
STARB
53
YEAH--
ROACH HOTEL
YOU WON'T WANT TO EVER LEAVE
--I COULD EAT A LITTLE SOMETHING.
NECTAR OF THE GODS

WELL, HANG ON TO YOUR *APPETITE.* WE'LL TAKE OUR BREAK RIGHT AFTER WE *RUN* THIS LEAD *DOWN.*

SWEET.

MAN, I DON'T KNOW HOW YOU CAN EVEN *THINK* OF FOOD RIGHT NOW. MY STOMACH'S ALL *TWISTED UP.* I PURELY *HATE* COMIN' TO BUGTOWN.

I'VE NEVER BEEN HERE *BEFORE,* BUT I FIND IT KIND OF-- *ALLURING.*

BUSY BEE DINER

WELL, YOU WON'T TOTE UP A *HELLUVA* LOT OF COMPANY ON *THAT* SCORE. MOST FOLKS PLAIN *REVILE* THIS PART OF TOWN. AH, HERE'S OUR STREET.

CHIGGER WAY

DRAGONFLY LN

CALL ME A *CHORDATE CHAUVINIST,* BUT I THINK THESE *CREEPY-CRAWLIES* BELONG IN THEIR OWN PART OF TOWN. AND A LOT OF REGU-LAR FOLKS *SYMPATHIZE* WITH ME.

THAT'S WHY *BUGTOWN* ENDED UP WITH THE WORST *REAL ESTATE* IN THE WHOLE DANG *RANCH.*

WHAT DO YOU MEAN?

CHIGGER WAY

HELL DITCH WAS HERE *BEFORE* NEOPOLIS WAS BUILT. THAT'S WHY THE *FEDS* GAVE AWAY THIS *LAND* TO THE *SCIENCE NAZIS* IN THE FIRST PLACE.

THAT'S THE *FLATLINERS DIS-TRICT* 'CROSS THE CANYON. ANOTHER BUNCHA *LOSERS...*

BITE MY THORAX

JOEY C HUFFS RAID

TRACI'S ONLY A LARVA BUT SHE BUZZES LIKE AN IMAGO

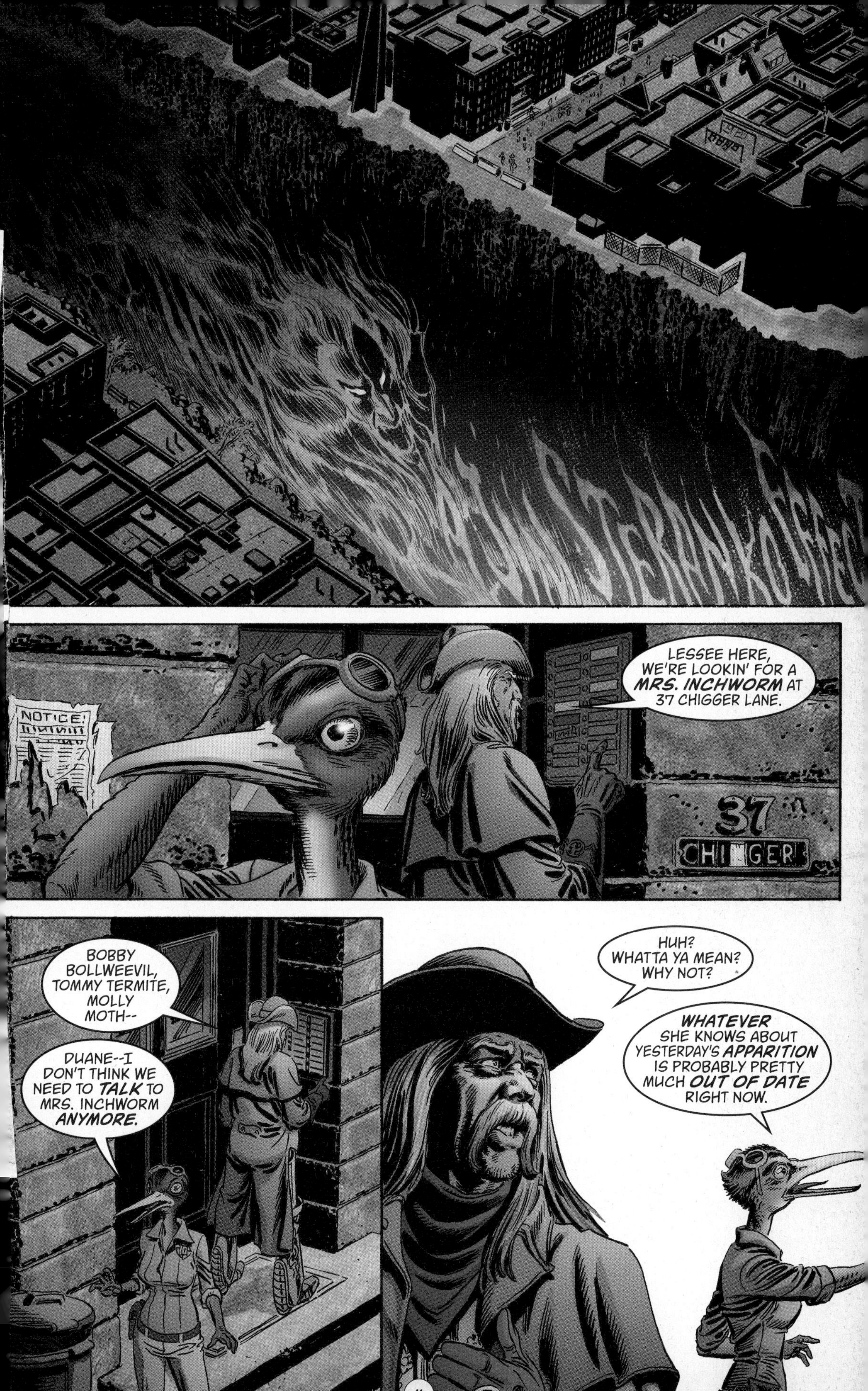
NOTICE!
LESSEE HERE, WE'RE LOOKIN' FOR A ***MRS. INCHWORM*** AT 37 CHIGGER LANE.
37
CHI GER
BOBBY BOLLWEEVIL, TOMMY TERMITE, MOLLY MOTH--
DUANE--I DON'T THINK WE NEED TO ***TALK*** TO MRS. INCHWORM ***ANYMORE.***
HUH? WHATTA YA MEAN? WHY NOT?
WHATEVER SHE KNOWS ABOUT YESTERDAY'S ***APPARITION*** IS PROBABLY PRETTY MUCH ***OUT OF DATE*** RIGHT NOW.

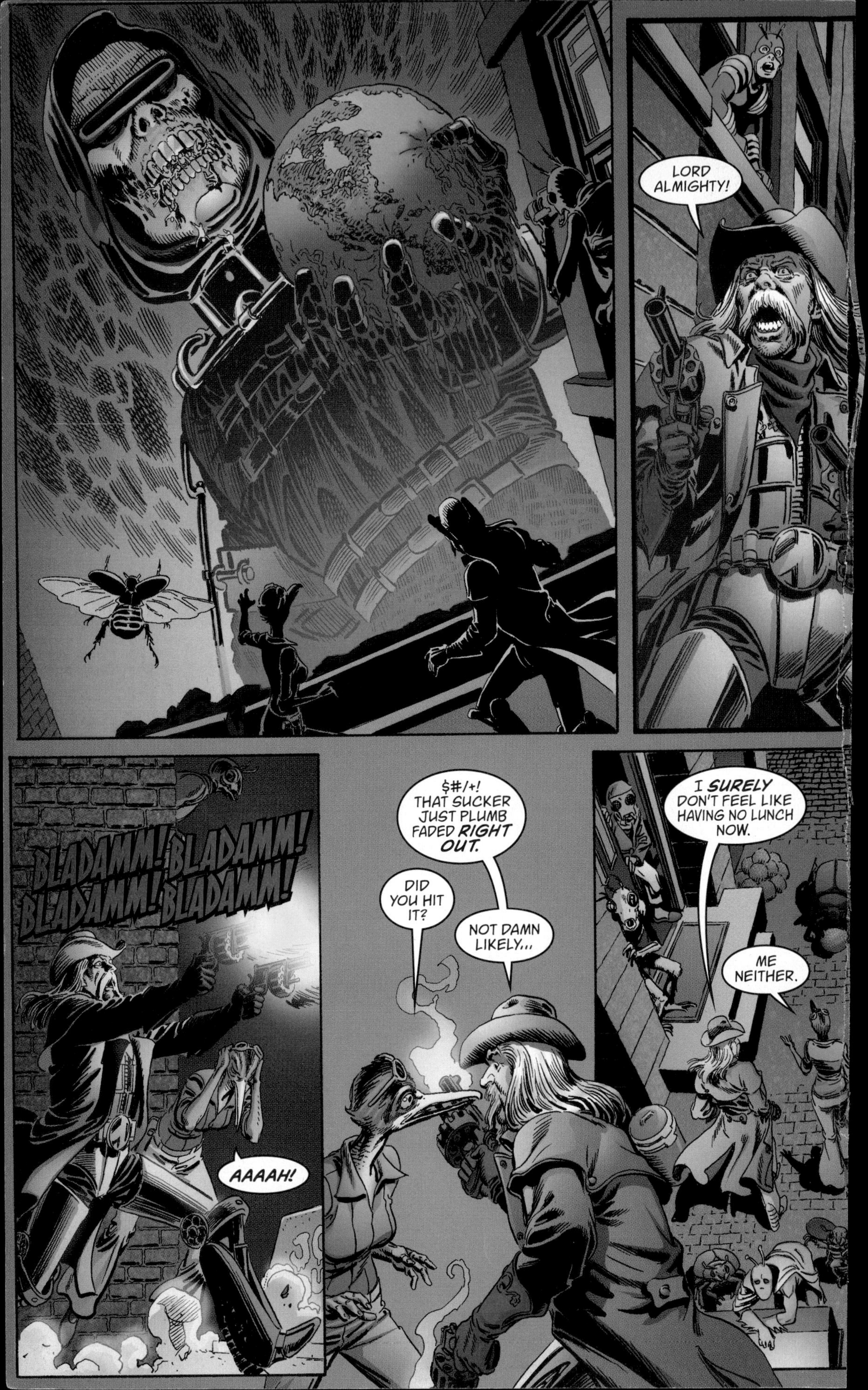

LORD ALMIGHTY!
BLADAMM! BLADAMM! BLADAMM! BLADAMM!
AAAAH!
$#/+! THAT SUCKER JUST PLUMB FADED RIGHT OUT.
DID YOU HIT IT?
NOT DAMN LIKELY...
I SURELY DON'T FEEL LIKE HAVING NO LUNCH NOW.
ME NEITHER.

VIVA SELENIA! LA REINA DE DIGI-TEJANO!

LOS ROBOTOS

ODE TO THE DEATHSTAR

EL BRUCE STEELSPRING

UM, YOU LIKE HER STUFF?

NAW, NOT REALLY. I'M MORE INTO *NARCOCORRIDO*.

OH...

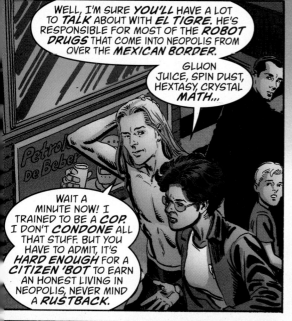

WELL, I'M SURE *YOU'LL* HAVE A LOT TO *TALK* ABOUT WITH *EL TIGRE*. HE'S RESPONSIBLE FOR MOST OF THE *ROBOT DRUGS* THAT COME INTO NEOPOLIS FROM OVER THE *MEXICAN BORDER*.

GLUON JUICE, SPIN DUST, HEXTASY, CRYSTAL *MATH*...

WAIT A MINUTE NOW! I TRAINED TO BE A *COP*. I DON'T *CONDONE* ALL THAT STUFF. BUT YOU HAVE TO ADMIT, IT'S *HARD ENOUGH* FOR A *CITIZEN 'BOT* TO EARN AN HONEST LIVING IN NEOPOLIS, NEVER MIND A *RUSTBACK*.

Petrol De Beber

ANYWAY, IF THIS *EL TIGRE* IS SUCH A BAD@$$, HOW COME WE DON'T *PULL HIM* OFF THE *STREETS?*

DON'T THINK WE HAVEN'T *TRIED*. BUT THE *D.A.* JUST HASN'T BEEN ABLE TO MAKE ANY CHARGES *STICK*. EL TIGRE IS AS SLIPPERY AS A *BUTTERED RAINBOW*.

Los Hermanos Hernand EMBARCADORES

PARTES DISPONIBLES

BUENAS DIAS. ¿TIENE UNA CITA?

PLEASE SPEAK ENGLISH. SPANISH SMELLS TOO MUCH LIKE *BULLS' BLOOD* TO ME.

"MACK"

LANGUAGE CHIPS

HOW MAY I HELP YOU?

TOP TEN, *CHICADROID*. WE NEED TO SEE EL TIGRE.

ONE MOMENT THEN...

CLICK!

"CHICADROID?"

HEY, WOMEN ARE **WOMEN**, WHETHER THEY'RE SILICON OR MEAT. THEY ALL APPRECIATE IT WHEN YOU COMMENT ON THEIR **GOOD LOOKS.**

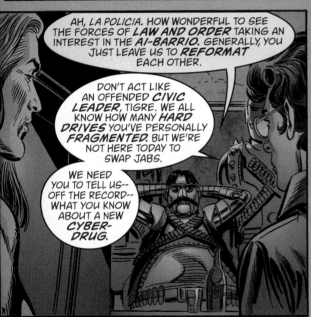

AH, *LA POLICIA.* HOW WONDERFUL TO SEE THE FORCES OF **LAW AND ORDER** TAKING AN INTEREST IN THE **AI-BARRIO.** GENERALLY, YOU JUST LEAVE US TO **REFORMAT** EACH OTHER.

DON'T ACT LIKE AN OFFENDED **CIVIC LEADER,** TIGRE. WE ALL KNOW HOW MANY **HARD DRIVES** YOU'VE PERSONALLY **FRAGMENTED.** BUT WE'RE NOT HERE TODAY TO SWAP JABS.

WE NEED YOU TO TELL US-- OFF THE RECORD-- WHAT YOU KNOW ABOUT A NEW **CYBER-DRUG.**

SO, YOU HAVE FINALLY STUMBLED ACROSS **DARKSHOTS.** THIS IS A RELATIVELY **NEW** DRUG I DO NOT TRADE IN. NOT BECAUSE I **OBJECT** TO ITS EXTREME POTENCY, BUT ONLY BECAUSE I HAVE NO **SOURCE** FOR IT.

POWERPC   SCARPANEL

INTEL
INSIDE

WHAT IS THE STUFF? WHAT'S IT DO?

EACH **DARKSHOT** IS NOTHING LESS THAN A SMALL CAPTURED QUANTITY OF **DARK ENERGY,** A CONCENTRATED CHARGE OF THE **VIRTUAL PARTICLES** THAT BIND THE **GALAXIES** TOGETHER. AS FOR ITS EFFECTS--

--IT APPEARS TO ALLOW **MACHINE CONSCIOUSNESS** TO ACCESS THE ROOT CONTROLS OF THE **MULTIVERSE** IN SOME FASHION.

AND BELIEVE ME, AMIGOS, THAT IS ONE **MUY PICANTE** KICK.

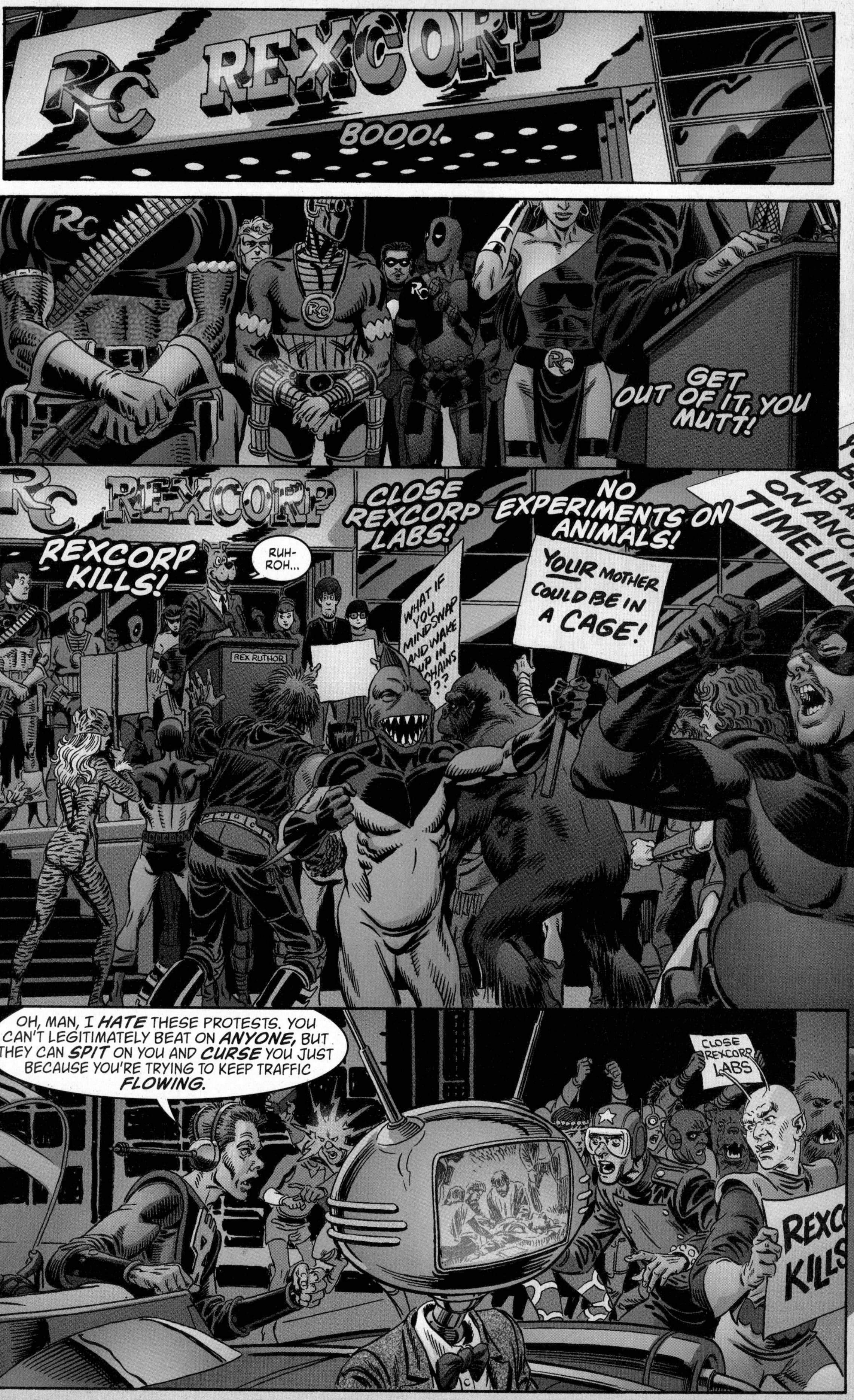
RC REXCORP
BOOO!
GET OUT OF IT, YOU MUTT!
RC REXCORP
REXCORP KILLS!
RUH-ROH...
CLOSE REXCORP LABS!
NO EXPERIMENTS ON ANIMALS!
REX RUTHOR
WHAT IF YOU MINDSWAP AND WAKE UP IN CHAINS??
YOUR MOTHER COULD BE IN A CAGE!
OH, MAN, I HATE THESE PROTESTS. YOU CAN'T LEGITIMATELY BEAT ON ANYONE, BUT THEY CAN SPIT ON YOU AND CURSE YOU JUST BECAUSE YOU'RE TRYING TO KEEP TRAFFIC FLOWING.
CLOSE REXCORP LABS

ANY THREATS OF *VIOLENCE* SO FAR? WE HAD A TIP THAT A NEW GROUP OF *ANARCHISTS* WAS PLANNING TO SHOW UP.

NOTHING YET, SIR.

YOU'D BE A LAB ANIMAL IN ANOTHER TIMELINE

HUH--?

VRRRRRRRRRRRRRRRRRRRRRRRRRRRRR

ONLY HIT THE *BAD GUYS!*

YAY!

OUCH!

WHAT THE--

TIK!

TIK!

THOK!

TIK!

THOK!

FREE JELLY BEANS!

WHO ARE THEY?

YAY!

DAMN, THEY GOT AWAY.

SWEETS FOR THE SOURPUSSES, COURTESY OF THE DERRIDADAISTS

IT'S A MATCH. OUR BOY IS *BAYOU BILLY.* WANTED FOR *MURDER* AND *ASSAULT* IN EVERY STATE THAT BORDERS THE *MISSISSIPPI.*

SUSPECT MATCH

"BAYOU BILLY" *ICTALURUS PUNCTATUS*

SIZE RATIO

I'M GOING TO HAVE TO CONSULT WITH *CAPTAIN TRAYNOR* ON OUR NEXT MOVE. PARSIFAL AND I CAN'T HANDLE THIS *ALONE...*

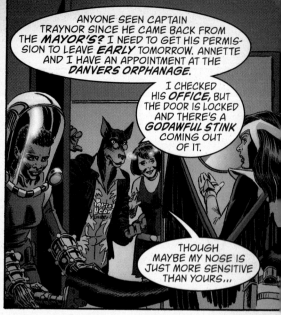

ANYONE SEEN CAPTAIN TRAYNOR SINCE HE CAME BACK FROM THE *MAYOR'S?* I NEED TO GET HIS PERMISSION TO LEAVE *EARLY* TOMORROW. ANNETTE AND I HAVE AN APPOINTMENT AT THE *DANVERS ORPHANAGE.*

I CHECKED HIS *OFFICE,* BUT THE DOOR IS LOCKED AND THERE'S A *GODAWFUL STINK* COMING OUT OF IT.

THOUGH MAYBE MY NOSE IS JUST MORE SENSITIVE THAN YOURS...

THAT DOESN'T *SOUND* RIGHT.

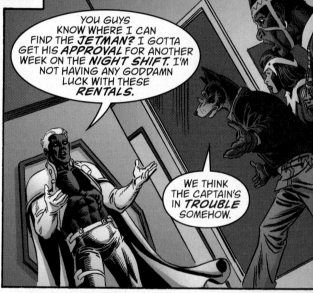

YOU GUYS KNOW WHERE I CAN FIND THE *JETMAN?* I GOTTA GET HIS *APPROVAL* FOR ANOTHER WEEK ON THE *NIGHT SHIFT.* I'M NOT HAVING ANY GODDAMN LUCK WITH THESE *RENTALS.*

WE THINK THE CAPTAIN'S IN *TROUBLE* SOMEHOW.

WHAT THE HELL ARE WE JABBERING ABOUT *PERSONAL PROBLEMS* FOR THEN?

CAPTAIN, CAN YOU HEAR ME? *OPEN UP!*

STEVE, ARE YOU *OKAY?*

WHO'S IN THERE? *REVEAL YOURSELF!*

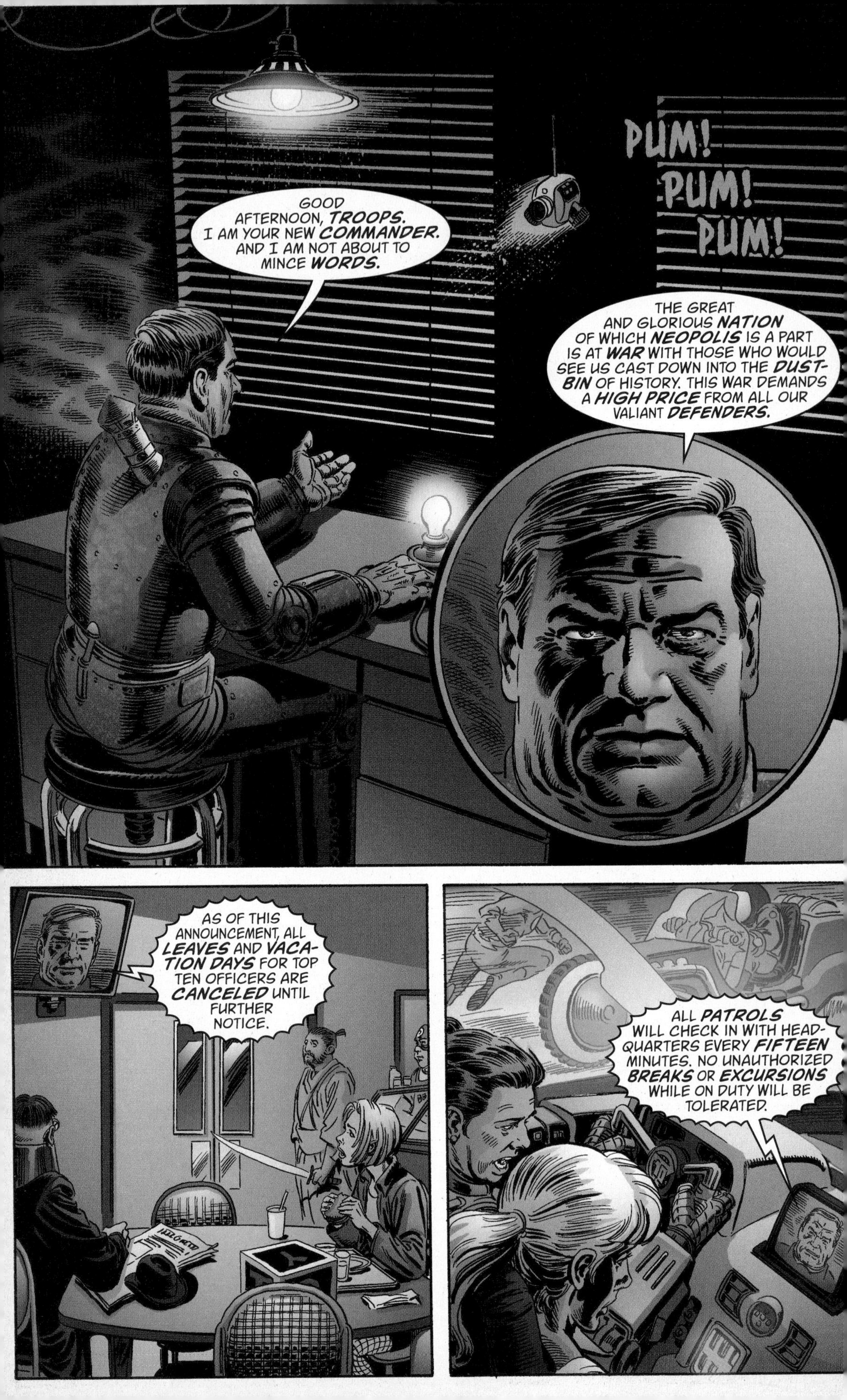
PUM! PUM! PUM!
GOOD AFTERNOON, TROOPS. I AM YOUR NEW COMMANDER. AND I AM NOT ABOUT TO MINCE WORDS.
THE GREAT AND GLORIOUS NATION OF WHICH NEOPOLIS IS A PART IS AT WAR WITH THOSE WHO WOULD SEE US CAST DOWN INTO THE DUST-BIN OF HISTORY. THIS WAR DEMANDS A HIGH PRICE FROM ALL OUR VALIANT DEFENDERS.
AS OF THIS ANNOUNCEMENT, ALL LEAVES AND VACA-TION DAYS FOR TOP TEN OFFICERS ARE CANCELED UNTIL FURTHER NOTICE.
ALL PATROLS WILL CHECK IN WITH HEAD-QUARTERS EVERY FIFTEEN MINUTES. NO UNAUTHORIZED BREAKS OR EXCURSIONS WHILE ON DUTY WILL BE TOLERATED.

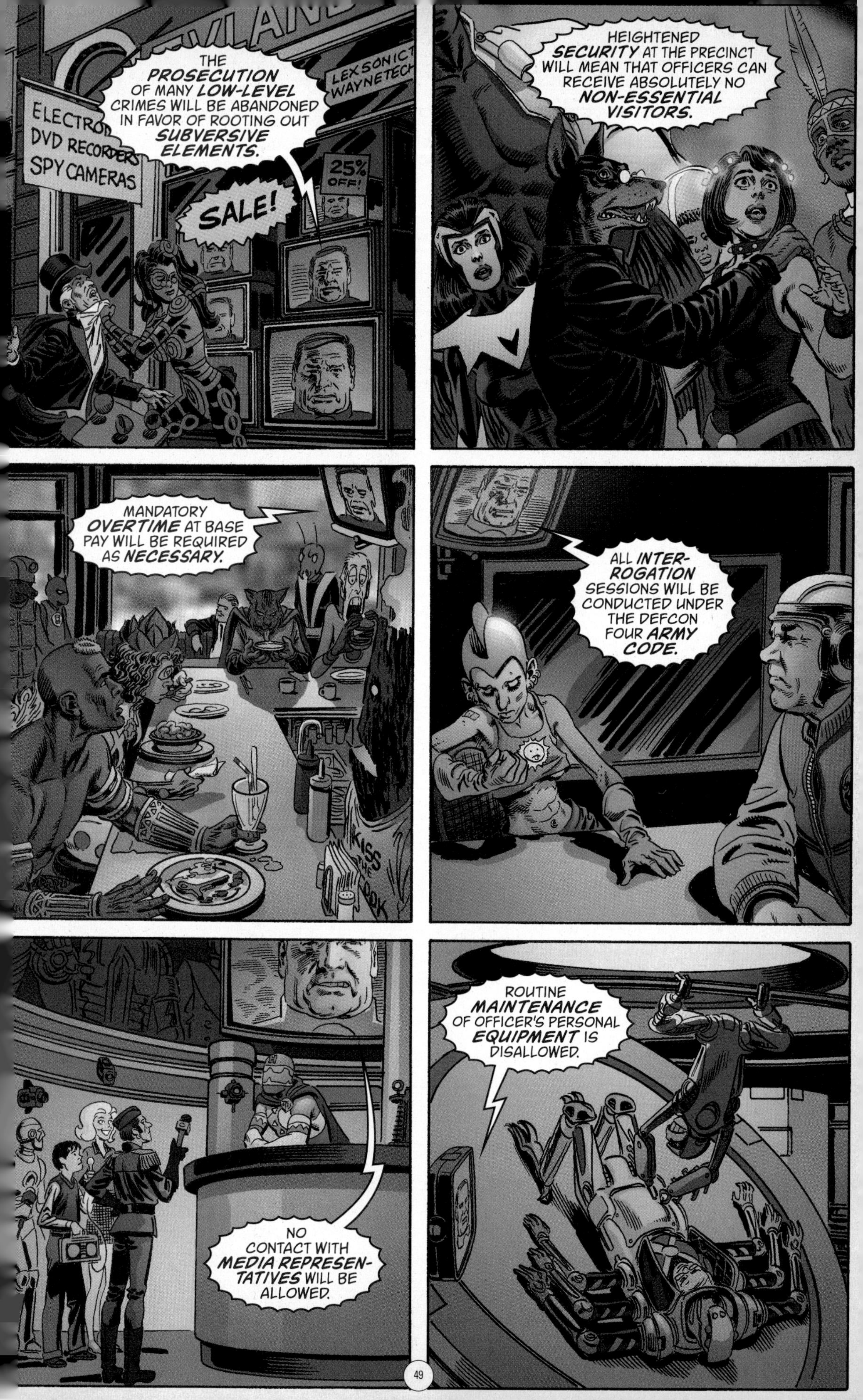

ELECTRO
DVD RECORDERS
SPY CAMERAS
LEXSONIC
WAYNETECH
THE PROSECUTION OF MANY LOW-LEVEL CRIMES WILL BE ABANDONED IN FAVOR OF ROOTING OUT SUBVERSIVE ELEMENTS.
25% OFF!
SALE!
HEIGHTENED SECURITY AT THE PRECINCT WILL MEAN THAT OFFICERS CAN RECEIVE ABSOLUTELY NO NON-ESSENTIAL VISITORS.
MANDATORY OVERTIME AT BASE PAY WILL BE REQUIRED AS NECESSARY.
KISS THE COOK
ALL INTER-ROGATION SESSIONS WILL BE CONDUCTED UNDER THE DEFCON FOUR ARMY CODE.
NO CONTACT WITH MEDIA REPRESEN-TATIVES WILL BE ALLOWED.
ROUTINE MAINTENANCE OF OFFICER'S PERSONAL EQUIPMENT IS DISALLOWED.

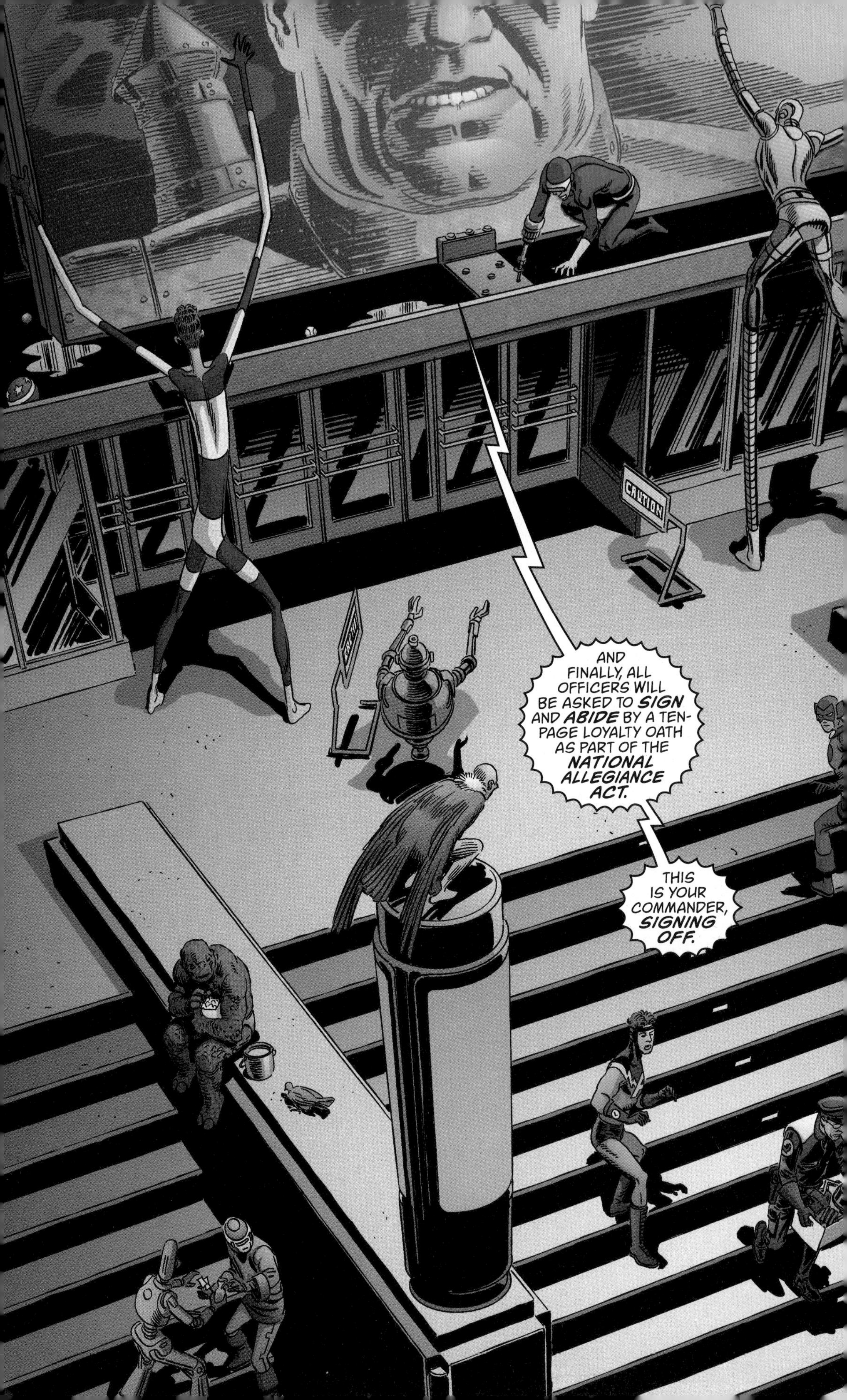
CAUTION
CAUTION
AND FINALLY, ALL OFFICERS WILL BE ASKED TO **SIGN** AND **ABIDE** BY A TEN-PAGE LOYALTY OATH AS PART OF THE **NATIONAL ALLEGIANCE ACT.**
THIS IS YOUR COMMANDER, **SIGNING OFF.**

CHAPTER #3

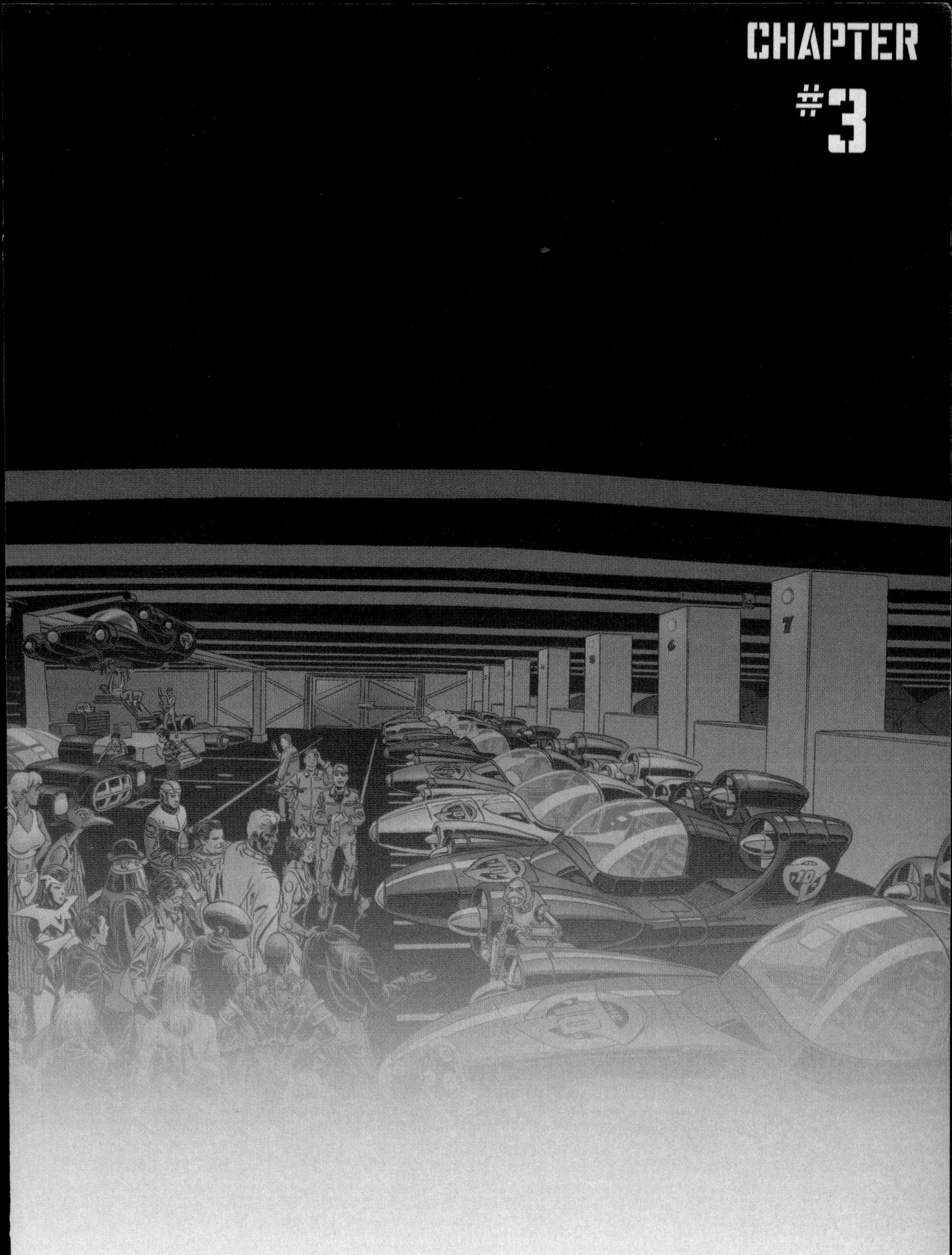

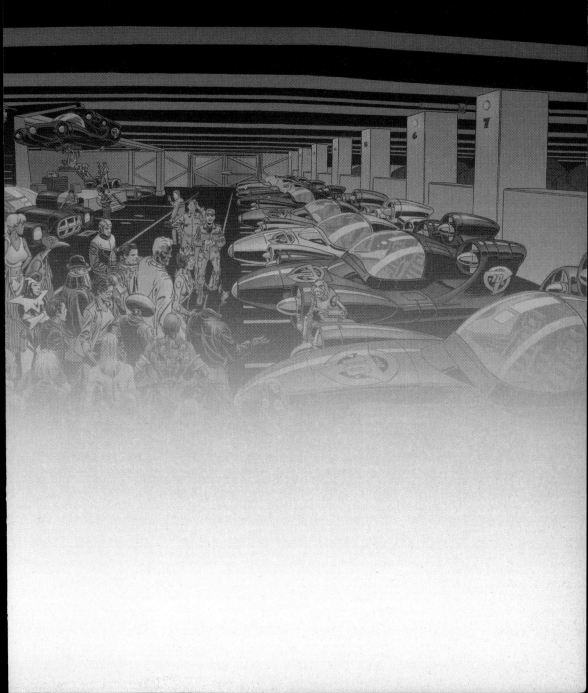

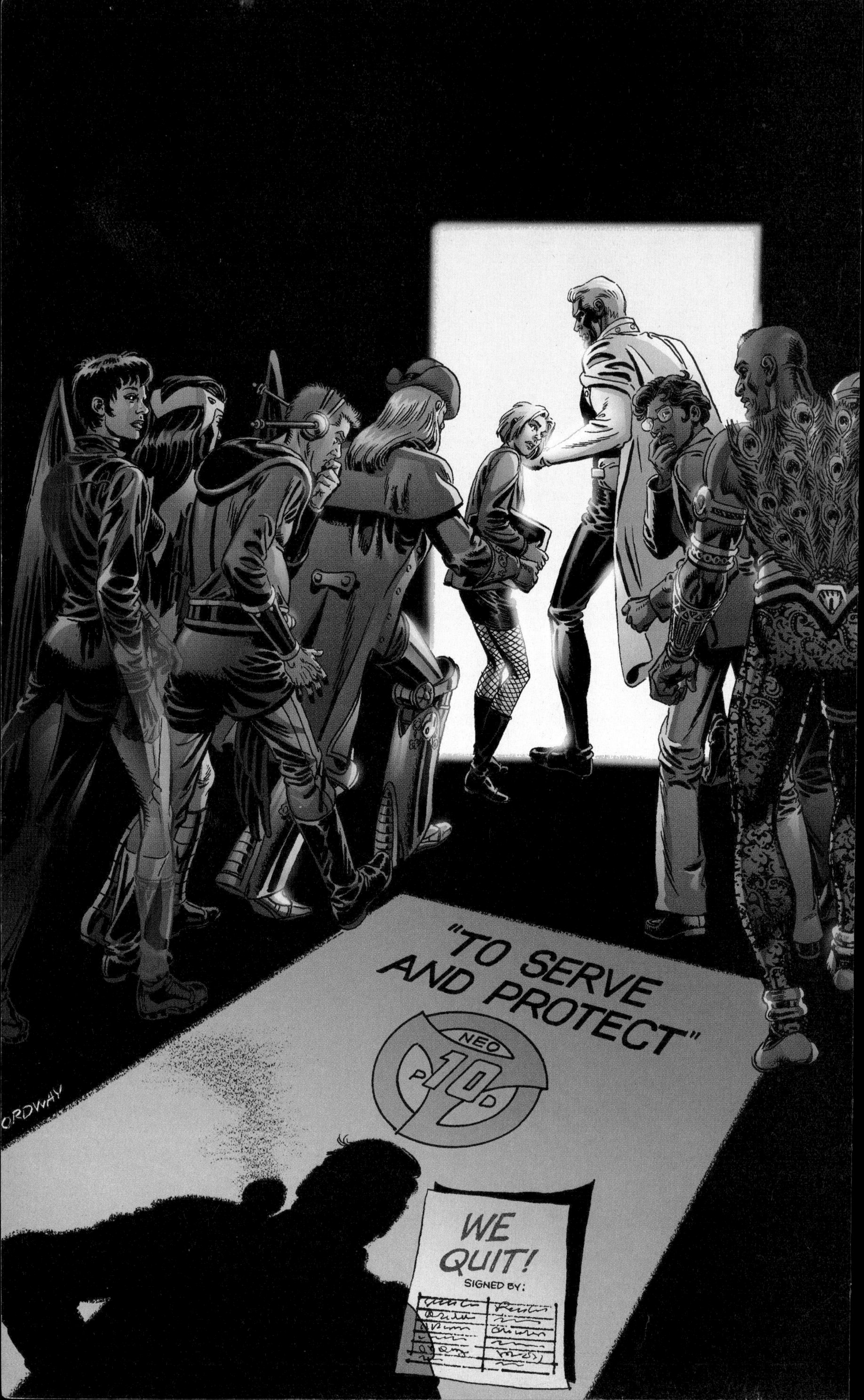
"TO SERVE AND PROTECT"
NEO
P 10 D
ORDWAY
WE QUIT!
SIGNED BY:

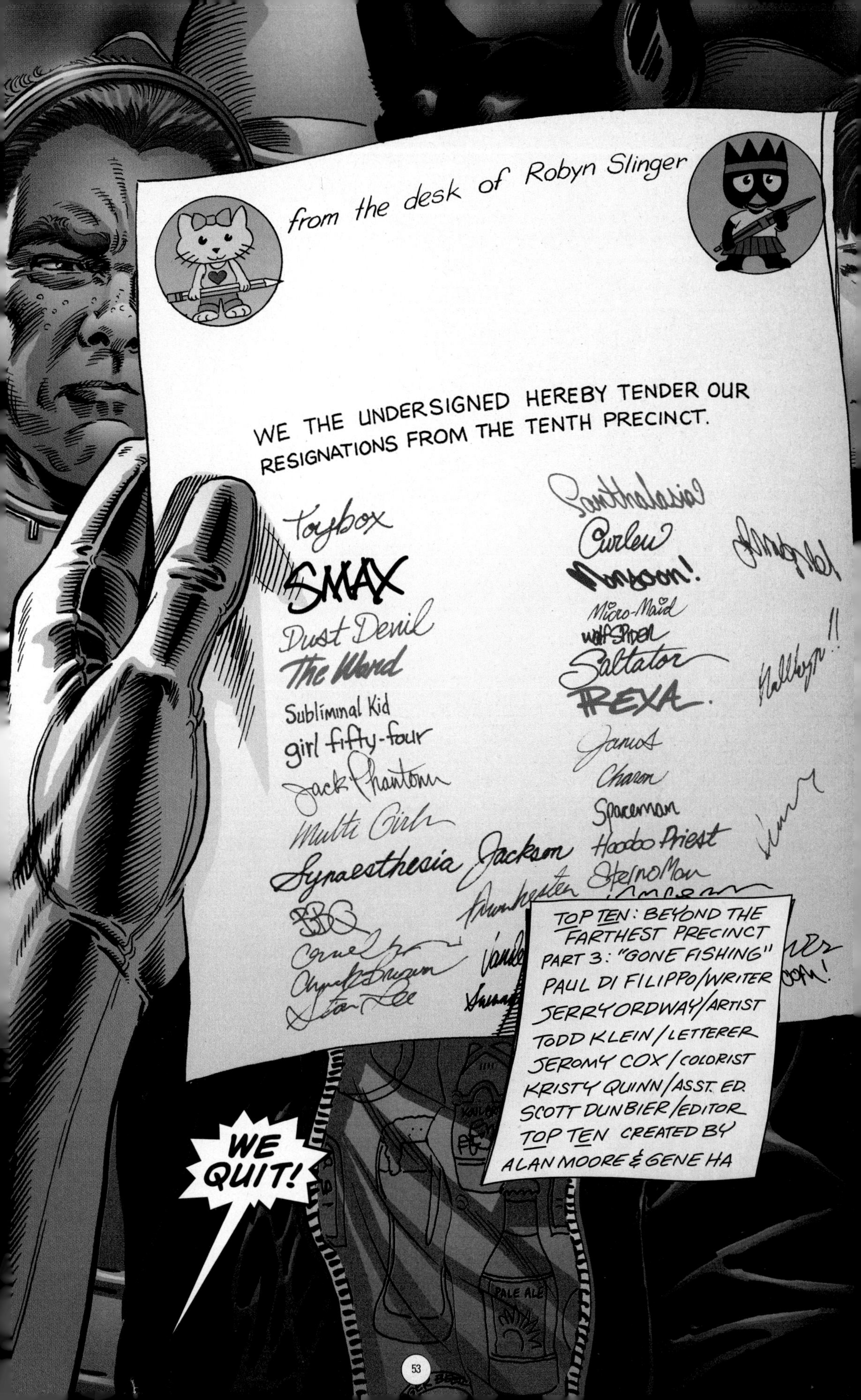
from the desk of Robyn Slinger
WE THE UNDERSIGNED HEREBY TENDER OUR RESIGNATIONS FROM THE TENTH PRECINCT.
Toybox
SMAX
Dust Devil
The Wand
Subliminal Kid
girl fifty-four
Jack Phantom
Multi Girl
Synaesthesia
Jackson
Curlew
Monsoon!
Micro-Maid
Wolf Spider
Saltator
TREXA
Janus
Charon
Spaceman
Hoodoo Priest
SternoMan
TOP TEN: BEYOND THE FARTHEST PRECINCT
PART 3: "GONE FISHING"
PAUL DI FILIPPO/WRITER
JERRY ORDWAY/ARTIST
TODD KLEIN/LETTERER
JEROMY COX/COLORIST
KRISTY QUINN/ASST. ED.
SCOTT DUNBIER/EDITOR
TOP TEN CREATED BY ALAN MOORE & GENE HA
WE QUIT!
PALE ALE

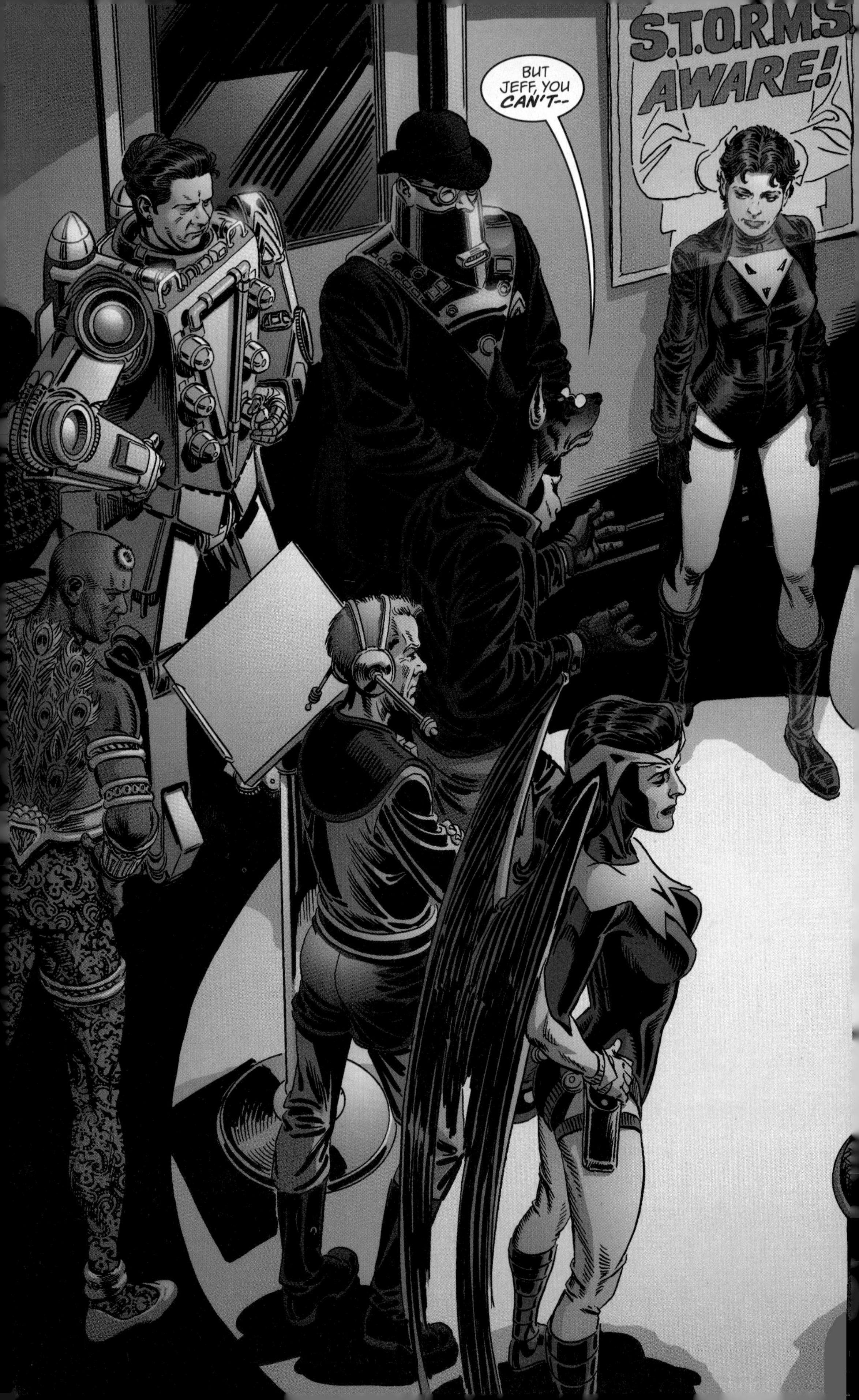
S.T.O.R.M.S.
AWARE!
BUT JEFF, YOU *CAN'T--*

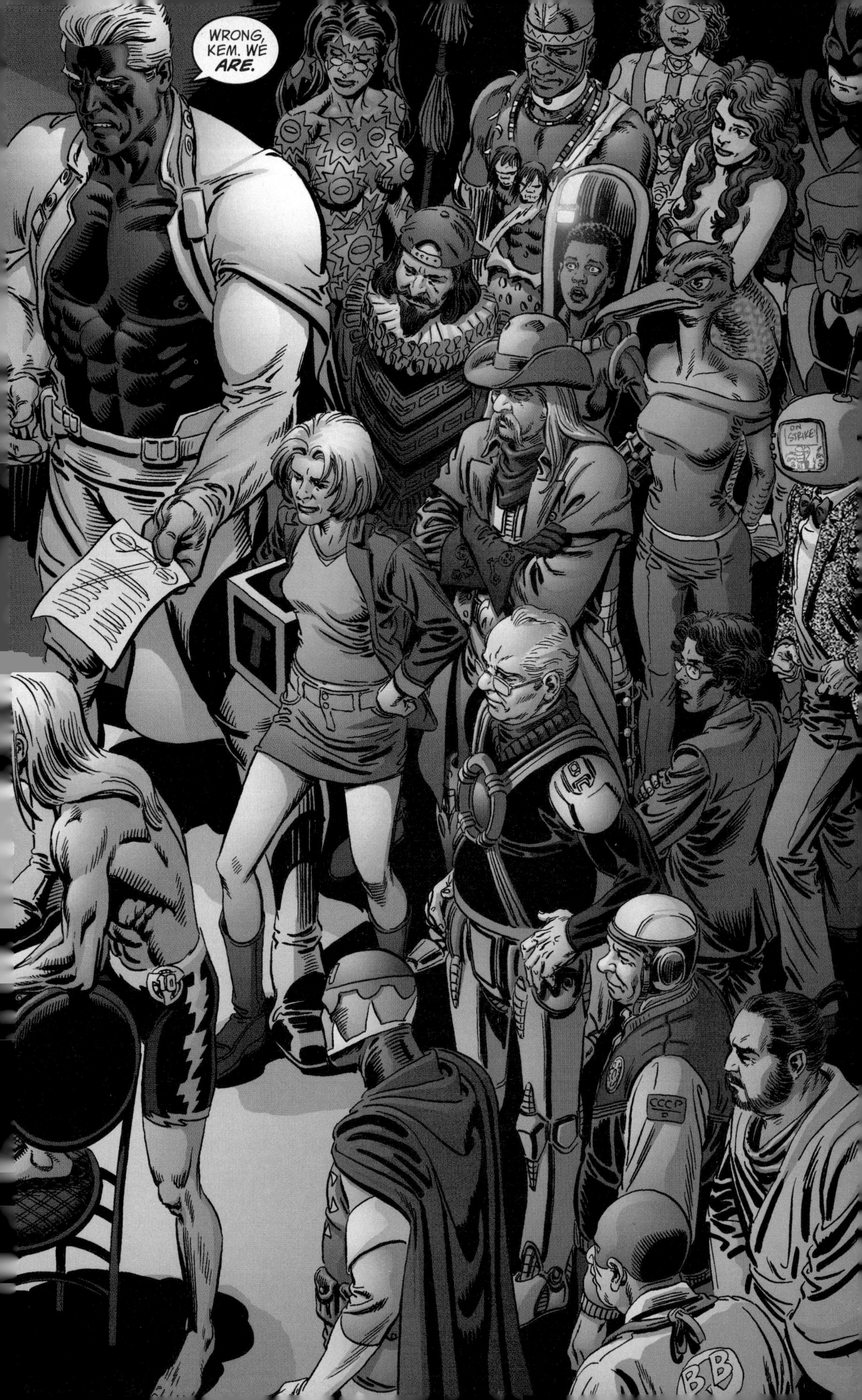
WRONG, KEM. WE ARE.
ON STRIKE!
CCCP
B.B

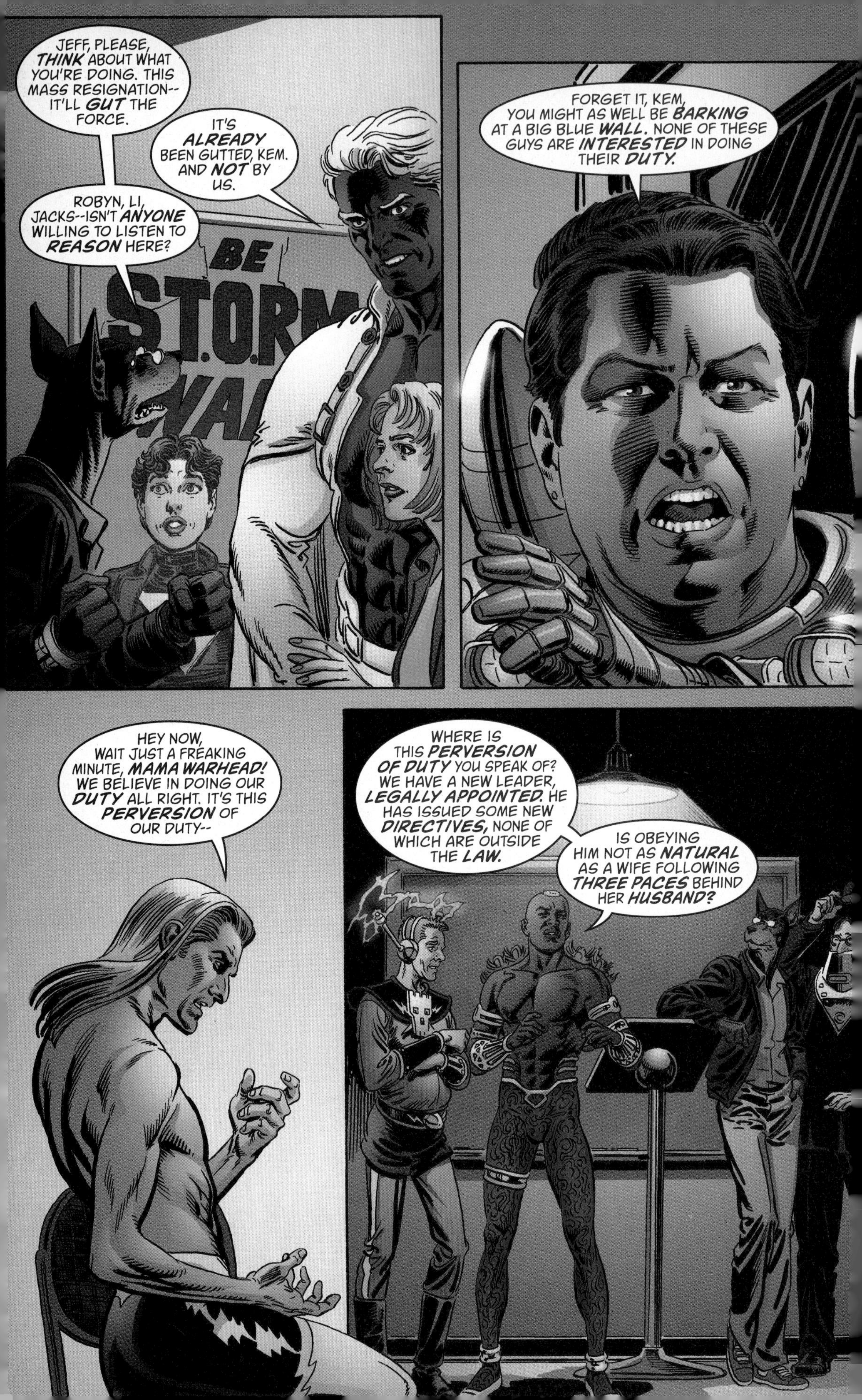
JEFF, PLEASE, THINK ABOUT WHAT YOU'RE DOING. THIS MASS RESIGNATION-- IT'LL GUT THE FORCE.
IT'S ALREADY BEEN GUTTED, KEM. AND NOT BY US.
ROBYN, LI, JACKS--ISN'T ANYONE WILLING TO LISTEN TO REASON HERE?
BE S.T.O.R.M.
FORGET IT, KEM, YOU MIGHT AS WELL BE BARKING AT A BIG BLUE WALL. NONE OF THESE GUYS ARE INTERESTED IN DOING THEIR DUTY.
HEY NOW, WAIT JUST A FREAKING MINUTE, MAMA WARHEAD! WE BELIEVE IN DOING OUR DUTY ALL RIGHT. IT'S THIS PERVERSION OF OUR DUTY--
WHERE IS THIS PERVERSION OF DUTY YOU SPEAK OF? WE HAVE A NEW LEADER, LEGALLY APPOINTED. HE HAS ISSUED SOME NEW DIRECTIVES, NONE OF WHICH ARE OUTSIDE THE LAW.
IS OBEYING HIM NOT AS NATURAL AS A WIFE FOLLOWING THREE PACES BEHIND HER HUSBAND?

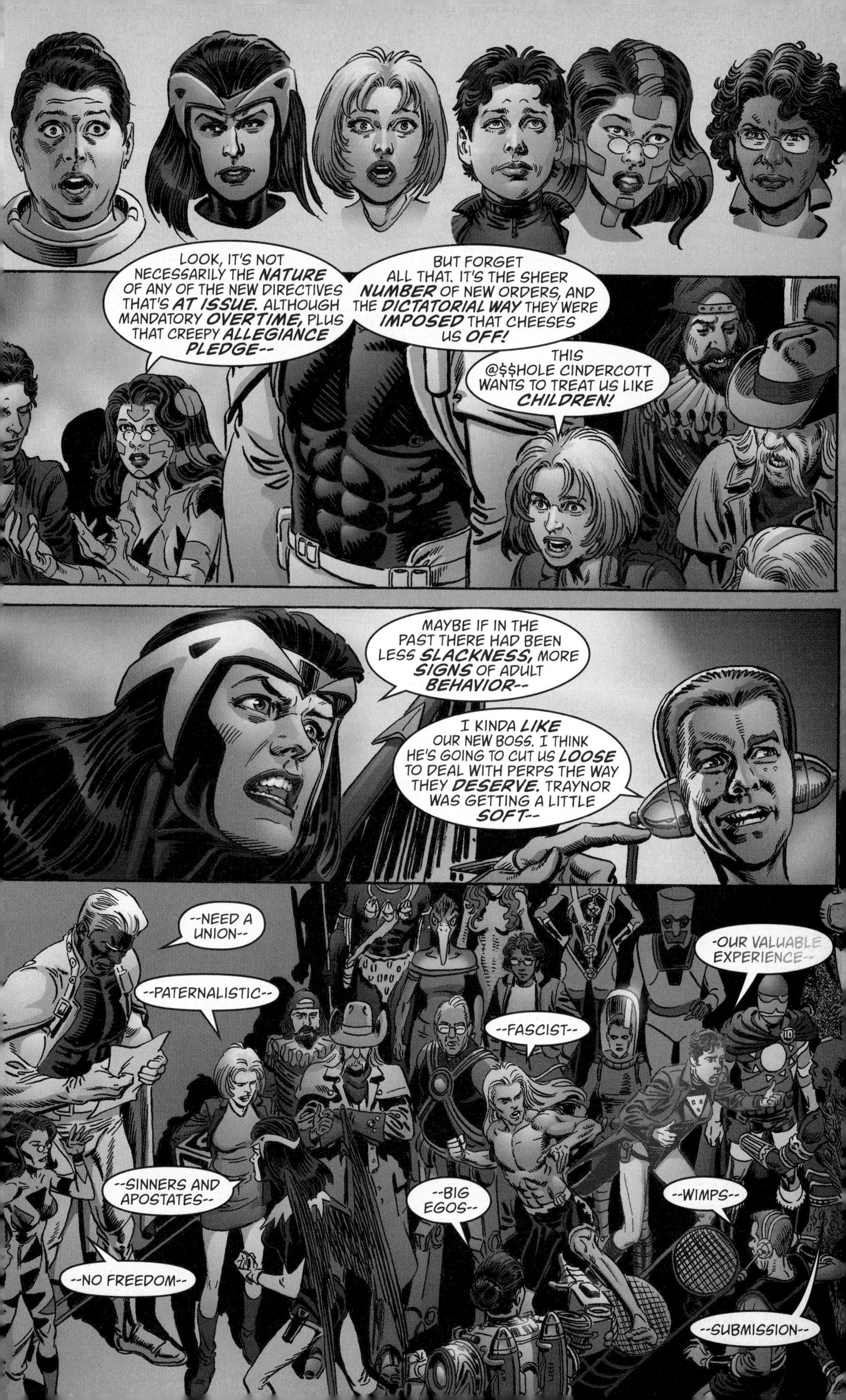
LOOK, IT'S NOT NECESSARILY THE NATURE OF ANY OF THE NEW DIRECTIVES THAT'S AT ISSUE. ALTHOUGH MANDATORY OVERTIME, PLUS THAT CREEPY ALLEGIANCE PLEDGE--
BUT FORGET ALL THAT. IT'S THE SHEER NUMBER OF NEW ORDERS, AND THE DICTATORIAL WAY THEY WERE IMPOSED THAT CHEESES US OFF!
THIS @$$HOLE CINDERCOTT WANTS TO TREAT US LIKE CHILDREN!
MAYBE IF IN THE PAST THERE HAD BEEN LESS SLACKNESS, MORE SIGNS OF ADULT BEHAVIOR--
I KINDA LIKE OUR NEW BOSS. I THINK HE'S GOING TO CUT US LOOSE TO DEAL WITH PERPS THE WAY THEY DESERVE. TRAYNOR WAS GETTING A LITTLE SOFT--
--NEED A UNION--
--PATERNALISTIC--
--FASCIST--
-OUR VALUABLE EXPERIENCE--
--SINNERS AND APOSTATES--
--BIG EGOS--
--WIMPS--
--NO FREEDOM--
--SUBMISSION--

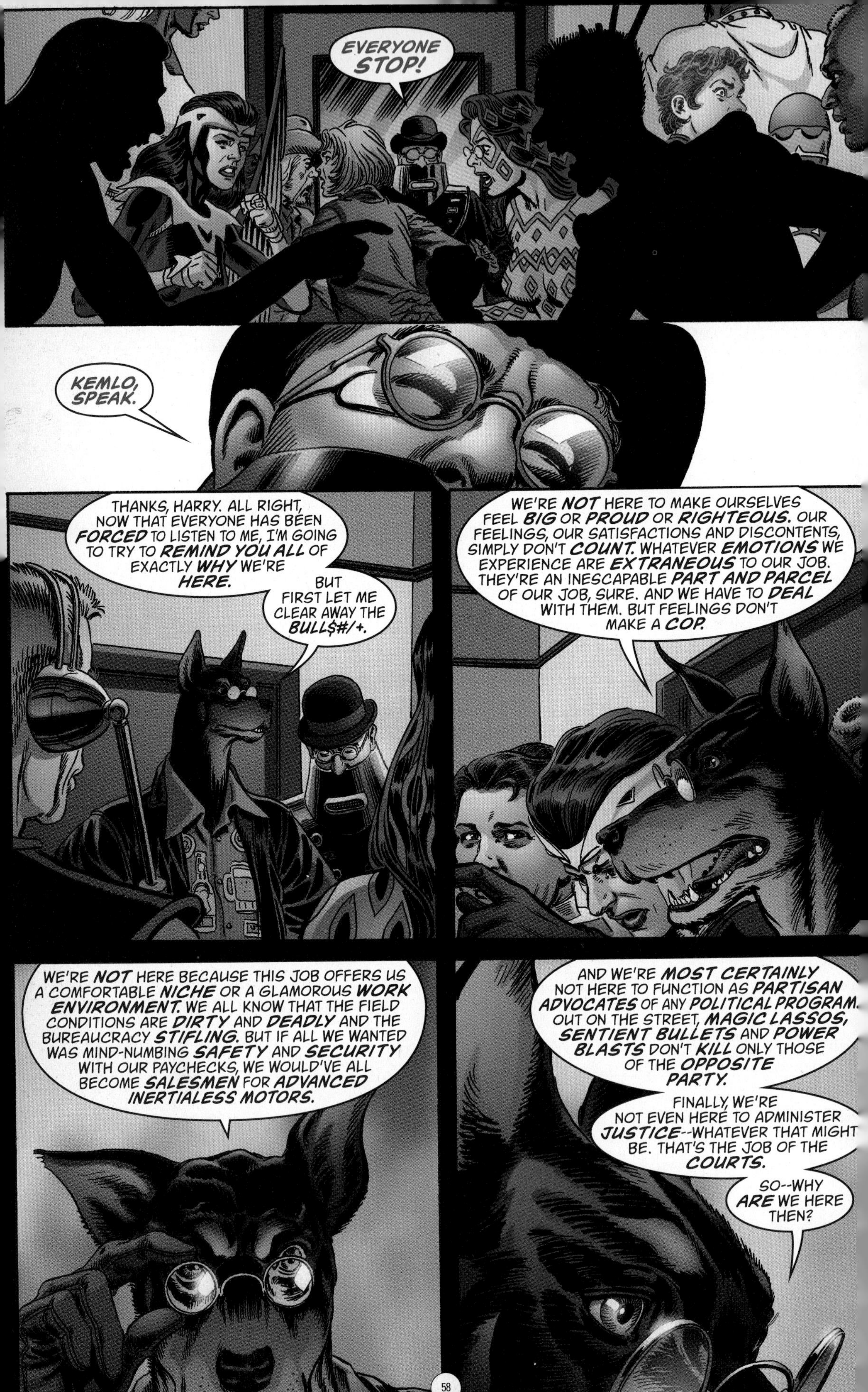
EVERYONE STOP!
KEMLO, SPEAK.
THANKS, HARRY. ALL RIGHT, NOW THAT EVERYONE HAS BEEN FORCED TO LISTEN TO ME, I'M GOING TO TRY TO REMIND YOU ALL OF EXACTLY WHY WE'RE HERE.
BUT FIRST LET ME CLEAR AWAY THE BULL$#/+.
WE'RE NOT HERE TO MAKE OURSELVES FEEL BIG OR PROUD OR RIGHTEOUS. OUR FEELINGS, OUR SATISFACTIONS AND DISCONTENTS, SIMPLY DON'T COUNT. WHATEVER EMOTIONS WE EXPERIENCE ARE EXTRANEOUS TO OUR JOB. THEY'RE AN INESCAPABLE PART AND PARCEL OF OUR JOB, SURE. AND WE HAVE TO DEAL WITH THEM. BUT FEELINGS DON'T MAKE A COP.
WE'RE NOT HERE BECAUSE THIS JOB OFFERS US A COMFORTABLE NICHE OR A GLAMOROUS WORK ENVIRONMENT. WE ALL KNOW THAT THE FIELD CONDITIONS ARE DIRTY AND DEADLY AND THE BUREAUCRACY STIFLING. BUT IF ALL WE WANTED WAS MIND-NUMBING SAFETY AND SECURITY WITH OUR PAYCHECKS, WE WOULD'VE ALL BECOME SALESMEN FOR ADVANCED INERTIALESS MOTORS.
AND WE'RE MOST CERTAINLY NOT HERE TO FUNCTION AS PARTISAN ADVOCATES OF ANY POLITICAL PROGRAM. OUT ON THE STREET, MAGIC LASSOS, SENTIENT BULLETS AND POWER BLASTS DON'T KILL ONLY THOSE OF THE OPPOSITE PARTY.
FINALLY, WE'RE NOT EVEN HERE TO ADMINISTER JUSTICE--WHATEVER THAT MIGHT BE. THAT'S THE JOB OF THE COURTS.
SO--WHY ARE WE HERE THEN?

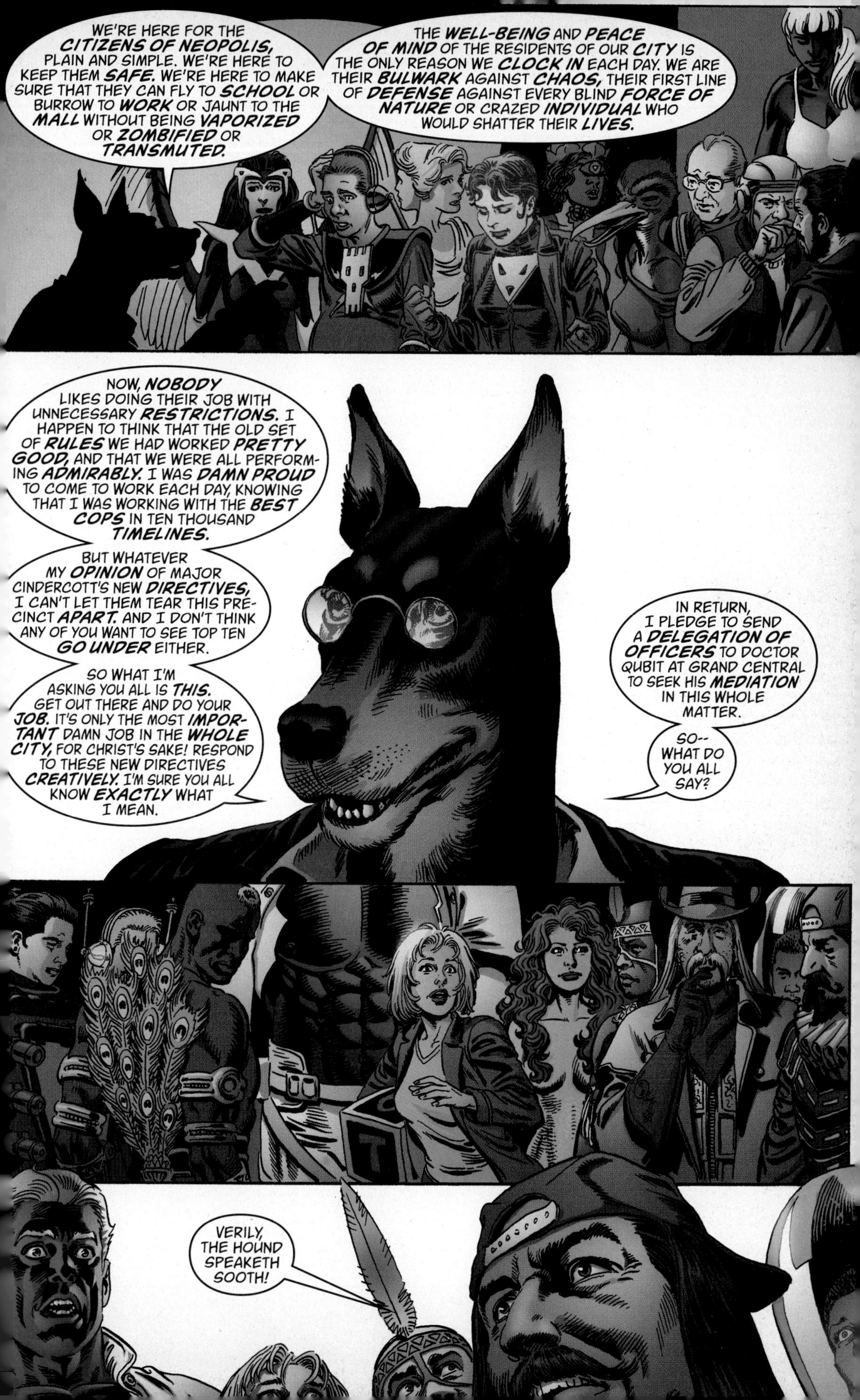
WE'RE HERE FOR THE CITIZENS OF NEOPOLIS, PLAIN AND SIMPLE. WE'RE HERE TO KEEP THEM SAFE. WE'RE HERE TO MAKE SURE THAT THEY CAN FLY TO SCHOOL OR BURROW TO WORK OR JAUNT TO THE MALL WITHOUT BEING VAPORIZED OR ZOMBIFIED OR TRANSMUTED.
THE WELL-BEING AND PEACE OF MIND OF THE RESIDENTS OF OUR CITY IS THE ONLY REASON WE CLOCK IN EACH DAY. WE ARE THEIR BULWARK AGAINST CHAOS, THEIR FIRST LINE OF DEFENSE AGAINST EVERY BLIND FORCE OF NATURE OR CRAZED INDIVIDUAL WHO WOULD SHATTER THEIR LIVES.
NOW, NOBODY LIKES DOING THEIR JOB WITH UNNECESSARY RESTRICTIONS. I HAPPEN TO THINK THAT THE OLD SET OF RULES WE HAD WORKED PRETTY GOOD, AND THAT WE WERE ALL PERFORMING ADMIRABLY. I WAS DAMN PROUD TO COME TO WORK EACH DAY, KNOWING THAT I WAS WORKING WITH THE BEST COPS IN TEN THOUSAND TIMELINES.
BUT WHATEVER MY OPINION OF MAJOR CINDERCOTT'S NEW DIRECTIVES, I CAN'T LET THEM TEAR THIS PRECINCT APART. AND I DON'T THINK ANY OF YOU WANT TO SEE TOP TEN GO UNDER EITHER.
SO WHAT I'M ASKING YOU ALL IS THIS. GET OUT THERE AND DO YOUR JOB. IT'S ONLY THE MOST IMPORTANT DAMN JOB IN THE WHOLE CITY, FOR CHRIST'S SAKE! RESPOND TO THESE NEW DIRECTIVES CREATIVELY. I'M SURE YOU ALL KNOW EXACTLY WHAT I MEAN.
IN RETURN, I PLEDGE TO SEND A DELEGATION OF OFFICERS TO DOCTOR QUBIT AT GRAND CENTRAL TO SEEK HIS MEDIATION IN THIS WHOLE MATTER.
SO-- WHAT DO YOU ALL SAY?
VERILY, THE HOUND SPEAKETH SOOTH!

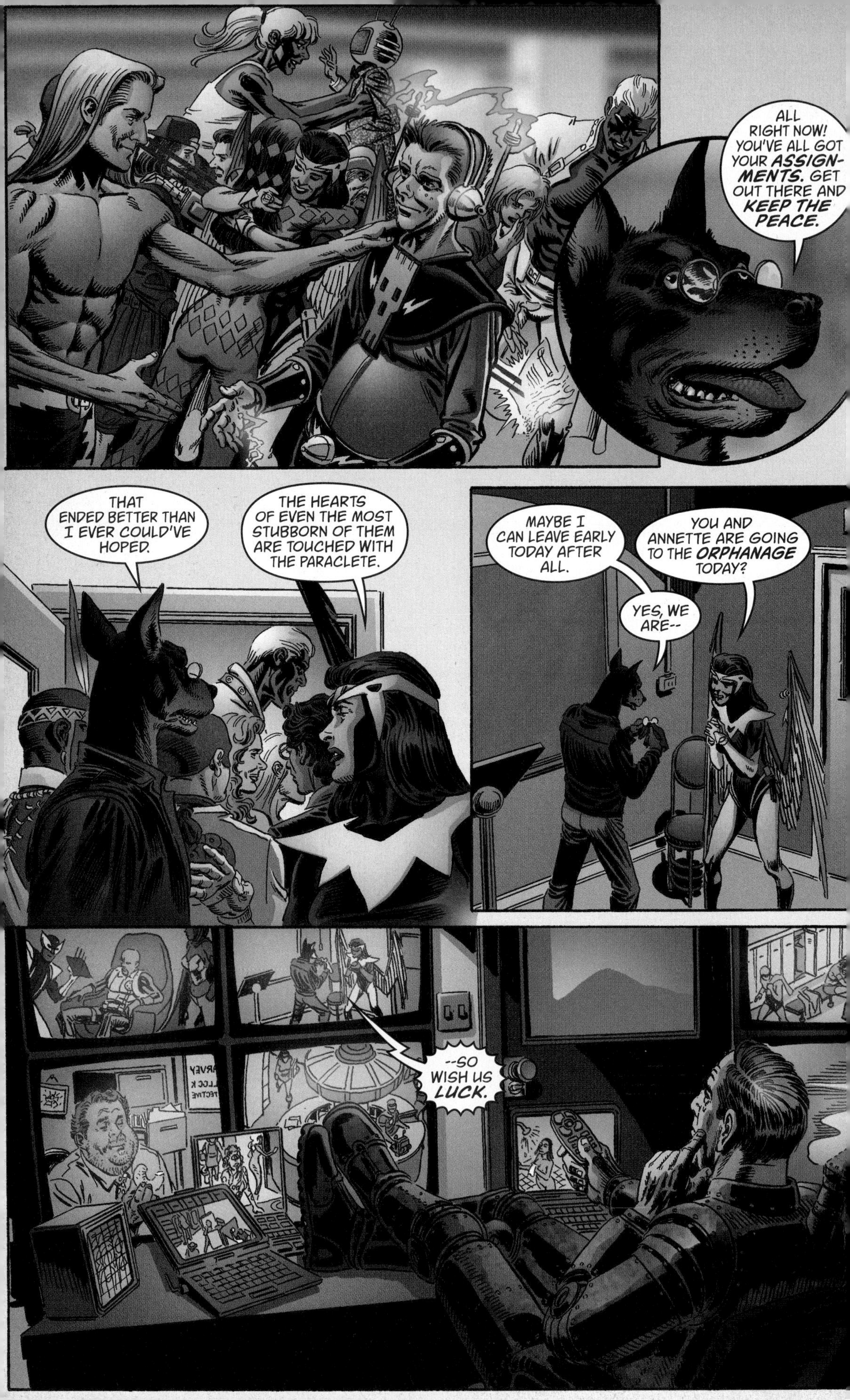

ALL RIGHT NOW! YOU'VE ALL GOT YOUR ASSIGNMENTS. GET OUT THERE AND KEEP THE PEACE.
THAT ENDED BETTER THAN I EVER COULD'VE HOPED.
THE HEARTS OF EVEN THE MOST STUBBORN OF THEM ARE TOUCHED WITH THE PARACLETE.
MAYBE I CAN LEAVE EARLY TODAY AFTER ALL.
YOU AND ANNETTE ARE GOING TO THE ORPHANAGE TODAY?
YES, WE ARE--
--SO WISH US LUCK.

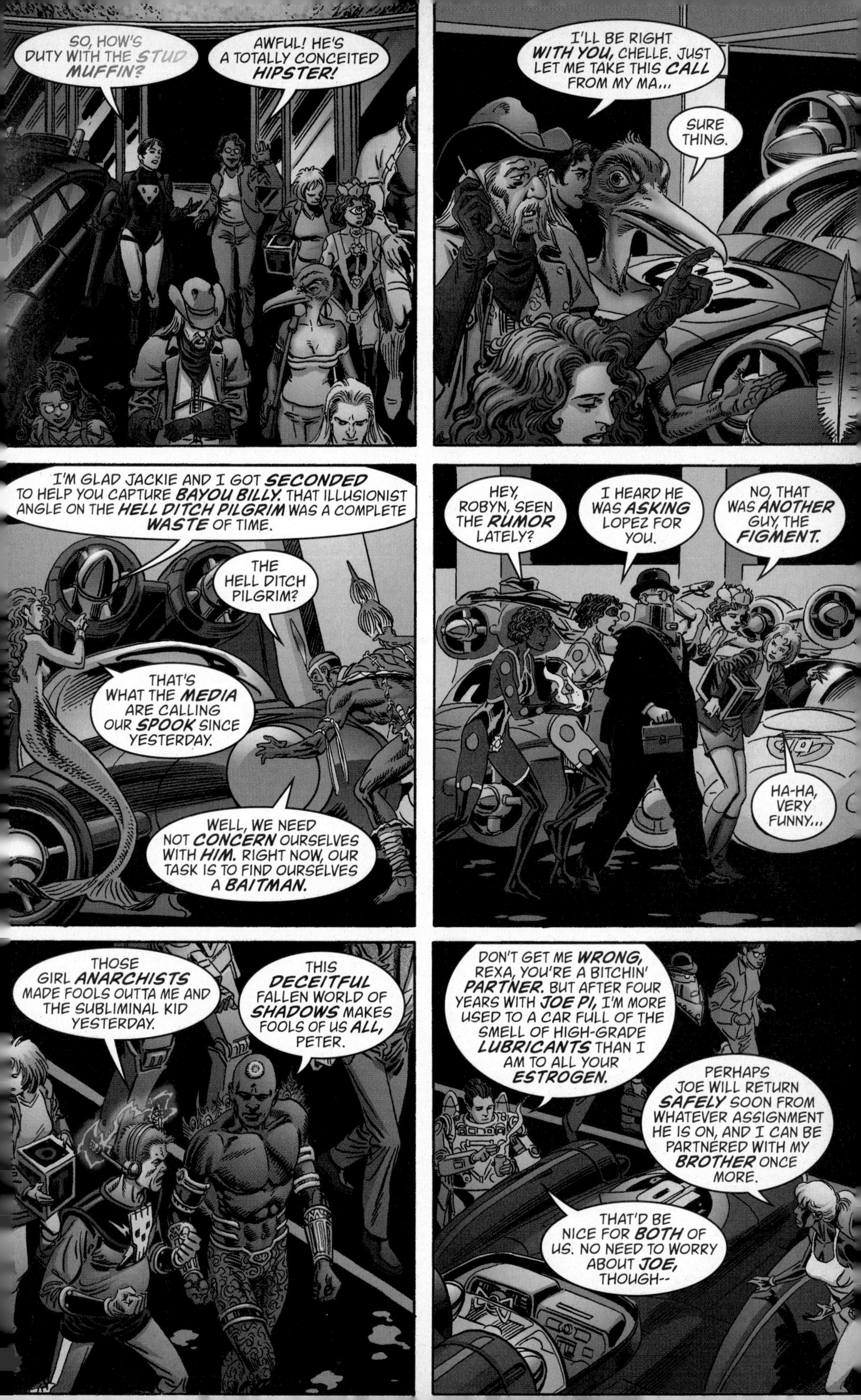
SO, HOW'S DUTY WITH THE STUD MUFFIN?
AWFUL! HE'S A TOTALLY CONCEITED HIPSTER!
I'LL BE RIGHT WITH YOU, CHELLE. JUST LET ME TAKE THIS CALL FROM MY MA...
SURE THING.
I'M GLAD JACKIE AND I GOT SECONDED TO HELP YOU CAPTURE BAYOU BILLY. THAT ILLUSIONIST ANGLE ON THE HELL DITCH PILGRIM WAS A COMPLETE WASTE OF TIME.
THE HELL DITCH PILGRIM?
THAT'S WHAT THE MEDIA ARE CALLING OUR SPOOK SINCE YESTERDAY.
WELL, WE NEED NOT CONCERN OURSELVES WITH HIM. RIGHT NOW, OUR TASK IS TO FIND OURSELVES A BAITMAN.
HEY, ROBYN, SEEN THE RUMOR LATELY?
I HEARD HE WAS ASKING LOPEZ FOR YOU.
NO, THAT WAS ANOTHER GUY, THE FIGMENT.
HA-HA, VERY FUNNY...
THOSE GIRL ANARCHISTS MADE FOOLS OUTTA ME AND THE SUBLIMINAL KID YESTERDAY.
THIS DECEITFUL FALLEN WORLD OF SHADOWS MAKES FOOLS OF US ALL, PETER.
DON'T GET ME WRONG, REXA, YOU'RE A BITCHIN' PARTNER. BUT AFTER FOUR YEARS WITH JOE PI, I'M MORE USED TO A CAR FULL OF THE SMELL OF HIGH-GRADE LUBRICANTS THAN I AM TO ALL YOUR ESTROGEN.
PERHAPS JOE WILL RETURN SAFELY SOON FROM WHATEVER ASSIGNMENT HE IS ON, AND I CAN BE PARTNERED WITH MY BROTHER ONCE MORE.
THAT'D BE NICE FOR BOTH OF US. NO NEED TO WORRY ABOUT JOE, THOUGH--

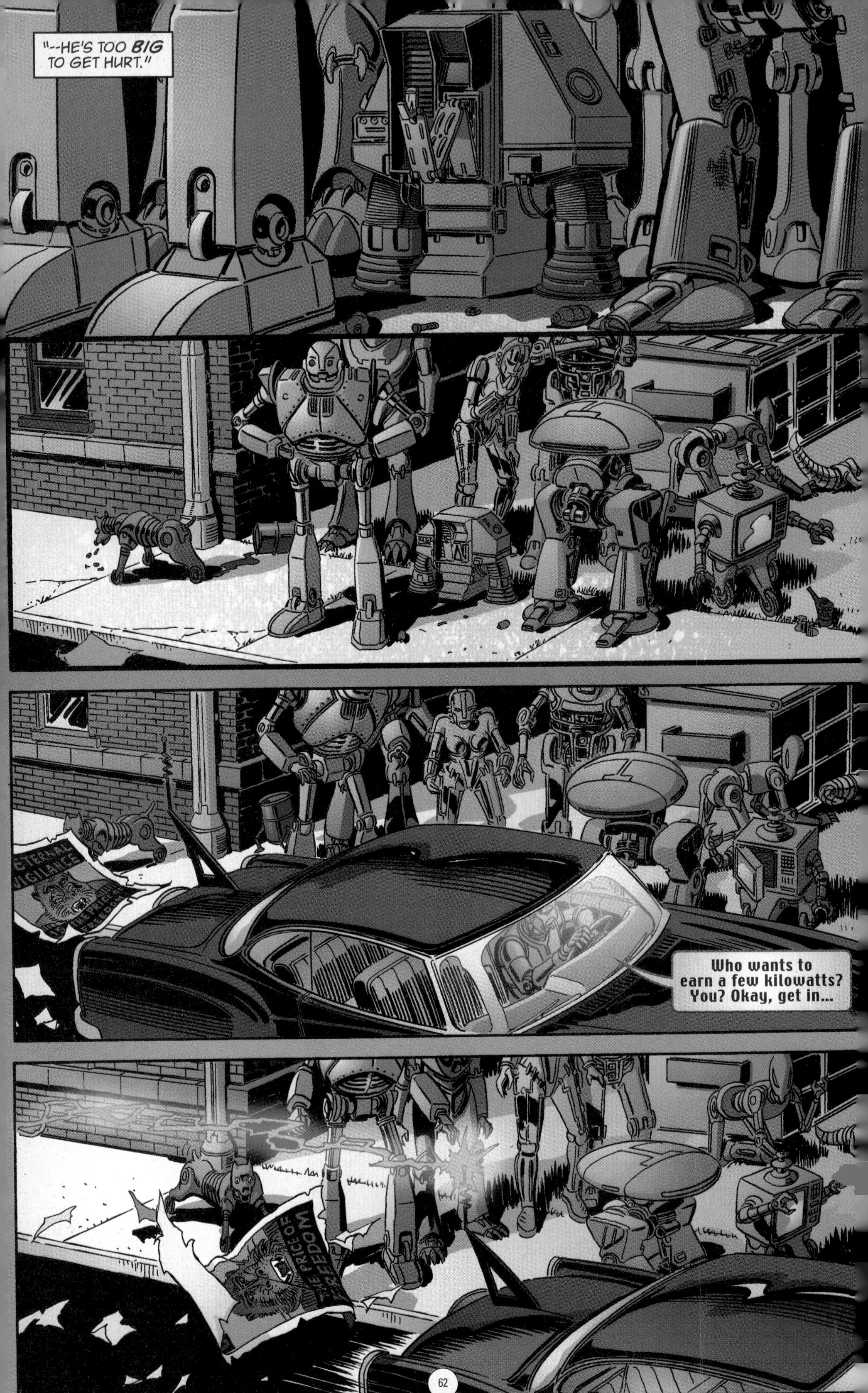
"--HE'S TOO BIG TO GET HURT."
ETERNAL VIGILANCE
Who wants to earn a few kilowatts? You? Okay, get in...
THE PRICE OF FREEDOM

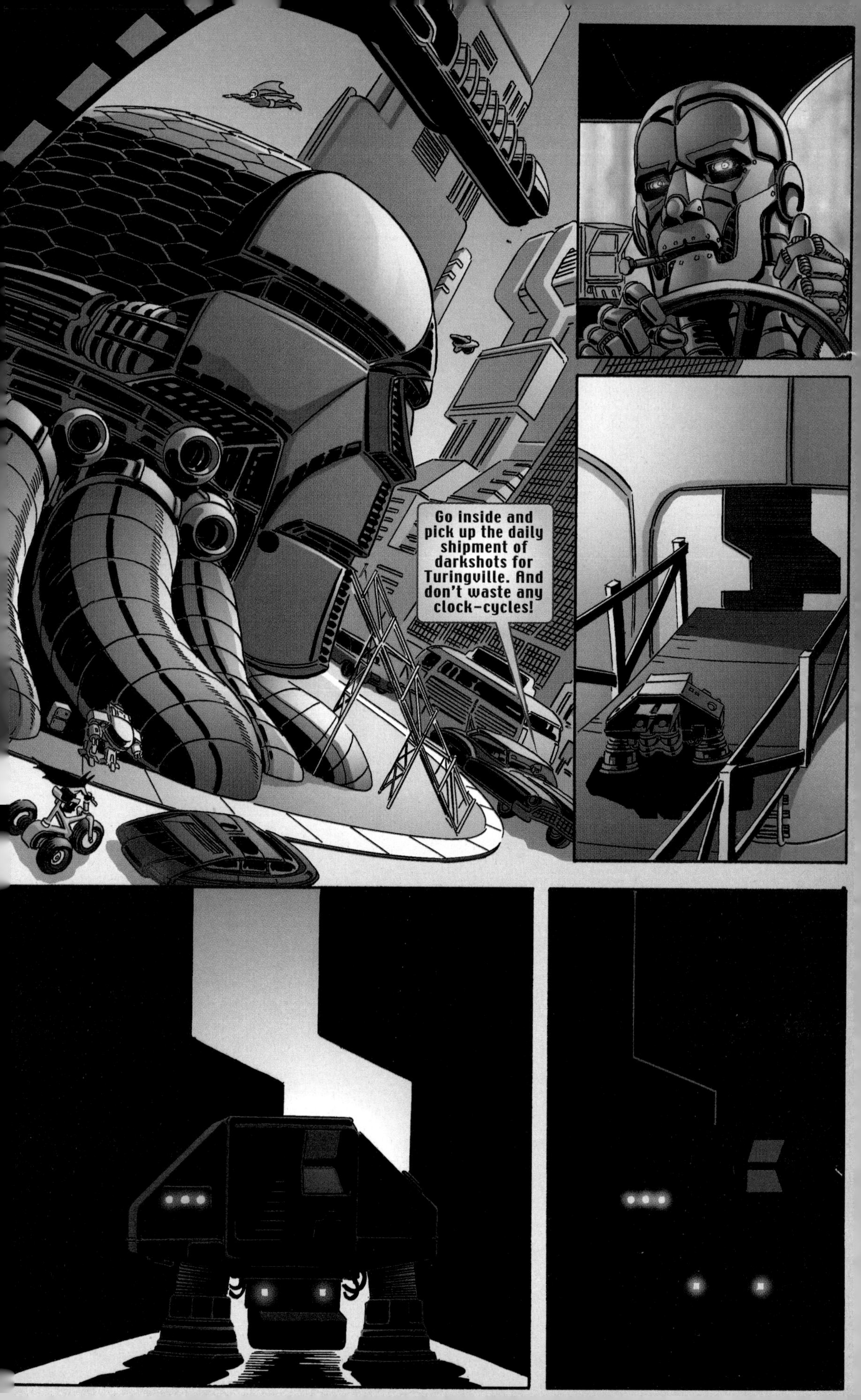
Go inside and pick up the daily shipment of darkshots for Turingville. And don't waste any clock-cycles!

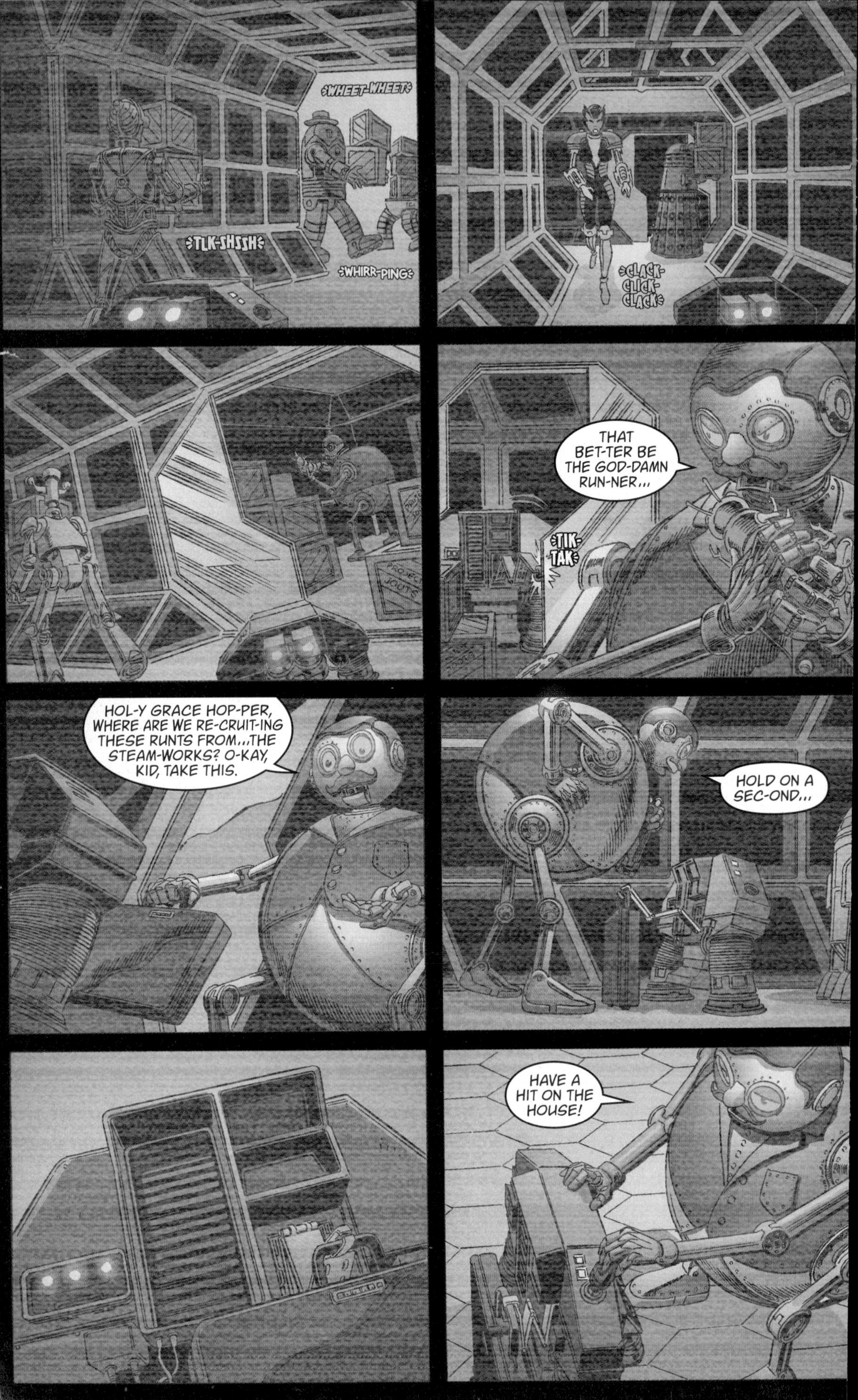
WHEET-WHEET
TLK-SHSSH
WHIRR-PING
CLACK-CLICK-CLACK
THAT BET-TER BE THE GOD-DAMN RUN-NER...
TIK-TAK
HOL-Y GRACE HOP-PER, WHERE ARE WE RE-CRUIT-ING THESE RUNTS FROM...THE STEAM-WORKS? O-KAY, KID, TAKE THIS.
HOLD ON A SEC-OND...
HAVE A HIT ON THE HOUSE!

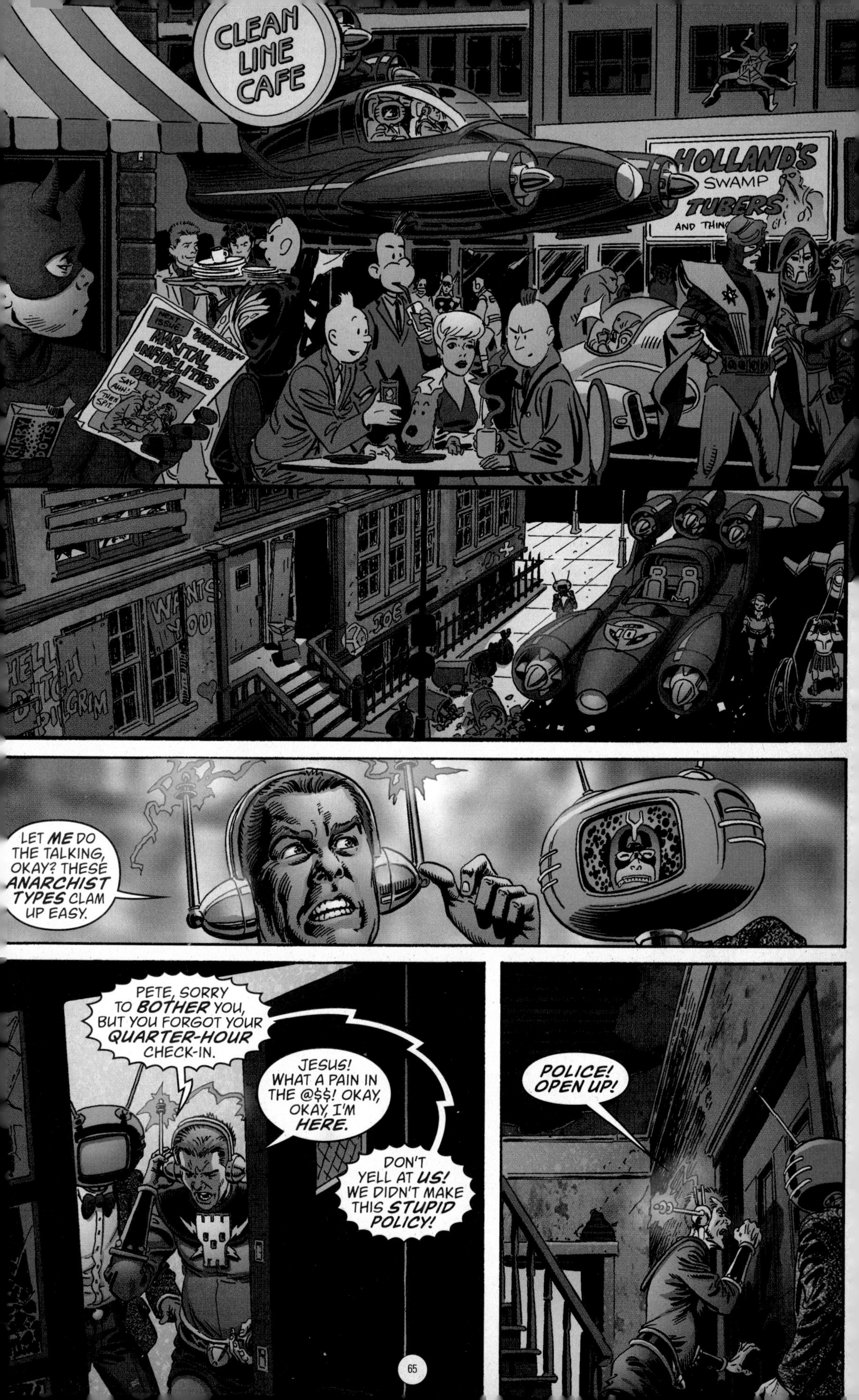
CLEAN LINE CAFE
HOLLAND'S SWAMP TUBERS AND THING
NEXT ISSUE: MARITAL INFIDELITIES OF A DENTIST
SAY AHH!
THEN SPIT.
KIRBY DOTS
WANTS YOU
JOE
LET ME DO THE TALKING, OKAY? THESE ANARCHIST TYPES CLAM UP EASY.
PETE, SORRY TO BOTHER YOU, BUT YOU FORGOT YOUR QUARTER-HOUR CHECK-IN.
JESUS! WHAT A PAIN IN THE @$$! OKAY, OKAY, I'M HERE.
DON'T YELL AT US! WE DIDN'T MAKE THIS STUPID POLICY!
POLICE! OPEN UP!

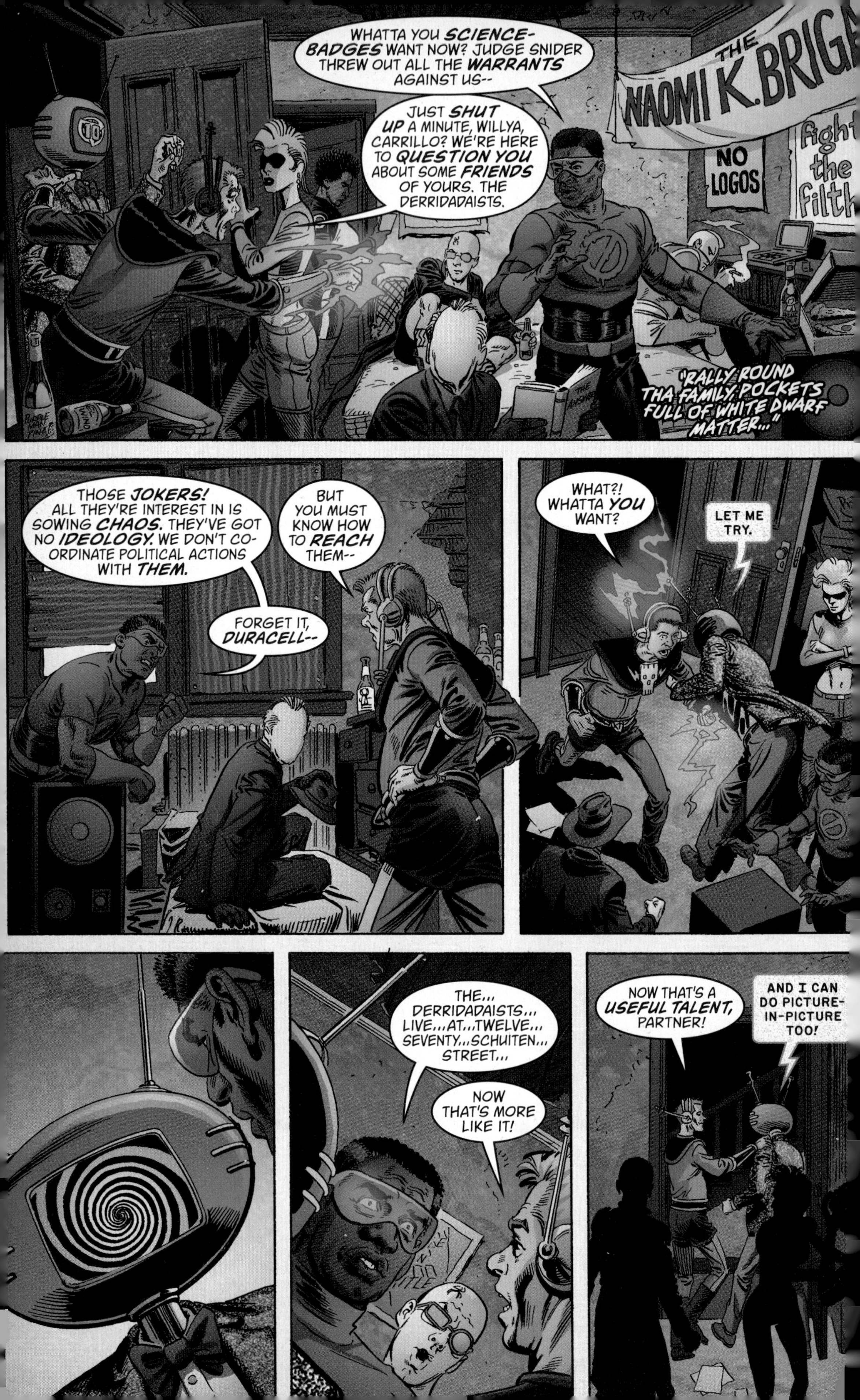
THE
NAOMI K. BRIGA
NO LOGOS
fight the filth
WHATTA YOU SCIENCE-BADGES WANT NOW? JUDGE SNIDER THREW OUT ALL THE WARRANTS AGAINST US--
JUST SHUT UP A MINUTE, WILLYA, CARRILLO? WE'RE HERE TO QUESTION YOU ABOUT SOME FRIENDS OF YOURS. THE DERRIDADAISTS.
"RALLY ROUND THA FAMILY, POCKETS FULL OF WHITE DWARF MATTER..."
THOSE JOKERS! ALL THEY'RE INTEREST IN IS SOWING CHAOS. THEY'VE GOT NO IDEOLOGY. WE DON'T CO-ORDINATE POLITICAL ACTIONS WITH THEM.
BUT YOU MUST KNOW HOW TO REACH THEM--
FORGET IT, DURACELL--
WHAT?! WHATTA YOU WANT?
LET ME TRY.
THE... DERRIDADAISTS... LIVE...AT...TWELVE... SEVENTY...SCHUITEN... STREET...
NOW THAT'S MORE LIKE IT!
NOW THAT'S A USEFUL TALENT, PARTNER!
AND I CAN DO PICTURE-IN-PICTURE TOO!

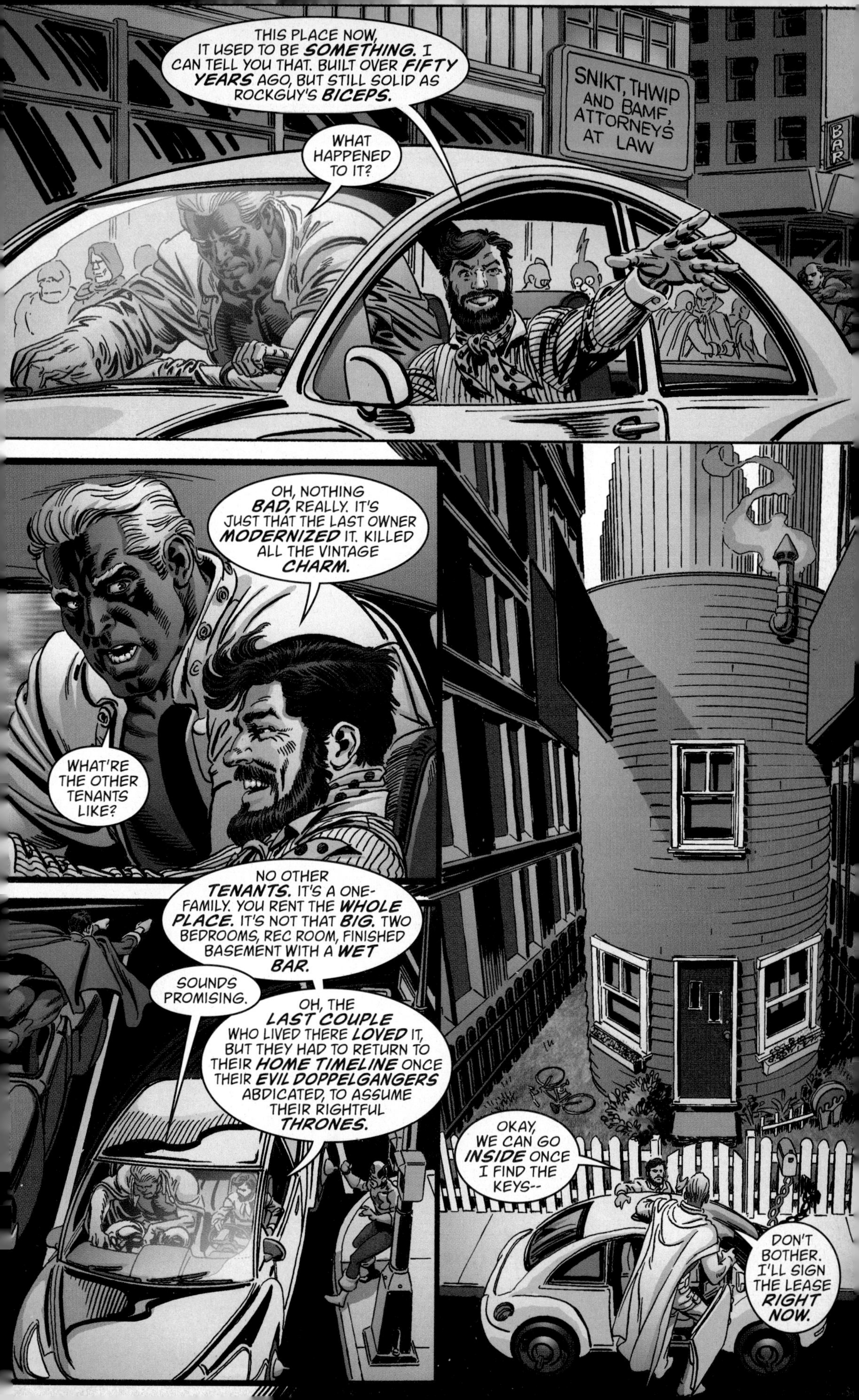
THIS PLACE NOW, IT USED TO BE SOMETHING. I CAN TELL YOU THAT. BUILT OVER FIFTY YEARS AGO, BUT STILL SOLID AS ROCKGUY'S BICEPS.
SNIKT, THWIP AND BAMF, ATTORNEYS AT LAW
BAR
WHAT HAPPENED TO IT?
OH, NOTHING BAD, REALLY. IT'S JUST THAT THE LAST OWNER MODERNIZED IT. KILLED ALL THE VINTAGE CHARM.
WHAT'RE THE OTHER TENANTS LIKE?
NO OTHER TENANTS. IT'S A ONE-FAMILY. YOU RENT THE WHOLE PLACE. IT'S NOT THAT BIG. TWO BEDROOMS, REC ROOM, FINISHED BASEMENT WITH A WET BAR.
SOUNDS PROMISING.
OH, THE LAST COUPLE WHO LIVED THERE LOVED IT, BUT THEY HAD TO RETURN TO THEIR HOME TIMELINE ONCE THEIR EVIL DOPPELGANGERS ABDICATED, TO ASSUME THEIR RIGHTFUL THRONES.
OKAY, WE CAN GO INSIDE ONCE I FIND THE KEYS--
DON'T BOTHER. I'LL SIGN THE LEASE RIGHT NOW.

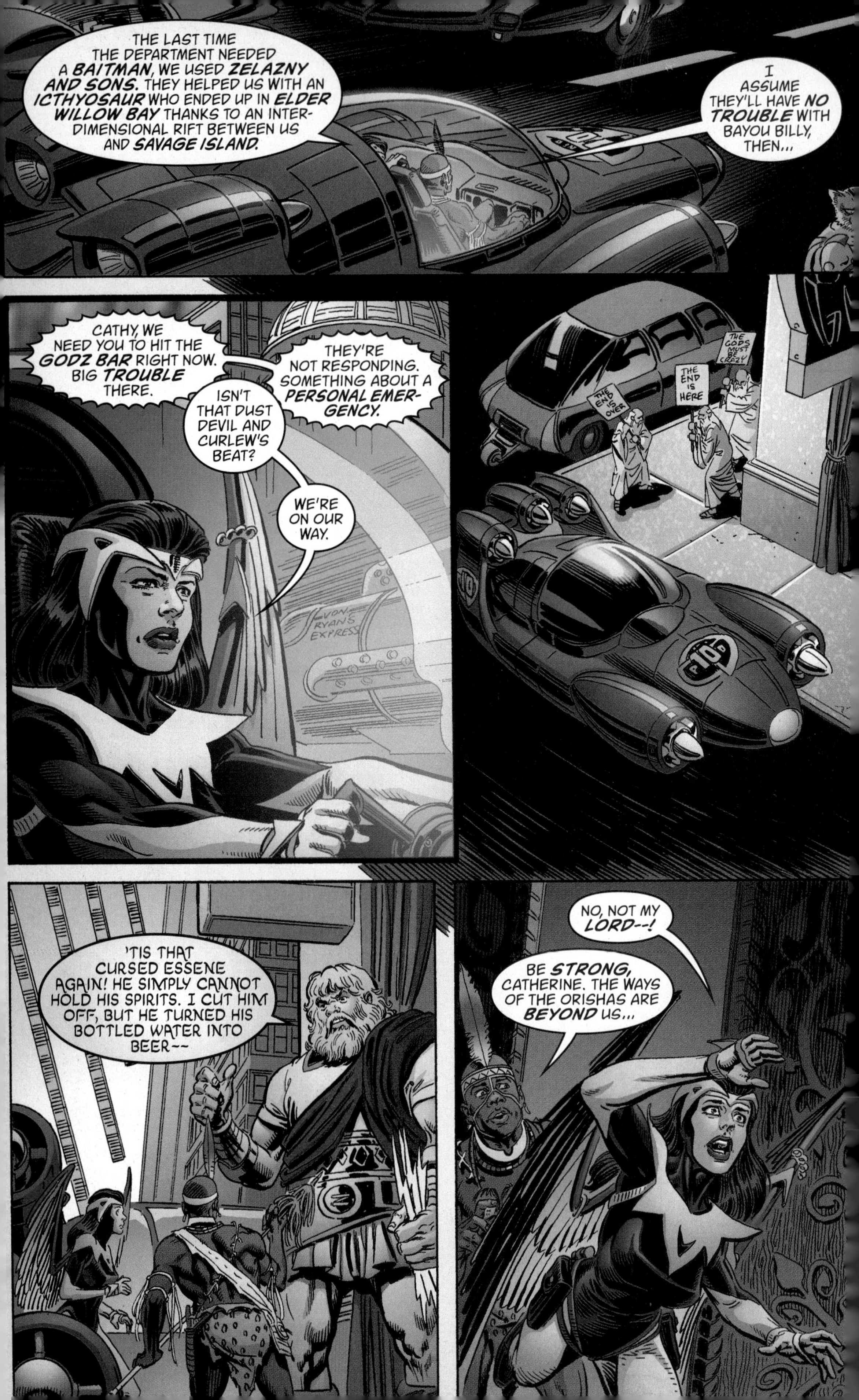

THE LAST TIME THE DEPARTMENT NEEDED A BAITMAN, WE USED ZELAZNY AND SONS. THEY HELPED US WITH AN ICTHYOSAUR WHO ENDED UP IN ELDER WILLOW BAY THANKS TO AN INTER-DIMENSIONAL RIFT BETWEEN US AND SAVAGE ISLAND.
I ASSUME THEY'LL HAVE NO TROUBLE WITH BAYOU BILLY, THEN...
CATHY, WE NEED YOU TO HIT THE GODZ BAR RIGHT NOW. BIG TROUBLE THERE.
ISN'T THAT DUST DEVIL AND CURLEW'S BEAT?
THEY'RE NOT RESPONDING. SOMETHING ABOUT A PERSONAL EMERGENCY.
WE'RE ON OUR WAY.
VON RYAN'S EXPRESS
THE GODS MUST BE CRAZY
THE END IS HERE
THE END IS OVER
'TIS THAT CURSED ESSENE AGAIN! HE SIMPLY CANNOT HOLD HIS SPIRITS. I CUT HIM OFF, BUT HE TURNED HIS BOTTLED WATER INTO BEER--
NO, NOT MY LORD--!
BE STRONG, CATHERINE. THE WAYS OF THE ORISHAS ARE BEYOND US...

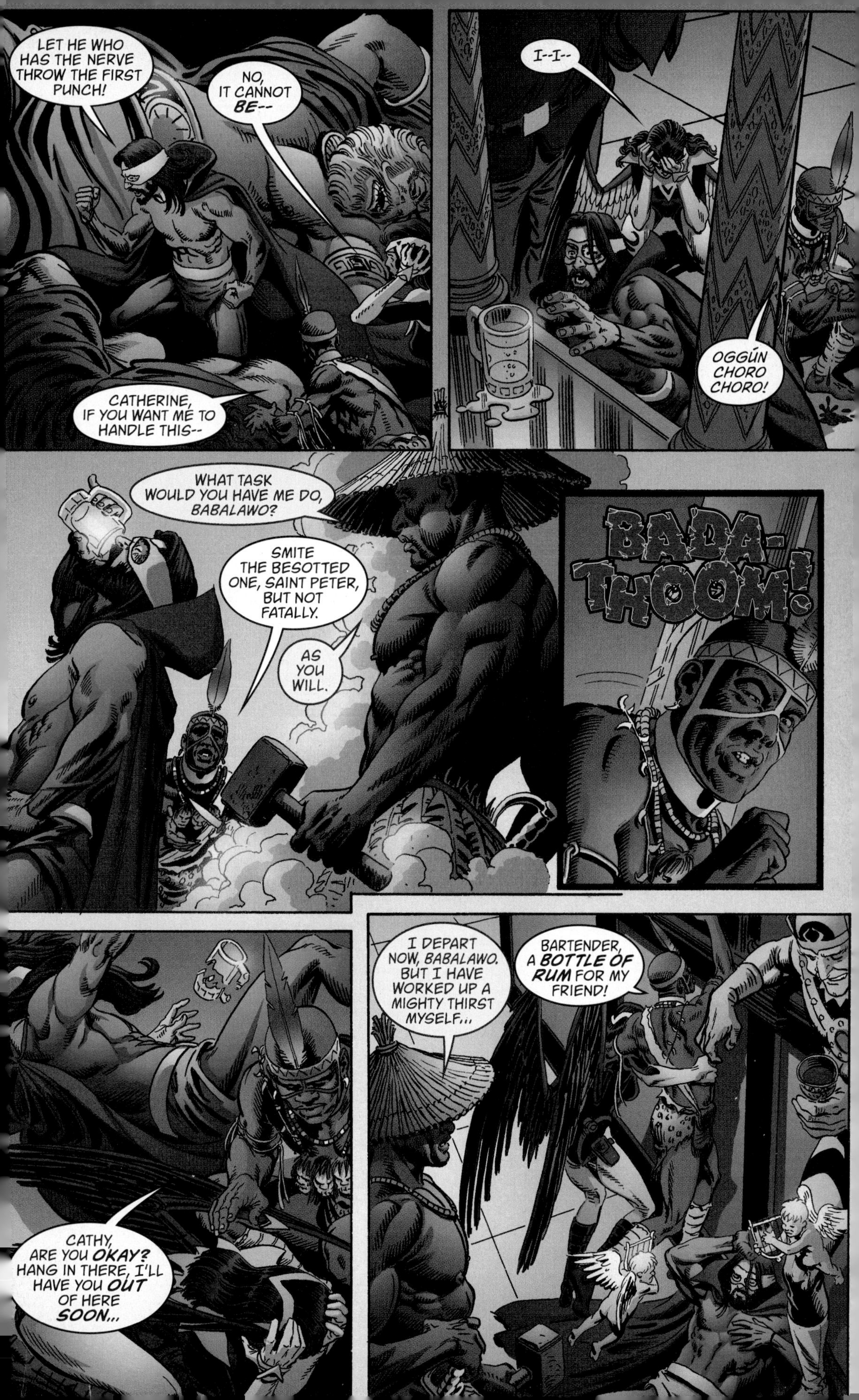

LET HE WHO HAS THE NERVE THROW THE FIRST PUNCH!
NO, IT CANNOT BE--
CATHERINE, IF YOU WANT ME TO HANDLE THIS--
I--I--
OGGÚN CHORO CHORO!
WHAT TASK WOULD YOU HAVE ME DO, BABALAWO?
SMITE THE BESOTTED ONE, SAINT PETER, BUT NOT FATALLY.
AS YOU WILL.
BADA-THOOM!
CATHY, ARE YOU OKAY? HANG IN THERE, I'LL HAVE YOU OUT OF HERE SOON...
I DEPART NOW, BABALAWO. BUT I HAVE WORKED UP A MIGHTY THIRST MYSELF...
BARTENDER, A BOTTLE OF RUM FOR MY FRIEND!

HERE I AM, MAJOR.

AND HERE YOU'LL STAY! WHAT'S THIS NONSENSE ABOUT LEAVING EARLY TODAY?

MAJOR SEAN CINDERCOTT

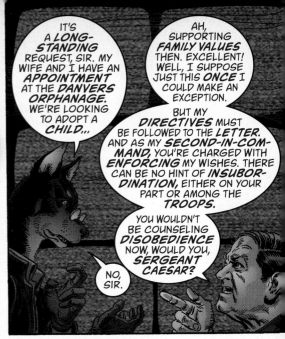

IT'S A LONG-STANDING REQUEST, SIR. MY WIFE AND I HAVE AN APPOINTMENT AT THE DANVERS ORPHANAGE. WE'RE LOOKING TO ADOPT A CHILD...

AH, SUPPORTING FAMILY VALUES THEN. EXCELLENT! WELL, I SUPPOSE JUST THIS ONCE I COULD MAKE AN EXCEPTION.

BUT MY DIRECTIVES MUST BE FOLLOWED TO THE LETTER. AND AS MY SECOND-IN-COMMAND, YOU'RE CHARGED WITH ENFORCING MY WISHES. THERE CAN BE NO HINT OF INSUBORDINATION, EITHER ON YOUR PART OR AMONG THE TROOPS.

YOU WOULDN'T BE COUNSELING DISOBEDIENCE NOW, WOULD YOU, SERGEANT CAESAR?

NO, SIR.

THAT'S VERY GOOD TO HEAR. A MOST WISE SURVIVAL STRATEGY ON YOUR PART. MAYOR FAMAILE AND I HAVE BIG PLANS FOR NEOPOLIS. AND THOSE WHO ARE OPPOSED TO US WILL BE IN FOR QUITE A SHOCK.

MAY I GO NOW, SIR?

CERTAINLY. BUT SERGEANT, I HAVE ONE FURTHER QUESTION.

YES?

IS YOUR MARRIAGE A...MIXED ONE?

WELL, WE'RE BOTH MAMMALS, SIR.

GOOD ENOUGH, THEN. DISMISSED!

666 DEADMAN'S ALLEY 666

DMAN'S ALLEY

DMAN'S ALLEY

ONLY YOU CAN STOP S.T.O.R.M.S. BETTER SAFE THAN SORRY!

RADIO FLYER

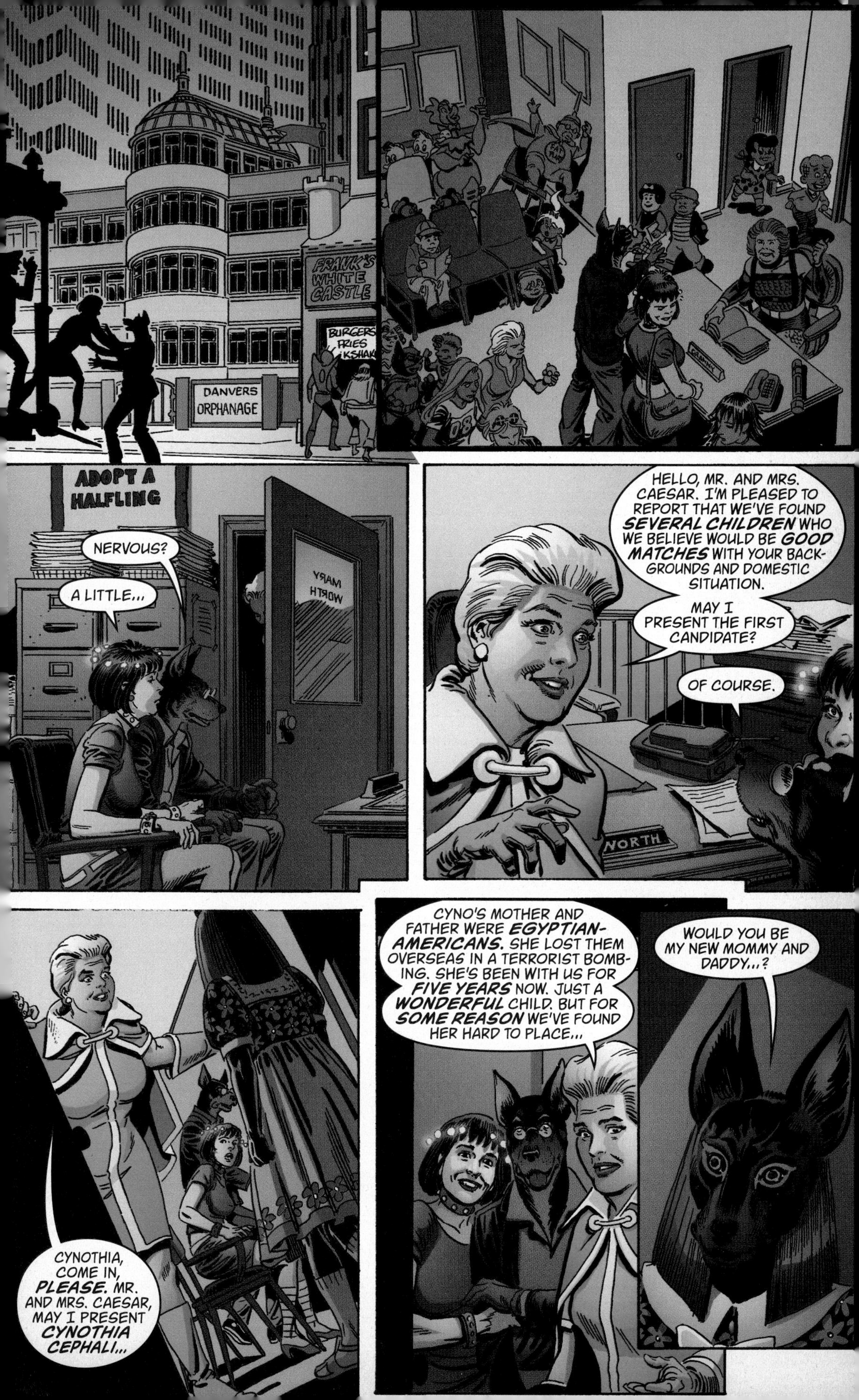
FRANK'S WHITE CASTLE
BURGERS FRIES
DANVERS ORPHANAGE
ADOPT A HALFLING
NERVOUS?
A LITTLE...
MARY WORTH
HELLO, MR. AND MRS. CAESAR. I'M PLEASED TO REPORT THAT WE'VE FOUND SEVERAL CHILDREN WHO WE BELIEVE WOULD BE GOOD MATCHES WITH YOUR BACKGROUNDS AND DOMESTIC SITUATION.
MAY I PRESENT THE FIRST CANDIDATE?
OF COURSE.
NORTH
CYNOTHIA, COME IN, PLEASE. MR. AND MRS. CAESAR, MAY I PRESENT CYNOTHIA CEPHALI...
CYNO'S MOTHER AND FATHER WERE EGYPTIAN-AMERICANS. SHE LOST THEM OVERSEAS IN A TERRORIST BOMBING. SHE'S BEEN WITH US FOR FIVE YEARS NOW. JUST A WONDERFUL CHILD. BUT FOR SOME REASON WE'VE FOUND HER HARD TO PLACE...
WOULD YOU BE MY NEW MOMMY AND DADDY...?

Zelazny and Sons

Baltmen since 1851

IS *PEREGRINE* GOING TO BE OKAY?

SURE, SHE'S JUST GOT A BAD CASE OF *GOD-SHOCK*. HAPPENS ALL THE TIME IN NEOPOLIS TO THE *FAITHFUL*. NOTHING WRONG *PHYSICALLY* WITH HER. SHE'LL BE UP AND AROUND IN *NO TIME.*

I DON'T KNOW. SOME-TIMES A CRISIS OF *FAITH* CAN BE WORSE THAN ANY *DISEASE...*

I AM READY NOW, OFFICERS. MY *PHEROMONE BOOSTERS* HAVE KICKED IN. OUR CATCH-WINDOW IS *TWO HOURS.*

ALL THE *EQUIPMENT'S* IN PLACE.

LET'S DO IT.

JANUS, TELL THE *SARGE* WE'RE ON YOUR WAY TO THE *MARS STREET DOCKS.*

WILL DO, JACKIE.

ANY WORD ON WHAT'S UP WITH *DUST DEVIL?*

NOTHING YET...

CAPTAIN DOUGH'S ANGLING EXPEDITIONS

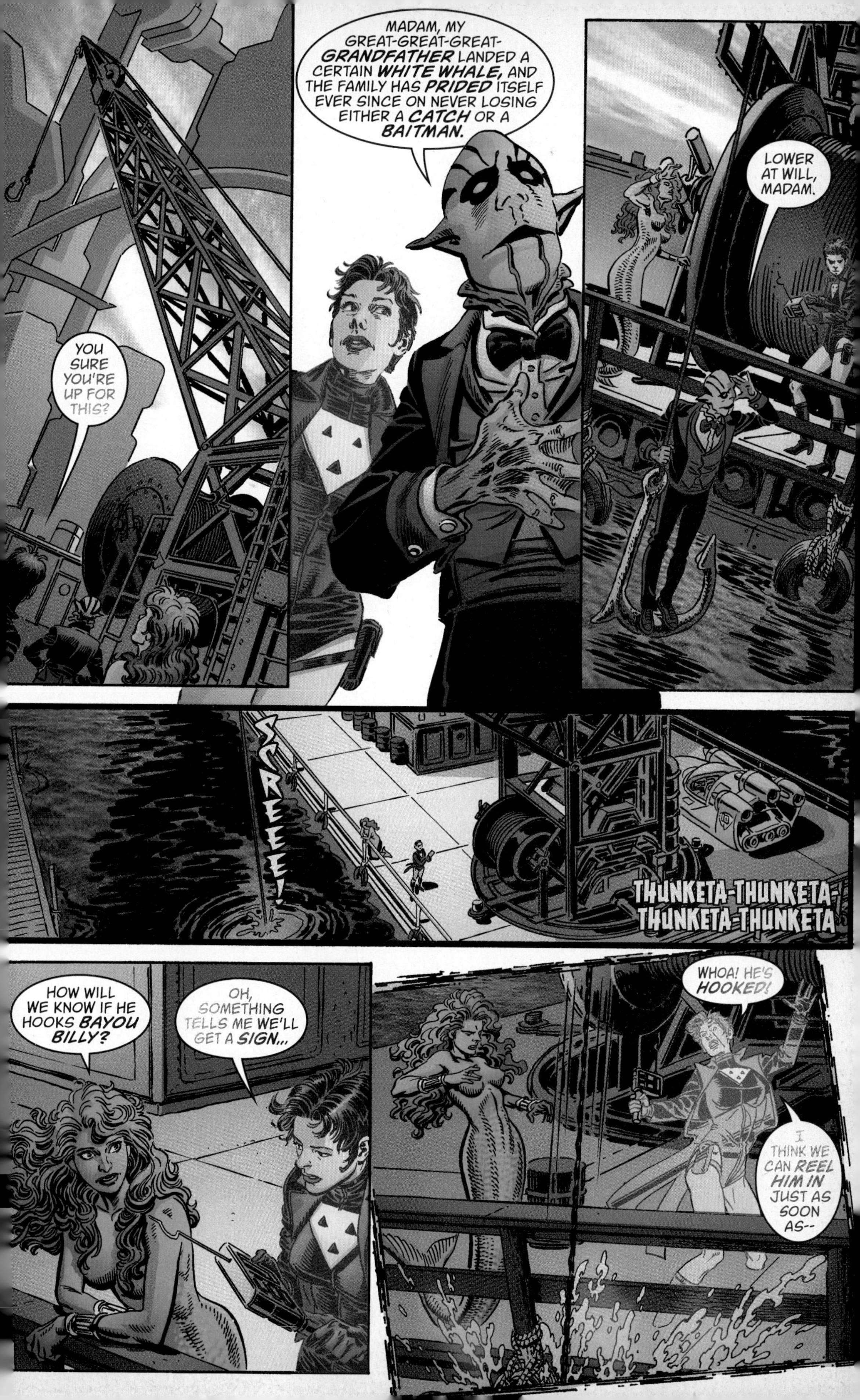
MADAM, MY GREAT-GREAT-GREAT-GRANDFATHER LANDED A CERTAIN WHITE WHALE, AND THE FAMILY HAS PRIDED ITSELF EVER SINCE ON NEVER LOSING EITHER A CATCH OR A BAITMAN.
YOU SURE YOU'RE UP FOR THIS?
LOWER AT WILL, MADAM.
SCREEE!
THUNKETA-THUNKETA-THUNKETA-THUNKETA
HOW WILL WE KNOW IF HE HOOKS BAYOU BILLY?
OH, SOMETHING TELLS ME WE'LL GET A SIGN...
WHOA! HE'S HOOKED!
I THINK WE CAN REEL HIM IN JUST AS SOON AS--

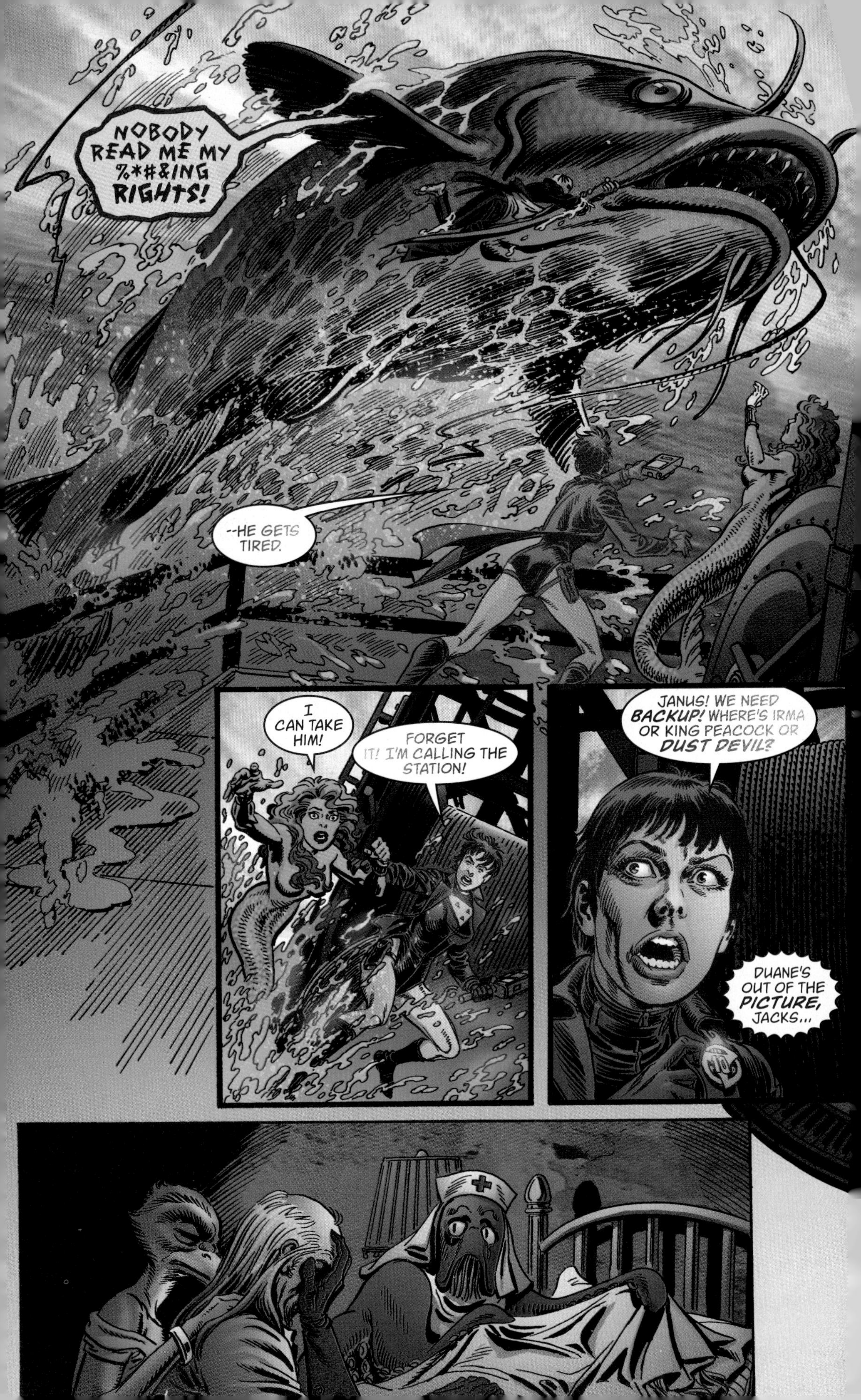
NOBODY READ ME MY %*#&ING RIGHTS!
--HE GETS TIRED.
I CAN TAKE HIM!
FORGET IT! I'M CALLING THE STATION!
JANUS! WE NEED BACKUP! WHERE'S IRMA OR KING PEACOCK OR DUST DEVIL?
DUANE'S OUT OF THE PICTURE, JACKS...

CHAPTER #4

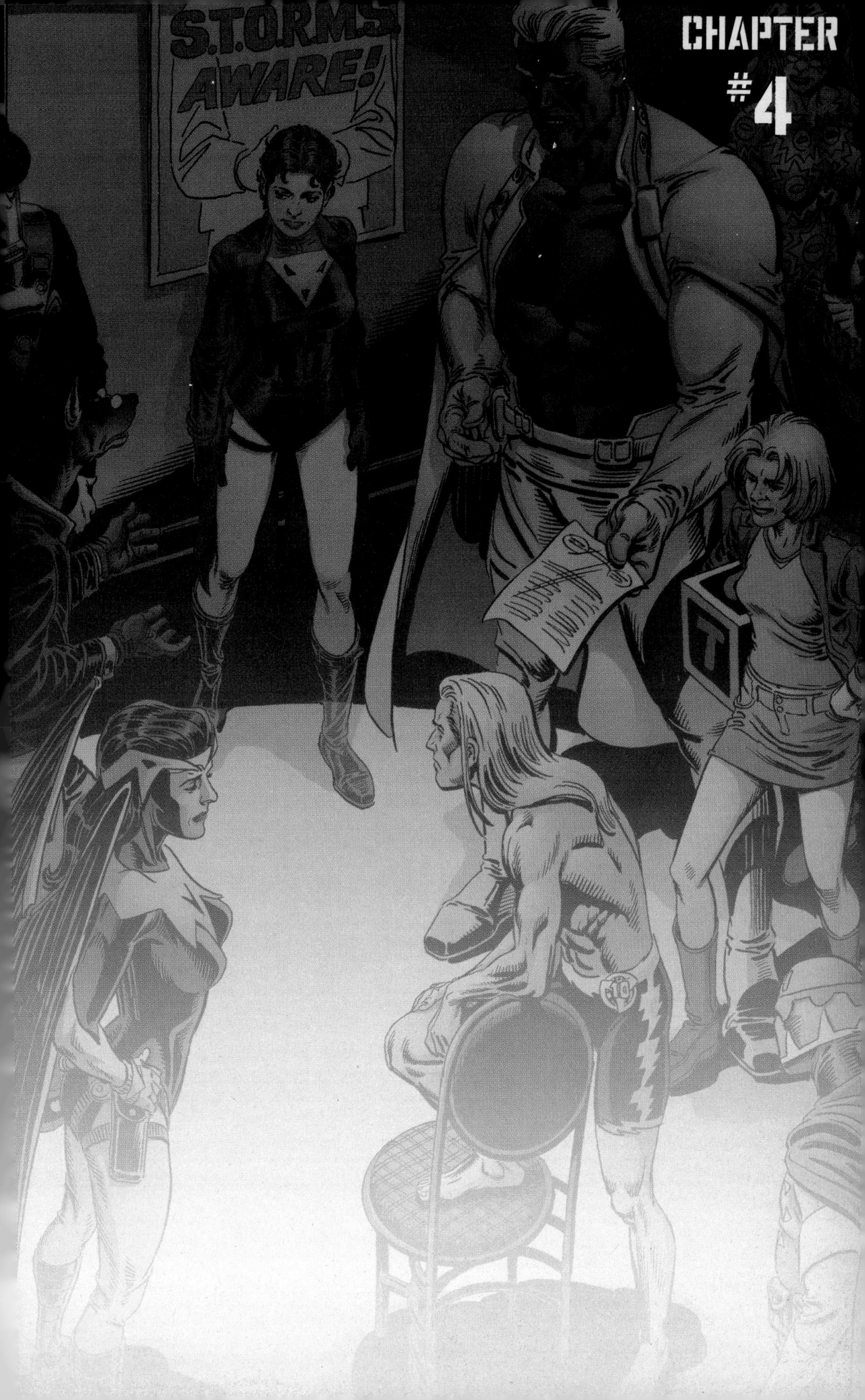
S.T.O.R.M.S.
AWARE!

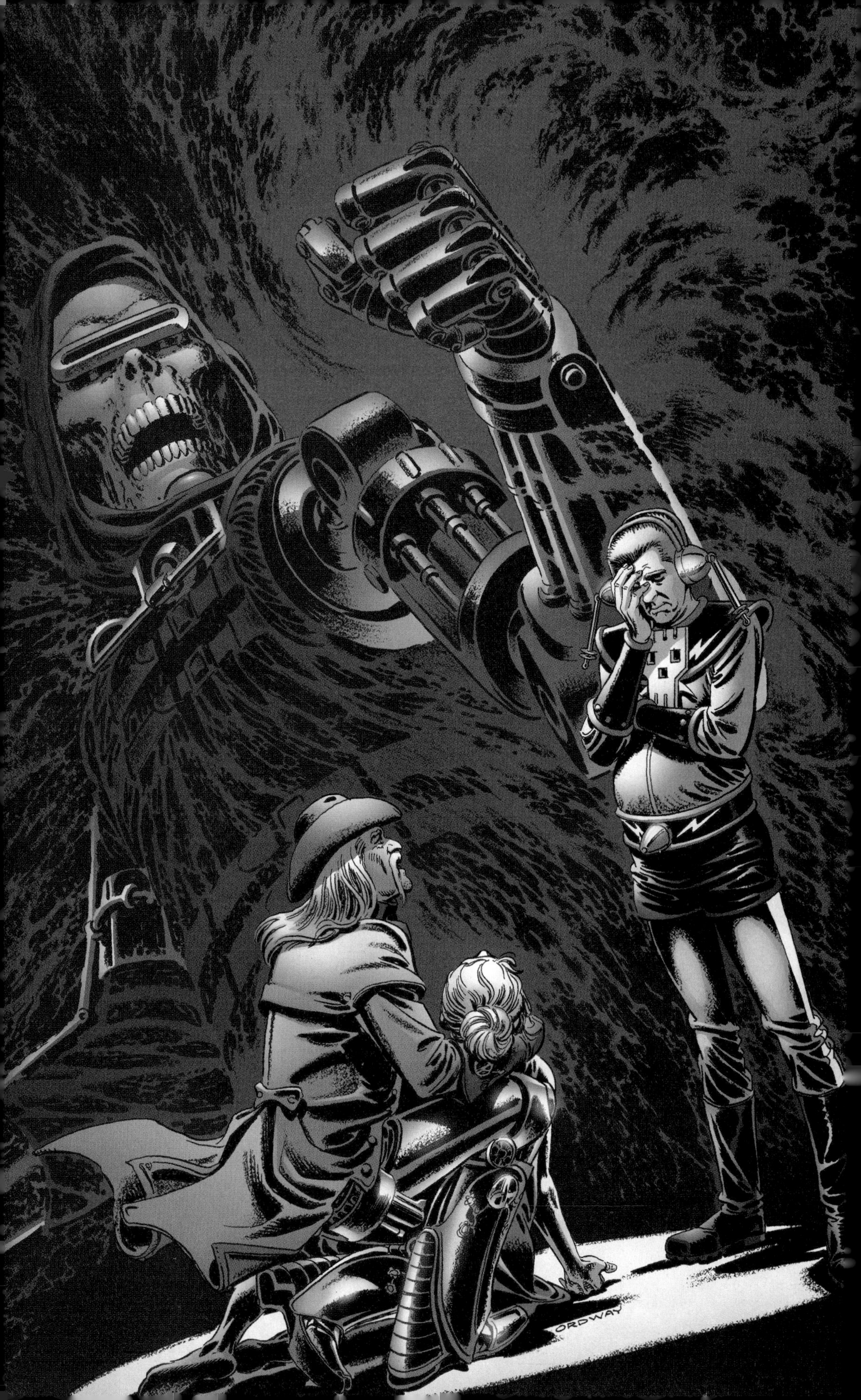
ORDWAY

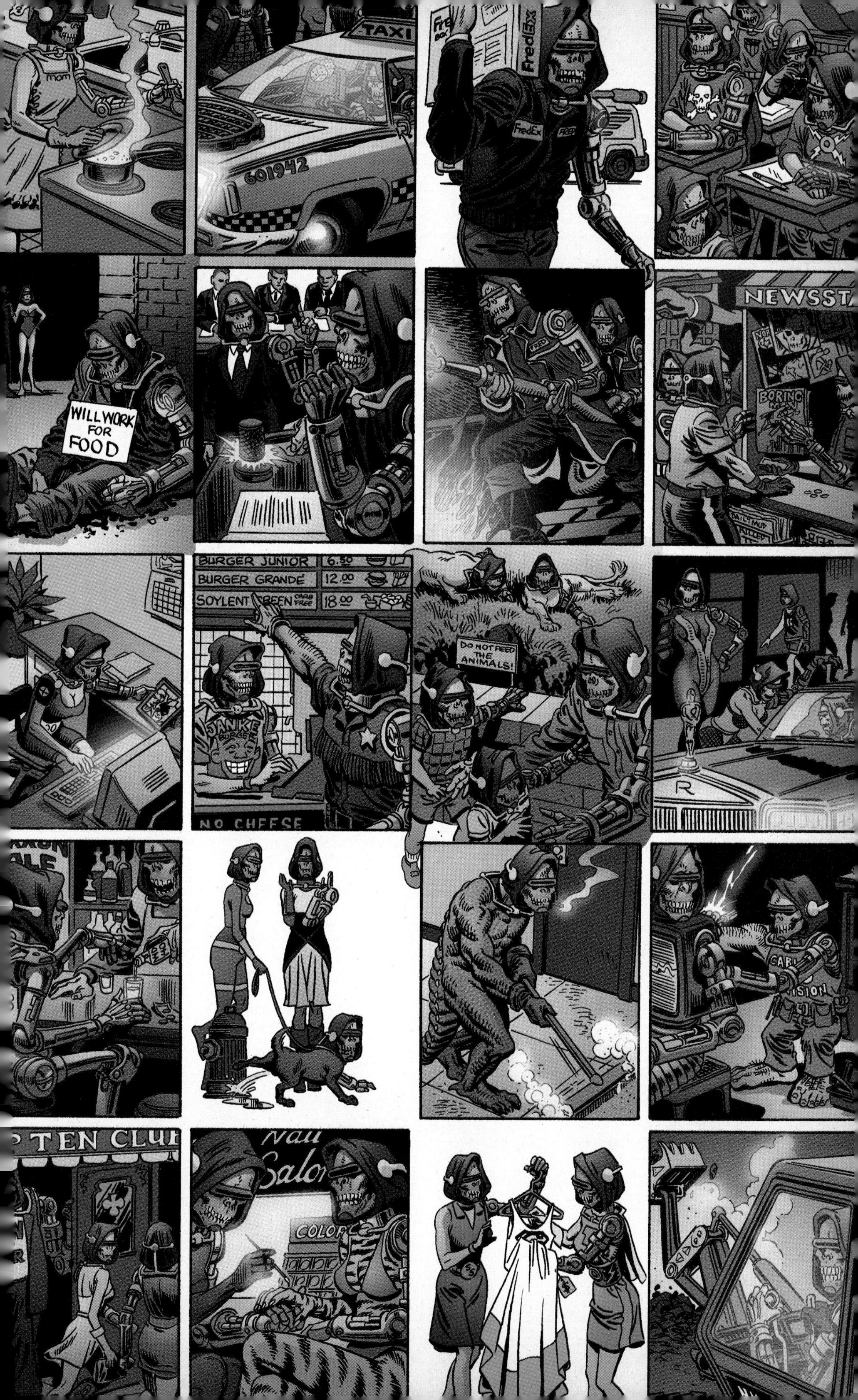
mom
TAXI
601942
FredEx
FredEx
WILL WORK FOR FOOD
NEWSSTA
BORING
BURGER JUNIOR 6.50
BURGER GRANDE 12.00
SOYLENT GREEN CARB FREE 18.00
JANKE BURGER
NO CHEESE
DO NOT FEED THE ANIMALS!
TEN CLUB
COLOR

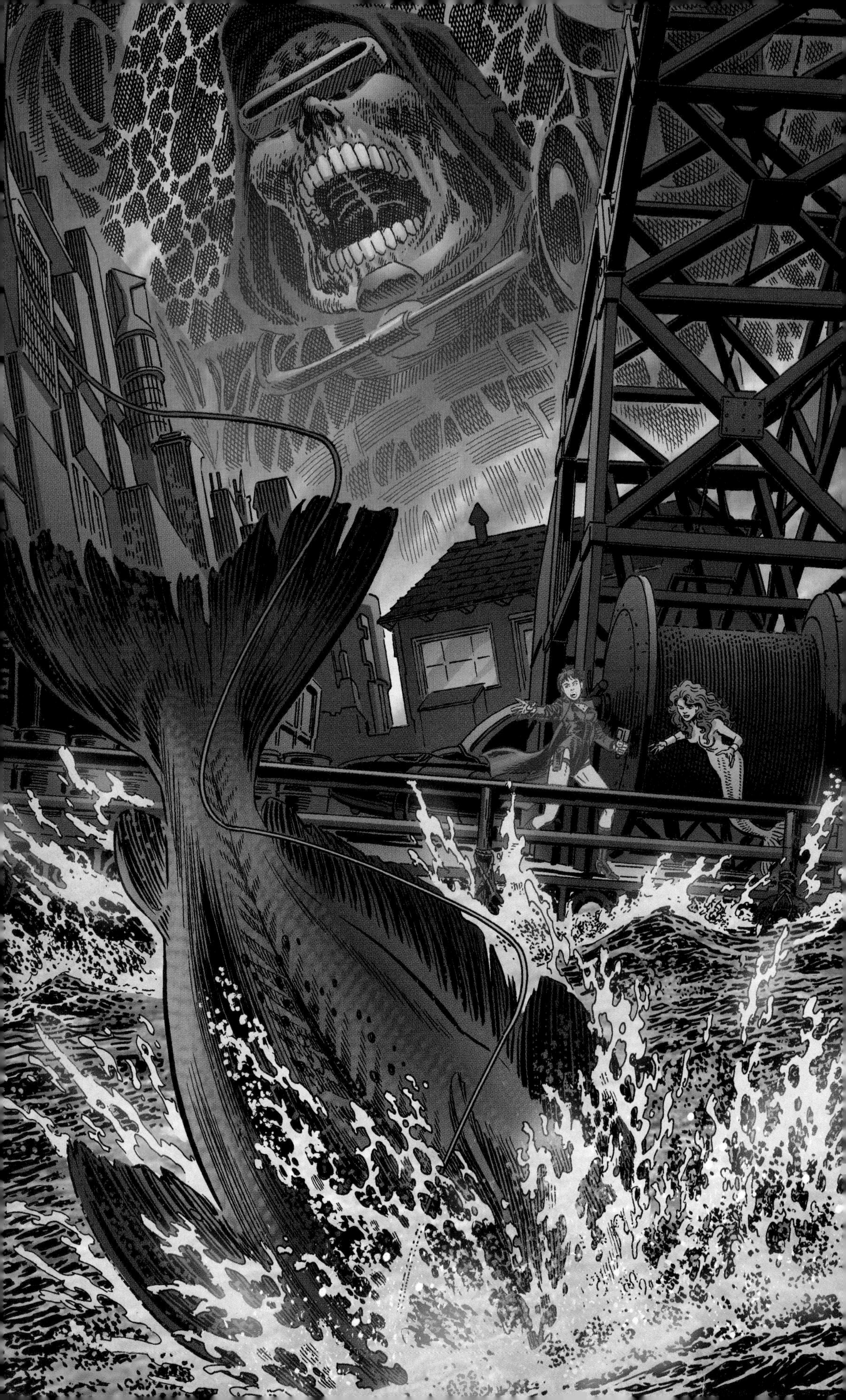

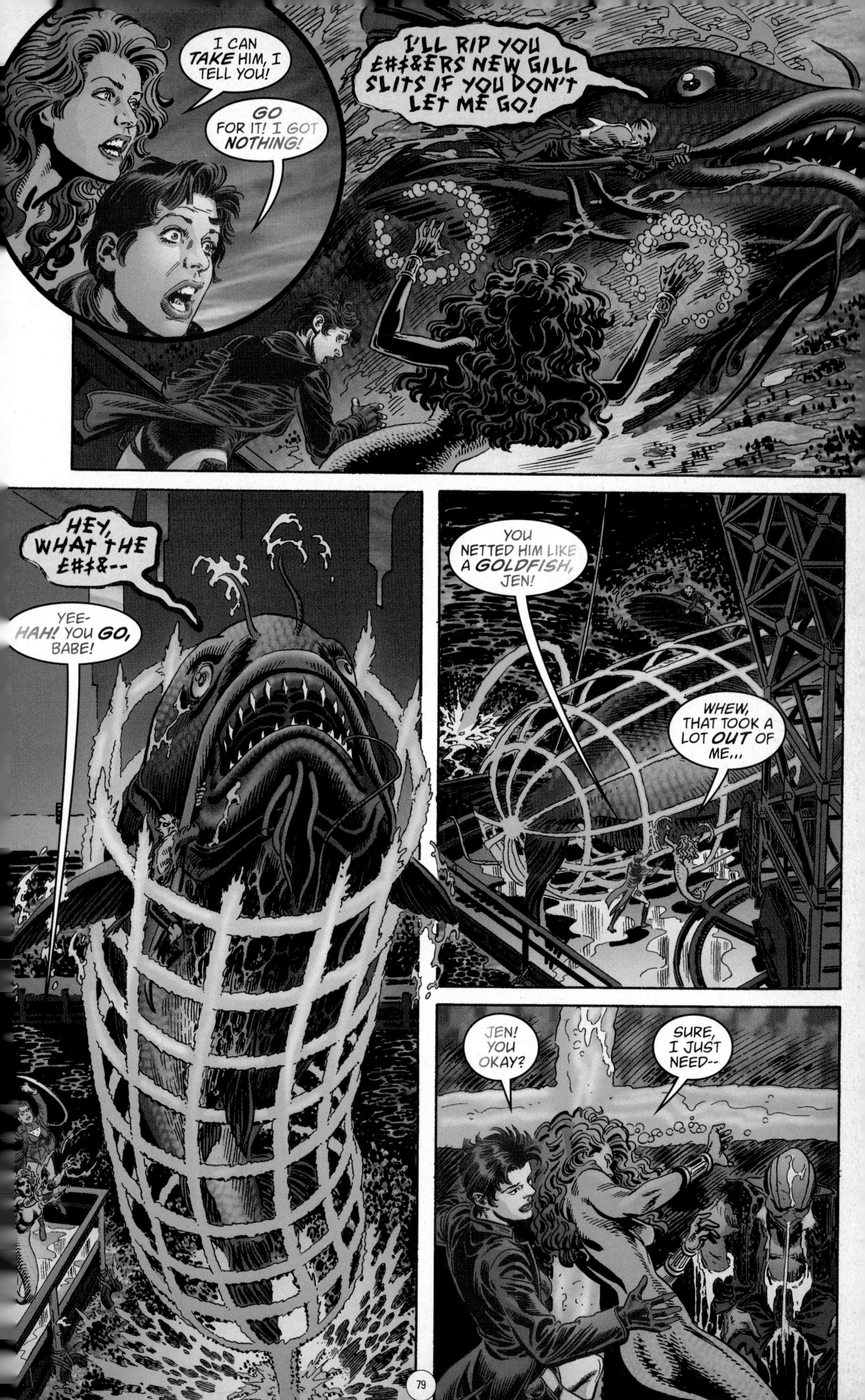
I CAN TAKE HIM, I TELL YOU!
GO FOR IT! I GOT NOTHING!
I'LL RIP YOU £#$&ERS NEW GILL SLITS IF YOU DON'T LET ME GO!
HEY, WHAT THE £#$&--
YEE-HAH! YOU GO, BABE!
YOU NETTED HIM LIKE A GOLDFISH, JEN!
WHEW, THAT TOOK A LOT OUT OF ME...
JEN! YOU OKAY?
SURE, I JUST NEED--

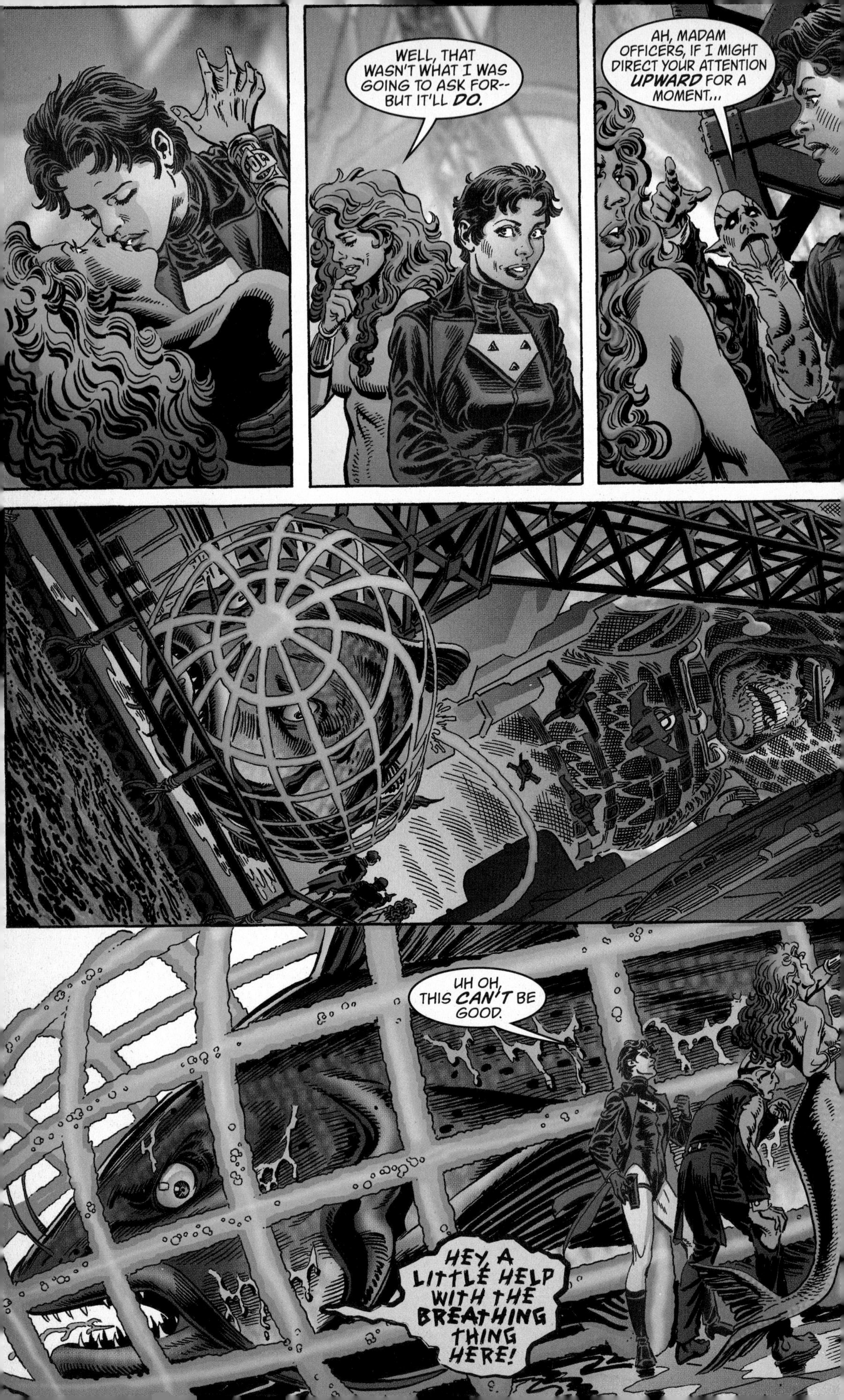
WELL, THAT WASN'T WHAT I WAS GOING TO ASK FOR-- BUT IT'LL DO.
AH, MADAM OFFICERS, IF I MIGHT DIRECT YOUR ATTENTION UPWARD FOR A MOMENT...
UH OH, THIS CAN'T BE GOOD.
HEY, A LITTLE HELP WITH THE BREATHING THING HERE!

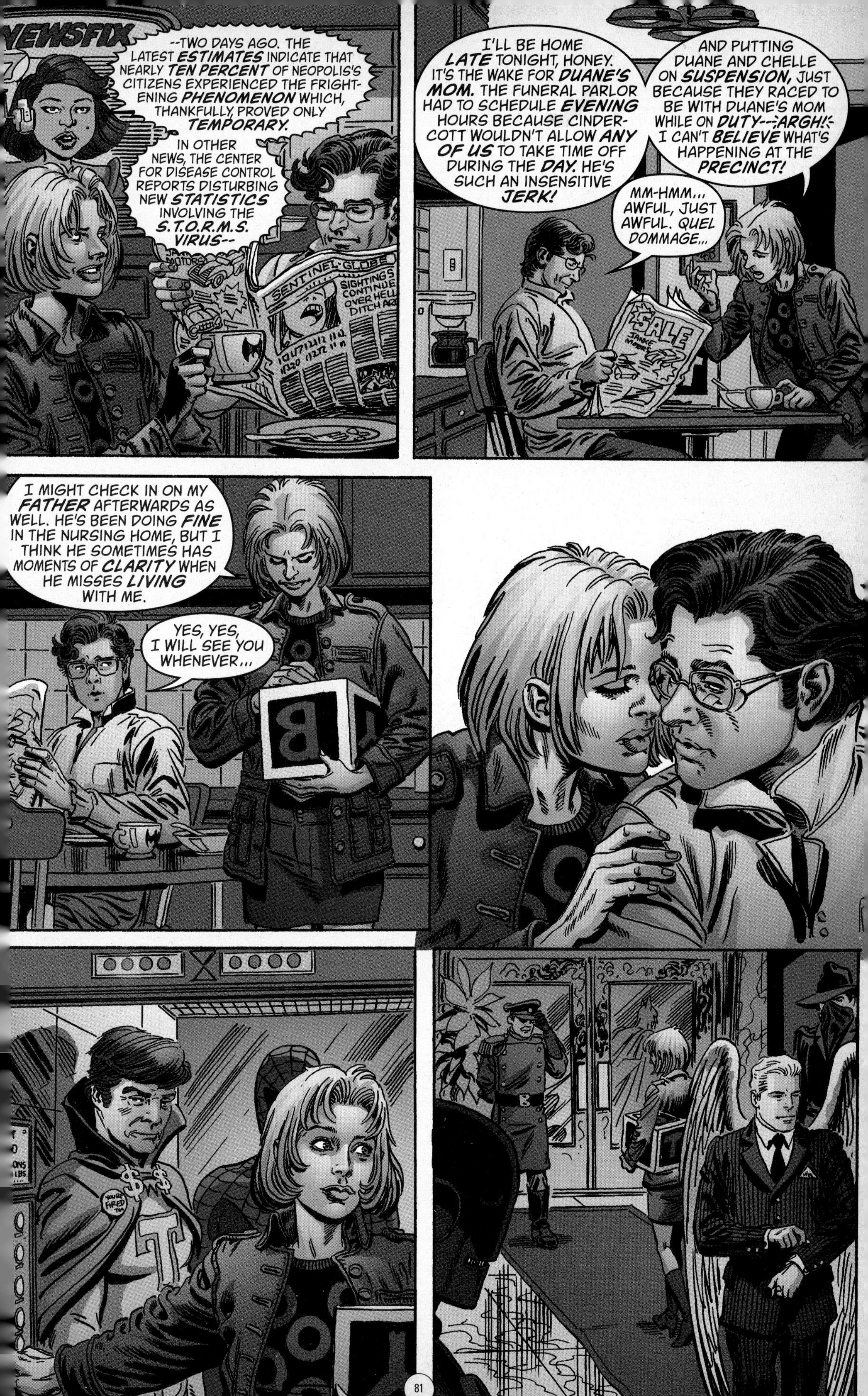
NEWSFIX
--TWO DAYS AGO. THE LATEST ESTIMATES INDICATE THAT NEARLY TEN PERCENT OF NEOPOLIS'S CITIZENS EXPERIENCED THE FRIGHTENING PHENOMENON WHICH, THANKFULLY, PROVED ONLY TEMPORARY.
IN OTHER NEWS, THE CENTER FOR DISEASE CONTROL REPORTS DISTURBING NEW STATISTICS INVOLVING THE S.T.O.R.M.S. VIRUS--
SENTINEL-GLOBE
SIGHTINGS CONTINUE OVER HELL DITCH
I'LL BE HOME LATE TONIGHT, HONEY. IT'S THE WAKE FOR DUANE'S MOM. THE FUNERAL PARLOR HAD TO SCHEDULE EVENING HOURS BECAUSE CINDERCOTT WOULDN'T ALLOW ANY OF US TO TAKE TIME OFF DURING THE DAY. HE'S SUCH AN INSENSITIVE JERK!
AND PUTTING DUANE AND CHELLE ON SUSPENSION, JUST BECAUSE THEY RACED TO BE WITH DUANE'S MOM WHILE ON DUTY--ARGH!! I CAN'T BELIEVE WHAT'S HAPPENING AT THE PRECINCT!
MM-HMM... AWFUL, JUST AWFUL. QUEL DOMMAGE...
SALE
I MIGHT CHECK IN ON MY FATHER AFTERWARDS AS WELL. HE'S BEEN DOING FINE IN THE NURSING HOME, BUT I THINK HE SOMETIMES HAS MOMENTS OF CLARITY WHEN HE MISSES LIVING WITH ME.
YES, YES, I WILL SEE YOU WHENEVER...
YOU'RE FIRED

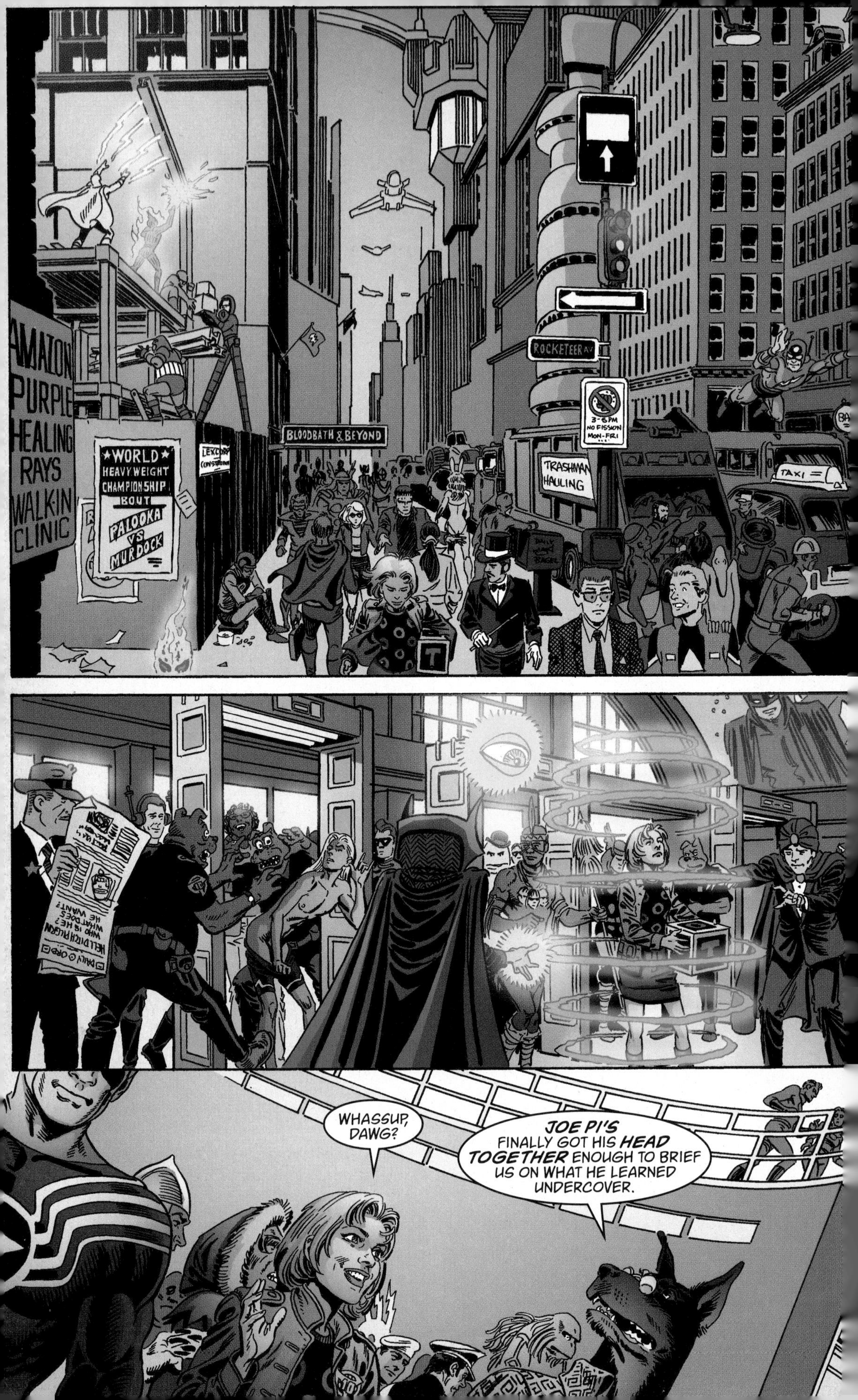
AMAZON PURPLE HEALING RAYS WALK-IN CLINIC
WORLD HEAVYWEIGHT CHAMPIONSHIP BOUT
PALOOKA VS MURDOCK
BLOODBATH & BEYOND
ROCKETEER AV
3-5PM NO FISSION MON-FRI
TRASHMAN HAULING
TAXI
WHASSUP, DAWG?
JOE PI'S FINALLY GOT HIS HEAD TOGETHER ENOUGH TO BRIEF US ON WHAT HE LEARNED UNDERCOVER.

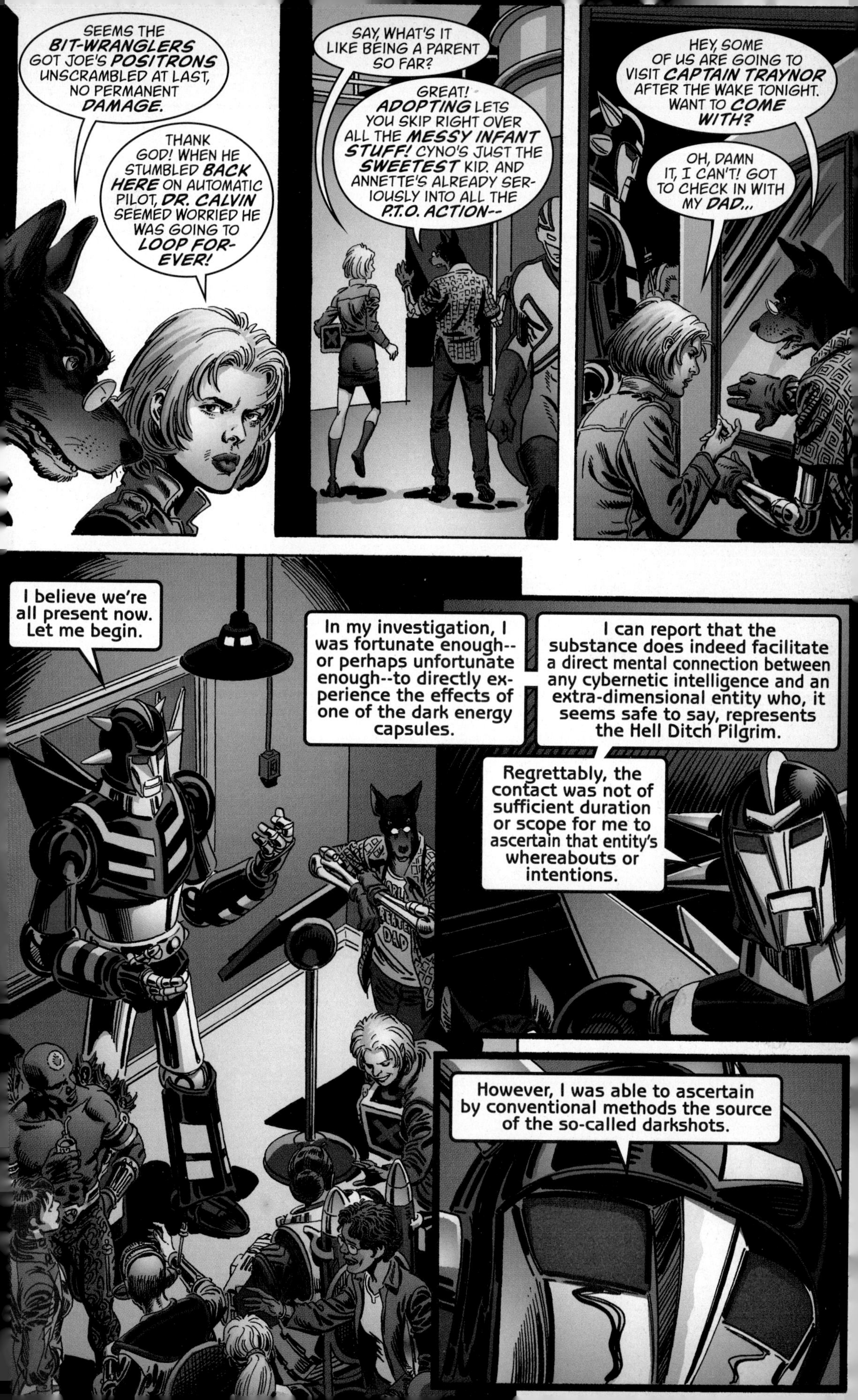

SEEMS THE BIT-WRANGLERS GOT JOE'S POSITRONS UNSCRAMBLED AT LAST, NO PERMANENT DAMAGE.
THANK GOD! WHEN HE STUMBLED BACK HERE ON AUTOMATIC PILOT, DR. CALVIN SEEMED WORRIED HE WAS GOING TO LOOP FOR-EVER!
SAY, WHAT'S IT LIKE BEING A PARENT SO FAR?
GREAT! ADOPTING LETS YOU SKIP RIGHT OVER ALL THE MESSY INFANT STUFF! CYNO'S JUST THE SWEETEST KID. AND ANNETTE'S ALREADY SER-IOUSLY INTO ALL THE P.T.O. ACTION--
HEY, SOME OF US ARE GOING TO VISIT CAPTAIN TRAYNOR AFTER THE WAKE TONIGHT. WANT TO COME WITH?
OH, DAMN IT, I CAN'T! GOT TO CHECK IN WITH MY DAD...
I believe we're all present now. Let me begin.
In my investigation, I was fortunate enough--or perhaps unfortunate enough--to directly ex-perience the effects of one of the dark energy capsules.
I can report that the substance does indeed facilitate a direct mental connection between any cybernetic intelligence and an extra-dimensional entity who, it seems safe to say, represents the Hell Ditch Pilgrim.
Regrettably, the contact was not of sufficient duration or scope for me to ascertain that entity's whereabouts or intentions.
However, I was able to ascertain by conventional methods the source of the so-called darkshots.

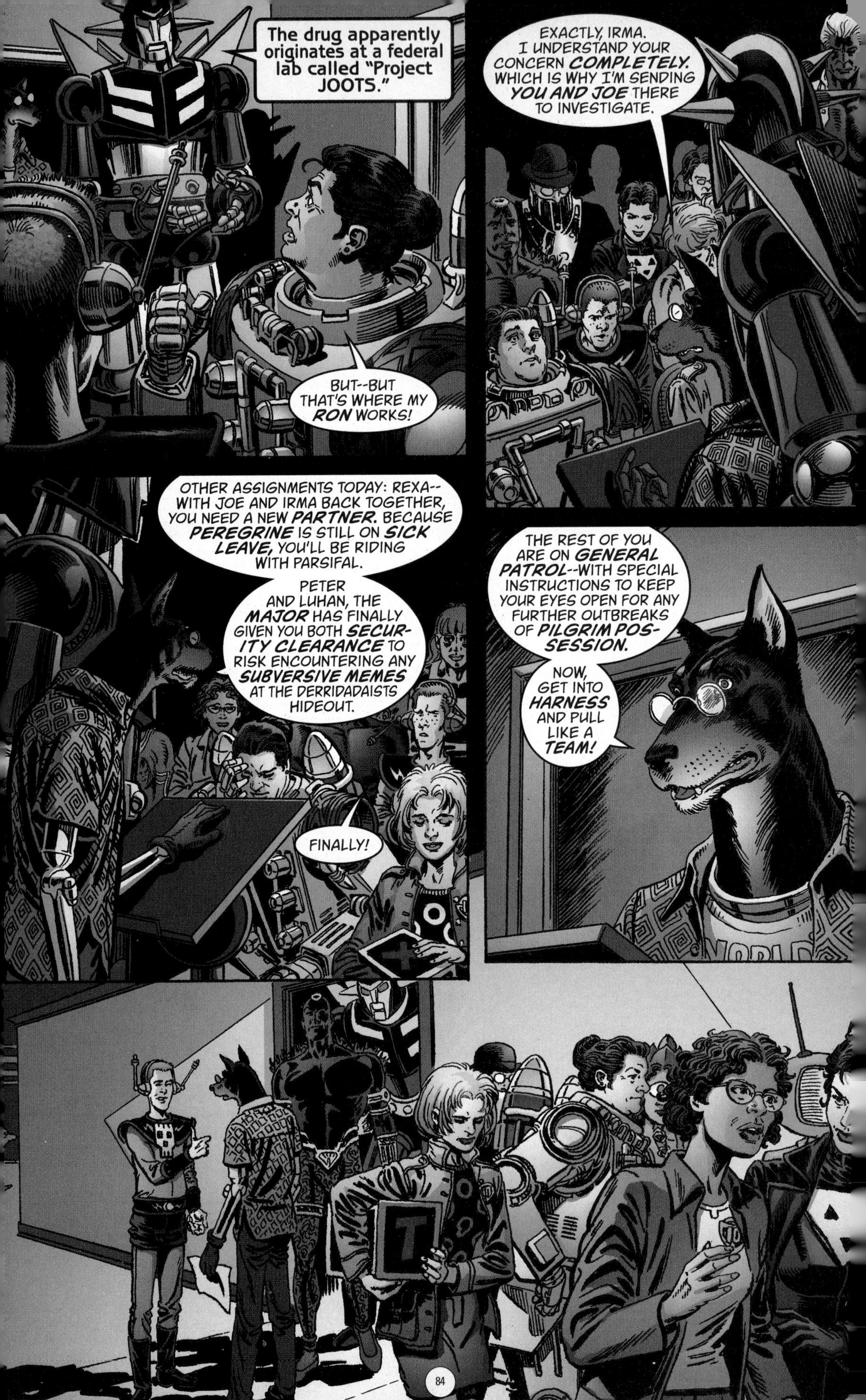

The drug apparently originates at a federal lab called "Project JOOTS."
BUT--BUT THAT'S WHERE MY RON WORKS!
EXACTLY, IRMA. I UNDERSTAND YOUR CONCERN COMPLETELY. WHICH IS WHY I'M SENDING YOU AND JOE THERE TO INVESTIGATE.
OTHER ASSIGNMENTS TODAY: REXA--WITH JOE AND IRMA BACK TOGETHER, YOU NEED A NEW PARTNER. BECAUSE PEREGRINE IS STILL ON SICK LEAVE, YOU'LL BE RIDING WITH PARSIFAL.
PETER AND LUHAN, THE MAJOR HAS FINALLY GIVEN YOU BOTH SECURITY CLEARANCE TO RISK ENCOUNTERING ANY SUBVERSIVE MEMES AT THE DERRIDADAISTS HIDEOUT.
FINALLY!
THE REST OF YOU ARE ON GENERAL PATROL--WITH SPECIAL INSTRUCTIONS TO KEEP YOUR EYES OPEN FOR ANY FURTHER OUTBREAKS OF PILGRIM POSSESSION.
NOW, GET INTO HARNESS AND PULL LIKE A TEAM!

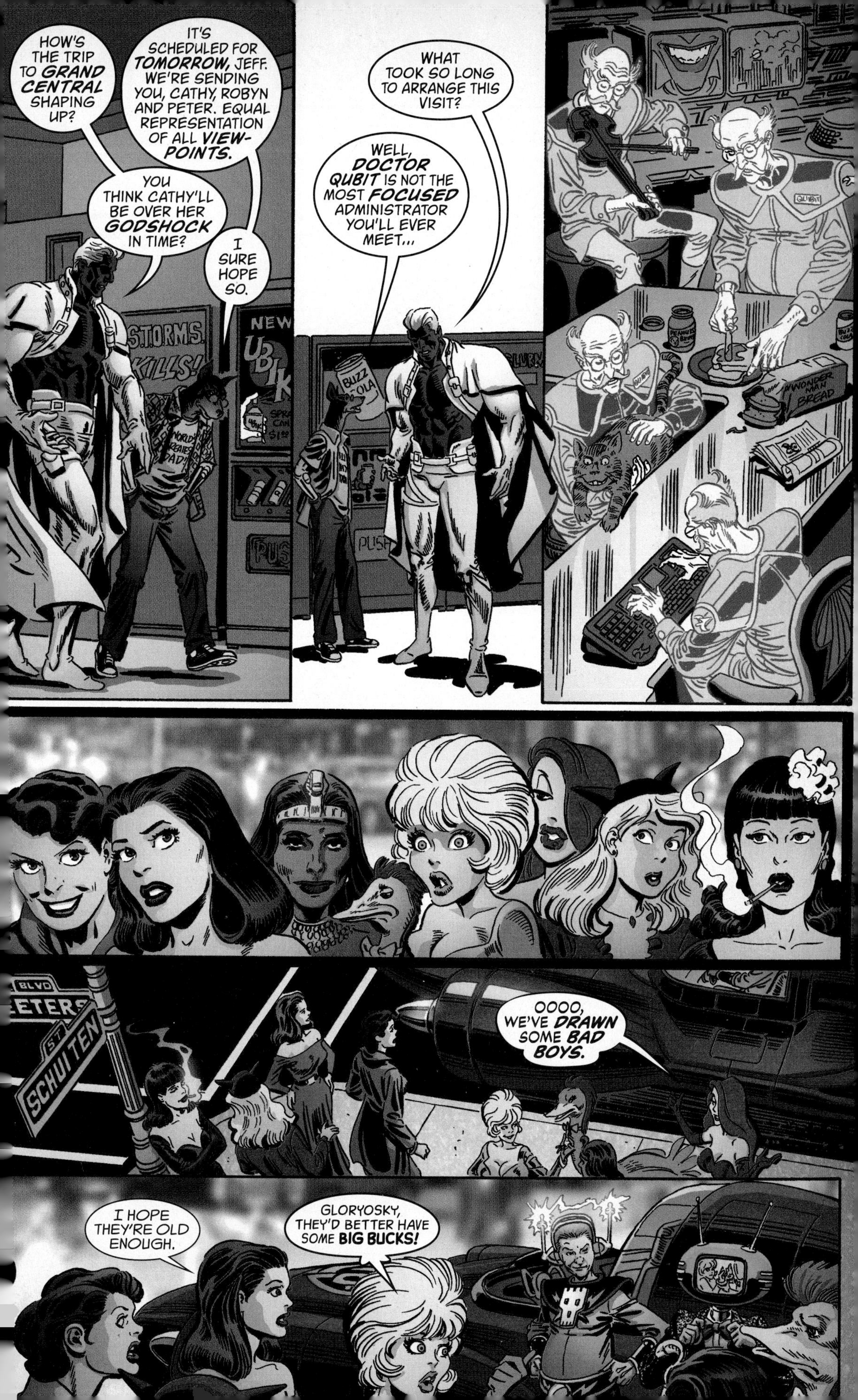
HOW'S THE TRIP TO GRAND CENTRAL SHAPING UP?
IT'S SCHEDULED FOR TOMORROW, JEFF. WE'RE SENDING YOU, CATHY, ROBYN AND PETER. EQUAL REPRESENTATION OF ALL VIEW-POINTS.
YOU THINK CATHY'LL BE OVER HER GODSHOCK IN TIME?
I SURE HOPE SO.
S.T.O.R.M.S.
KILLS!
NEW
UBIK
WORLD'S GREATEST DAD!
PUSH
WHAT TOOK SO LONG TO ARRANGE THIS VISIT?
WELL, DOCTOR QUBIT IS NOT THE MOST FOCUSED ADMINISTRATOR YOU'LL EVER MEET...
BUZZ COLA
PUSH
QUBIT
WONDER MAN BREAD
BLVD
PEETERS
ST
SCHUITEN
OOOO, WE'VE DRAWN SOME BAD BOYS.
I HOPE THEY'RE OLD ENOUGH.
GLORYOSKY, THEY'D BETTER HAVE SOME BIG BUCKS!

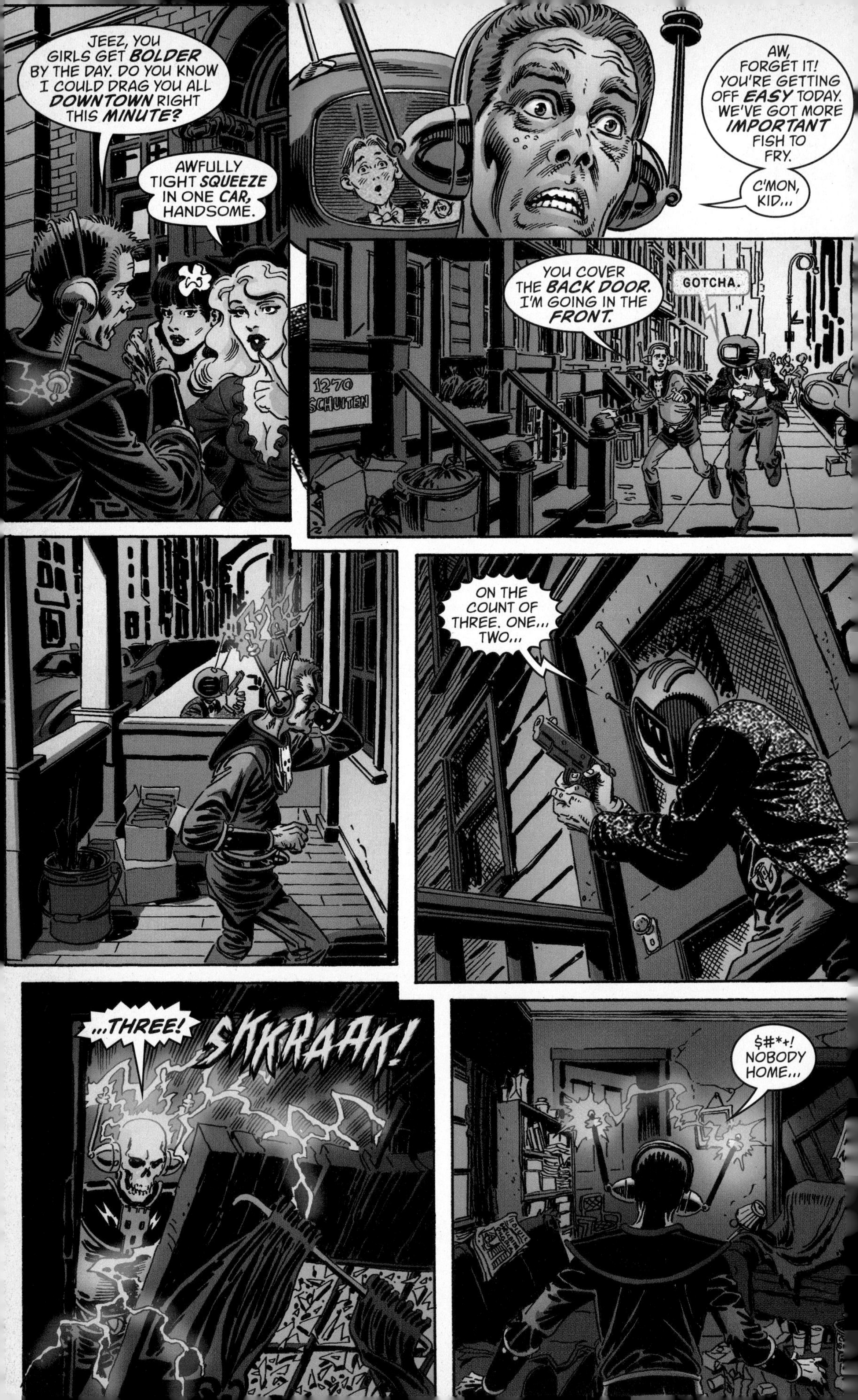
JEEZ, YOU GIRLS GET BOLDER BY THE DAY. DO YOU KNOW I COULD DRAG YOU ALL DOWNTOWN RIGHT THIS MINUTE?
AWFULLY TIGHT SQUEEZE IN ONE CAR, HANDSOME.
AW, FORGET IT! YOU'RE GETTING OFF EASY TODAY. WE'VE GOT MORE IMPORTANT FISH TO FRY.
C'MON, KID...
YOU COVER THE BACK DOOR. I'M GOING IN THE FRONT.
GOTCHA.
1270 SCHUITEN
ON THE COUNT OF THREE. ONE... TWO...
...THREE!
SKKRAAK!
$#*+! NOBODY HOME...

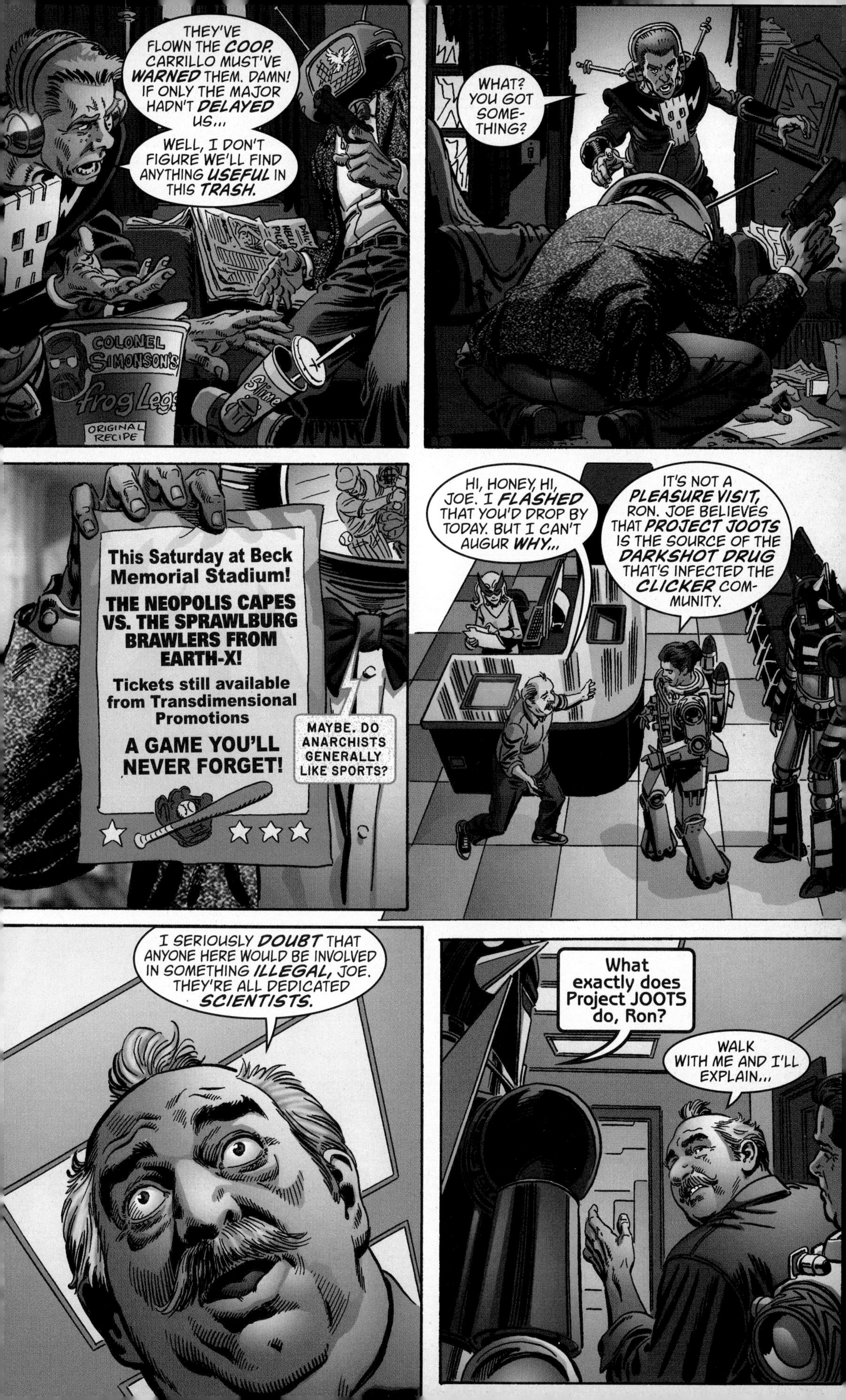
THEY'VE FLOWN THE COOP. CARRILLO MUST'VE WARNED THEM. DAMN! IF ONLY THE MAJOR HADN'T DELAYED US...
WELL, I DON'T FIGURE WE'LL FIND ANYTHING USEFUL IN THIS TRASH.
COLONEL SIMONSON'S Frog Legs ORIGINAL RECIPE
Slime
WHAT? YOU GOT SOME-THING?
This Saturday at Beck Memorial Stadium!
THE NEOPOLIS CAPES VS. THE SPRAWLBURG BRAWLERS FROM EARTH-X!
Tickets still available from Transdimensional Promotions
A GAME YOU'LL NEVER FORGET!
MAYBE. DO ANARCHISTS GENERALLY LIKE SPORTS?
HI, HONEY, HI, JOE. I FLASHED THAT YOU'D DROP BY TODAY. BUT I CAN'T AUGUR WHY...
IT'S NOT A PLEASURE VISIT, RON. JOE BELIEVES THAT PROJECT JOOTS IS THE SOURCE OF THE DARKSHOT DRUG THAT'S INFECTED THE CLICKER COM-MUNITY.
I SERIOUSLY DOUBT THAT ANYONE HERE WOULD BE INVOLVED IN SOMETHING ILLEGAL, JOE. THEY'RE ALL DEDICATED SCIENTISTS.
What exactly does Project JOOTS do, Ron?
WALK WITH ME AND I'LL EXPLAIN...

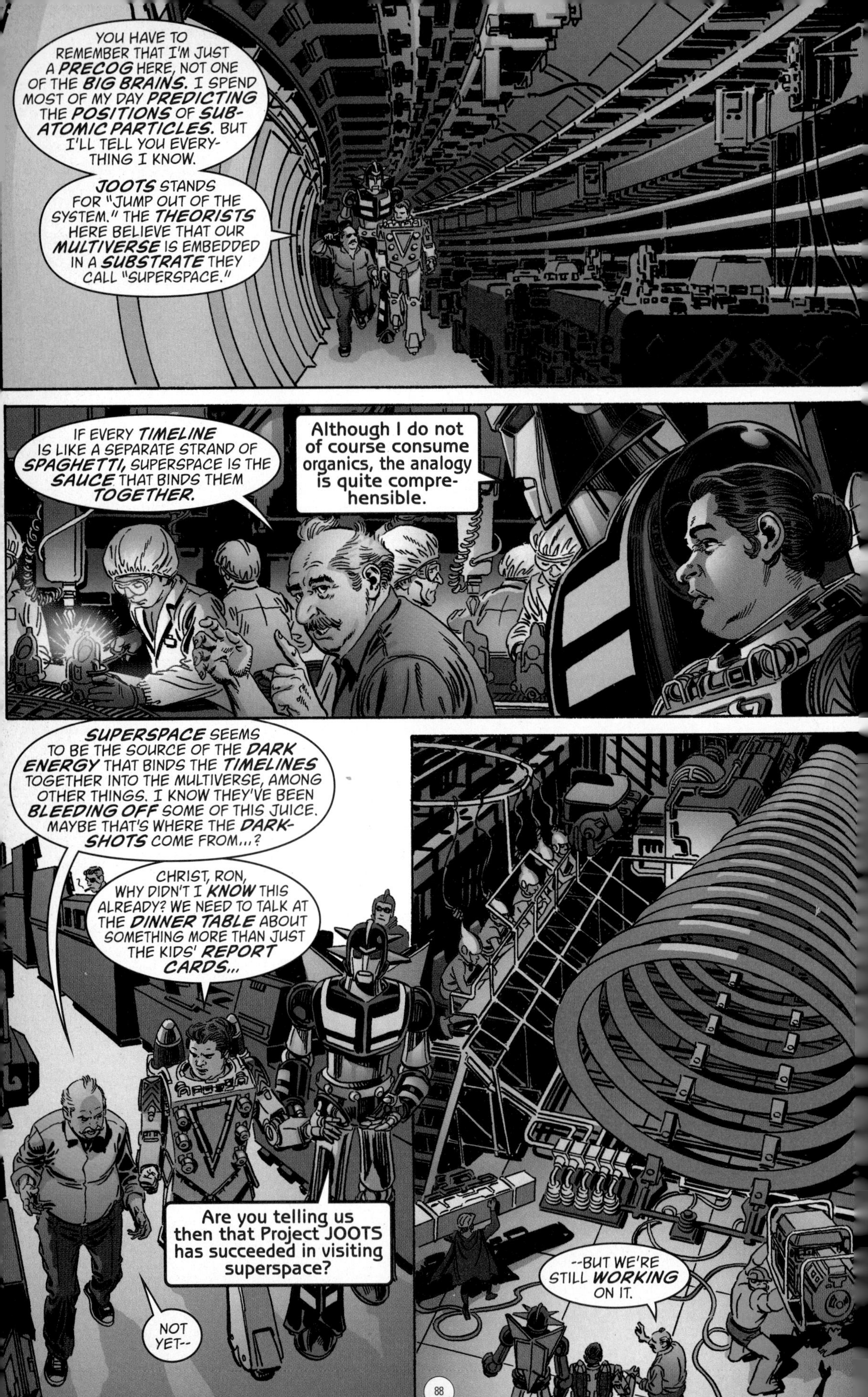
YOU HAVE TO REMEMBER THAT I'M JUST A PRECOG HERE, NOT ONE OF THE BIG BRAINS. I SPEND MOST OF MY DAY PREDICTING THE POSITIONS OF SUB-ATOMIC PARTICLES. BUT I'LL TELL YOU EVERY-THING I KNOW.
JOOTS STANDS FOR "JUMP OUT OF THE SYSTEM." THE THEORISTS HERE BELIEVE THAT OUR MULTIVERSE IS EMBEDDED IN A SUBSTRATE THEY CALL "SUPERSPACE."
IF EVERY TIMELINE IS LIKE A SEPARATE STRAND OF SPAGHETTI, SUPERSPACE IS THE SAUCE THAT BINDS THEM TOGETHER.
Although I do not of course consume organics, the analogy is quite compre-hensible.
SUPERSPACE SEEMS TO BE THE SOURCE OF THE DARK ENERGY THAT BINDS THE TIMELINES TOGETHER INTO THE MULTIVERSE, AMONG OTHER THINGS. I KNOW THEY'VE BEEN BLEEDING OFF SOME OF THIS JUICE. MAYBE THAT'S WHERE THE DARK-SHOTS COME FROM...?
CHRIST, RON, WHY DIDN'T I KNOW THIS ALREADY? WE NEED TO TALK AT THE DINNER TABLE ABOUT SOMETHING MORE THAN JUST THE KIDS' REPORT CARDS...
Are you telling us then that Project JOOTS has succeeded in visiting superspace?
NOT YET--
--BUT WE'RE STILL WORKING ON IT.

Ron, who is in charge of bleeding off the dark energy?

WHY, THAT WOULD BE RIKBY-2001.

A non-organic citizen?

SURE.

Let's find this individual...

STAY BACK, RON.

Rikby-2001, I am Officer Pi from the Tenth Precinct, with my partner Officer Warnow. We wish to speak with you.

§TOK-TOK§

SAFETY NOTICE: NEURAL INHIBITORS INSTALLED AT THIS POINT

My sensors reveal you're in there, citizen. We are now about to enter forcibly--

OH, CHRIST, JOE, JUST STAND ASIDE!

STEP AWAY FROM THE ENERGY FEED, CLICKER!

BOOM!

$#*&! HE OVERDOSED RATHER THAN TALK.

I'm afraid this is my fault, Irma. But then, I am just a dumb clicker.

AW, CHRIST, JOE, SORRY...

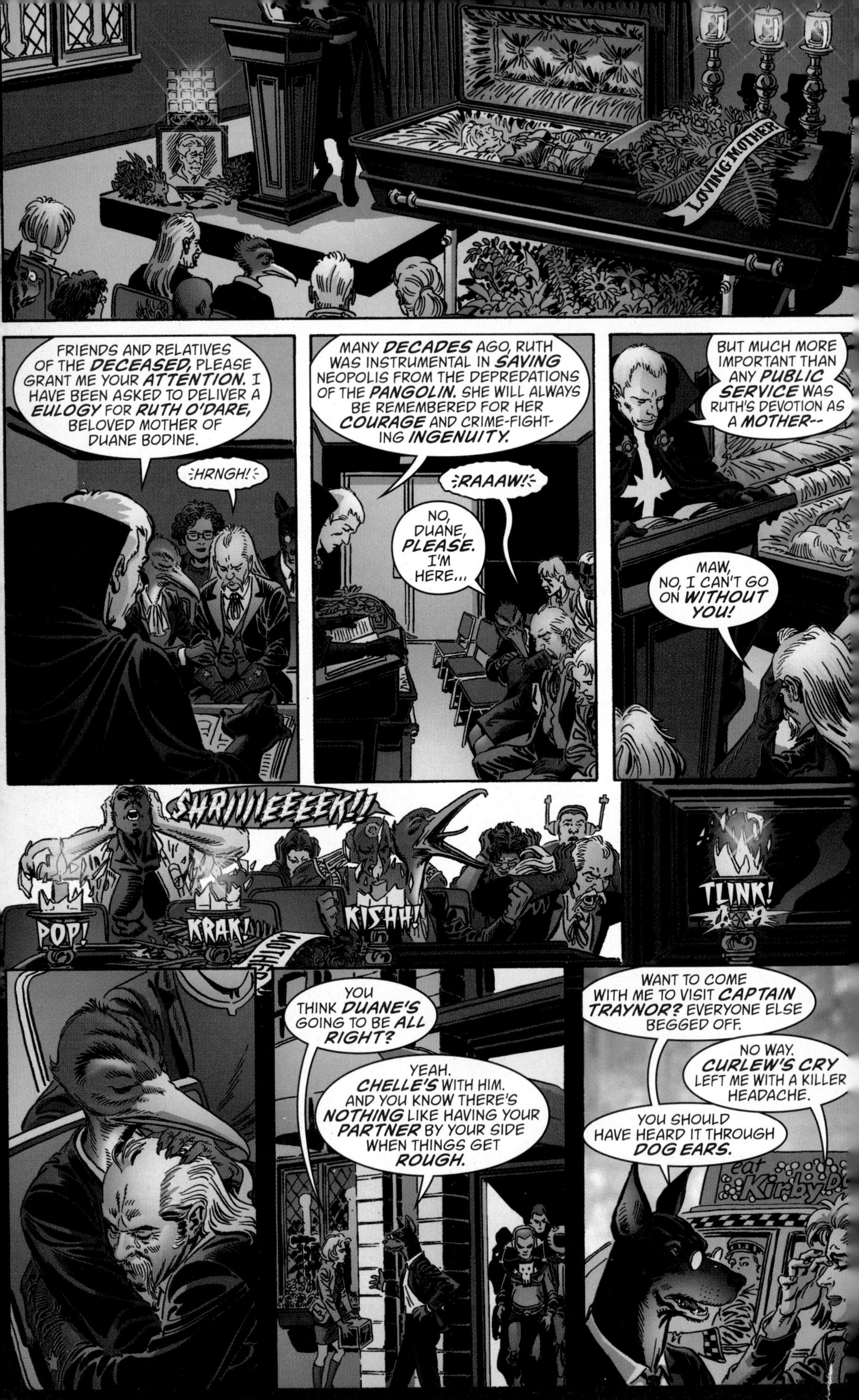
LOVING MOTHER
FRIENDS AND RELATIVES OF THE DECEASED, PLEASE GRANT ME YOUR ATTENTION. I HAVE BEEN ASKED TO DELIVER A EULOGY FOR RUTH O'DARE, BELOVED MOTHER OF DUANE BODINE.
HRNGH!
MANY DECADES AGO, RUTH WAS INSTRUMENTAL IN SAVING NEOPOLIS FROM THE DEPREDATIONS OF THE PANGOLIN. SHE WILL ALWAYS BE REMEMBERED FOR HER COURAGE AND CRIME-FIGHTING INGENUITY.
RAAAW!
NO, DUANE, PLEASE. I'M HERE...
BUT MUCH MORE IMPORTANT THAN ANY PUBLIC SERVICE WAS RUTH'S DEVOTION AS A MOTHER--
MAW, NO, I CAN'T GO ON WITHOUT YOU!
SHRIIIIEEEEK!!
POP!
KRAK!
KISHH!
TLINK!
YOU THINK DUANE'S GOING TO BE ALL RIGHT?
YEAH. CHELLE'S WITH HIM. AND YOU KNOW THERE'S NOTHING LIKE HAVING YOUR PARTNER BY YOUR SIDE WHEN THINGS GET ROUGH.
WANT TO COME WITH ME TO VISIT CAPTAIN TRAYNOR? EVERYONE ELSE BEGGED OFF.
NO WAY. CURLEW'S CRY LEFT ME WITH A KILLER HEADACHE.
YOU SHOULD HAVE HEARD IT THROUGH DOG EARS.

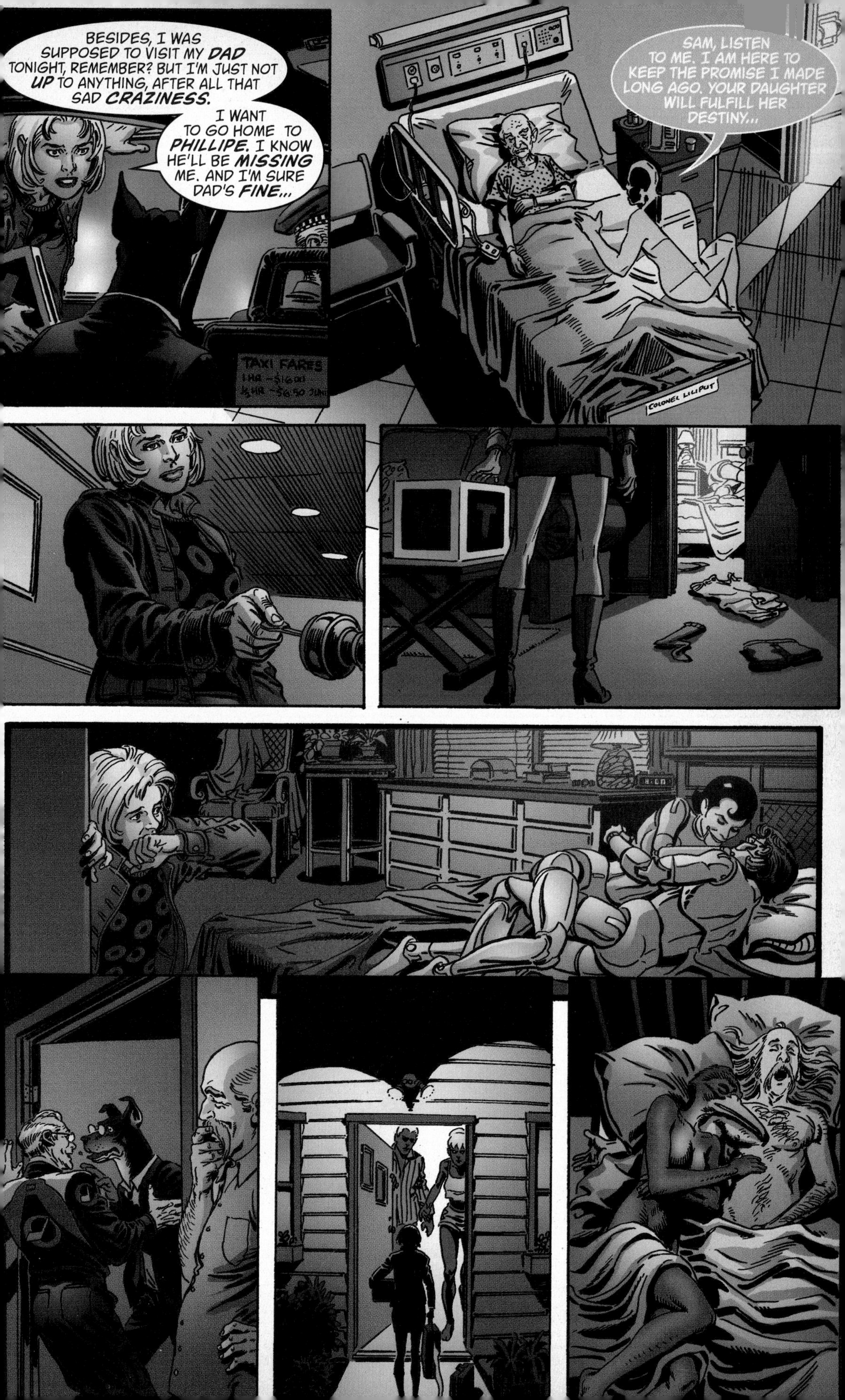
BESIDES, I WAS SUPPOSED TO VISIT MY DAD TONIGHT, REMEMBER? BUT I'M JUST NOT UP TO ANYTHING, AFTER ALL THAT SAD CRAZINESS.
I WANT TO GO HOME TO PHILLIPE. I KNOW HE'LL BE MISSING ME. AND I'M SURE DAD'S FINE...
TAXI FARES
SAM, LISTEN TO ME. I AM HERE TO KEEP THE PROMISE I MADE LONG AGO. YOUR DAUGHTER WILL FULFILL HER DESTINY...
COLONEL LILIPUT

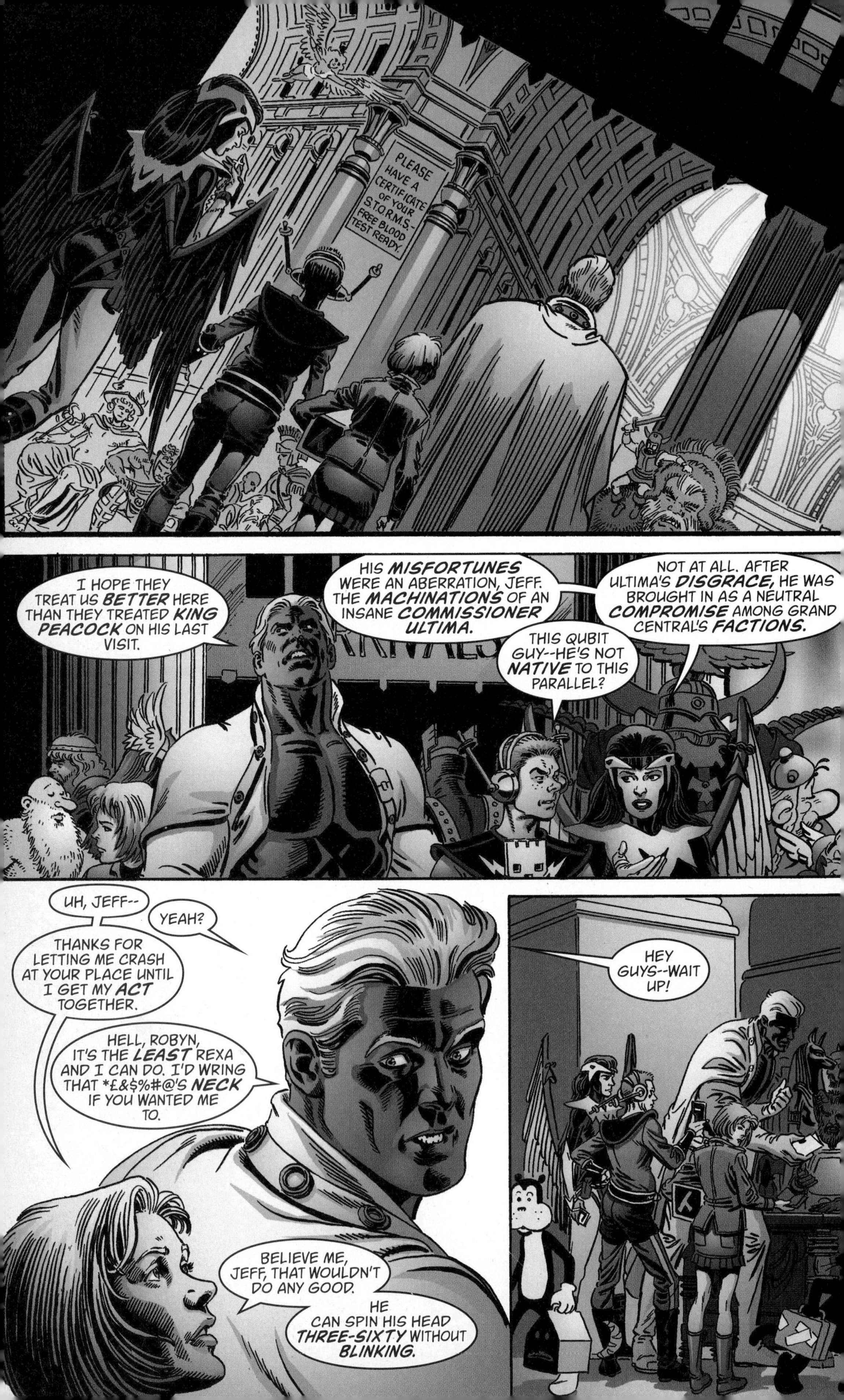

PLEASE HAVE A CERTIFICATE OF YOUR S.T.O.R.M.S.-FREE BLOOD TEST READY.
I HOPE THEY TREAT US BETTER HERE THAN THEY TREATED KING PEACOCK ON HIS LAST VISIT.
HIS MISFORTUNES WERE AN ABERRATION, JEFF. THE MACHINATIONS OF AN INSANE COMMISSIONER ULTIMA.
NOT AT ALL. AFTER ULTIMA'S DISGRACE, HE WAS BROUGHT IN AS A NEUTRAL COMPROMISE AMONG GRAND CENTRAL'S FACTIONS.
THIS QUBIT GUY--HE'S NOT NATIVE TO THIS PARALLEL?
UH, JEFF--
YEAH?
THANKS FOR LETTING ME CRASH AT YOUR PLACE UNTIL I GET MY ACT TOGETHER.
HELL, ROBYN, IT'S THE LEAST REXA AND I CAN DO. I'D WRING THAT *£&$%#@'S NECK IF YOU WANTED ME TO.
BELIEVE ME, JEFF, THAT WOULDN'T DO ANY GOOD.
HE CAN SPIN HIS HEAD THREE-SIXTY WITHOUT BLINKING.
HEY GUYS--WAIT UP!

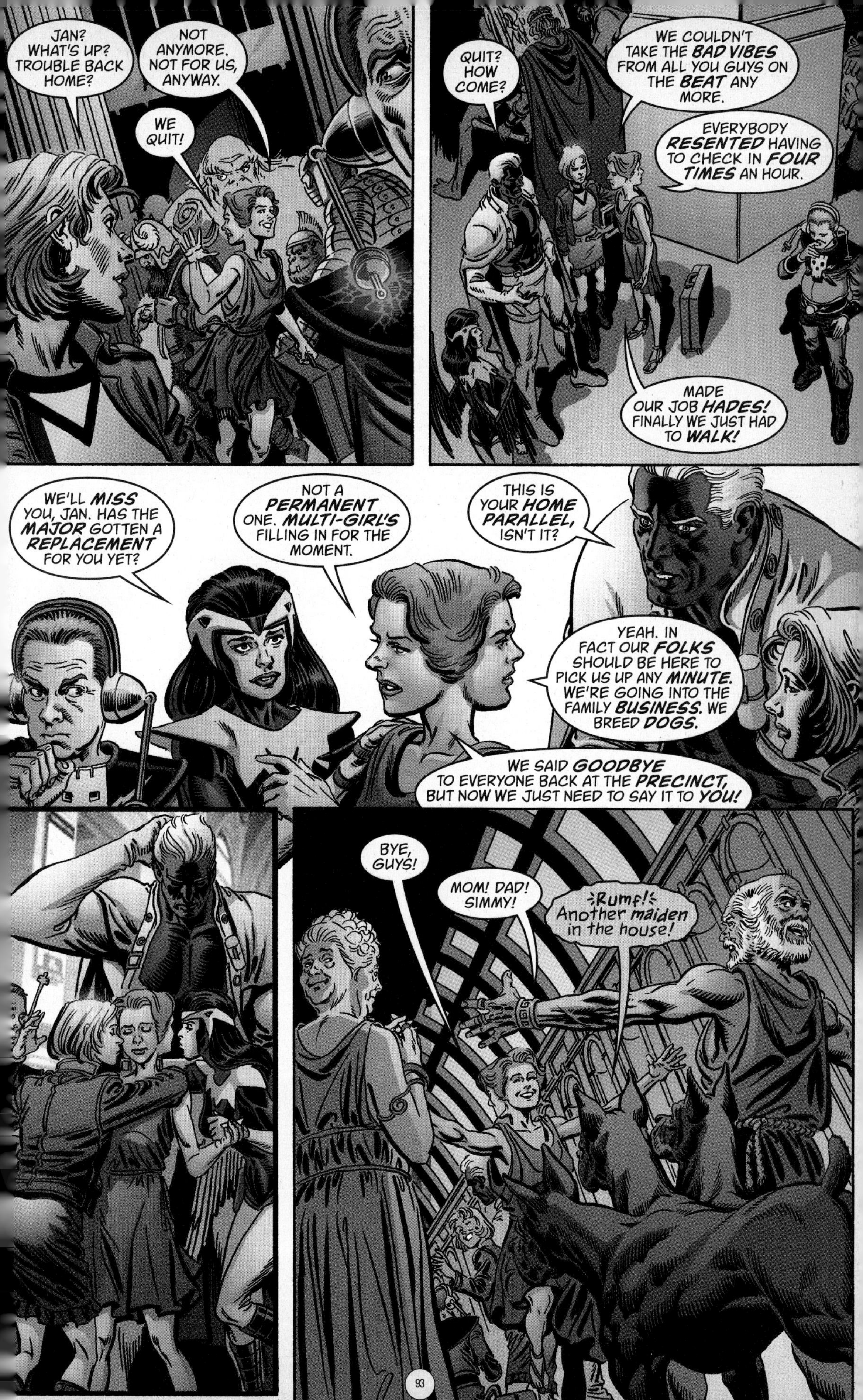

JAN? WHAT'S UP? TROUBLE BACK HOME?
NOT ANYMORE. NOT FOR US, ANYWAY.
WE QUIT!
QUIT? HOW COME?
WE COULDN'T TAKE THE BAD VIBES FROM ALL YOU GUYS ON THE BEAT ANY MORE.
EVERYBODY RESENTED HAVING TO CHECK IN FOUR TIMES AN HOUR.
MADE OUR JOB HADES! FINALLY WE JUST HAD TO WALK!
WE'LL MISS YOU, JAN. HAS THE MAJOR GOTTEN A REPLACEMENT FOR YOU YET?
NOT A PERMANENT ONE. MULTI-GIRL'S FILLING IN FOR THE MOMENT.
THIS IS YOUR HOME PARALLEL, ISN'T IT?
YEAH. IN FACT OUR FOLKS SHOULD BE HERE TO PICK US UP ANY MINUTE. WE'RE GOING INTO THE FAMILY BUSINESS. WE BREED DOGS.
WE SAID GOODBYE TO EVERYONE BACK AT THE PRECINCT, BUT NOW WE JUST NEED TO SAY IT TO YOU!
BYE, GUYS!
MOM! DAD! SIMMY!
Rumf! Another maiden in the house!

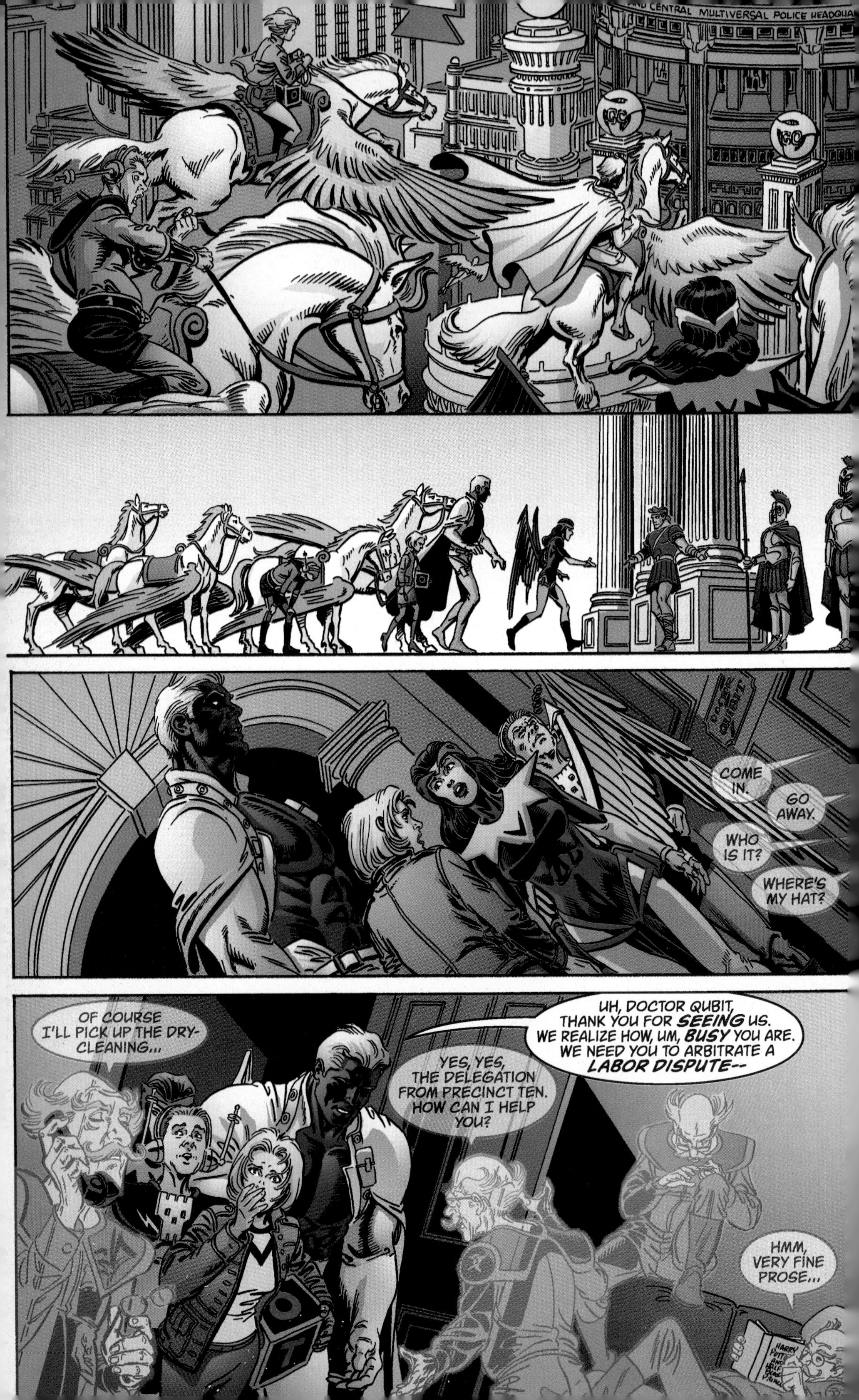
CENTRAL MULTIVERSAL POLICE
DOCTOR QUBIT
COME IN.
GO AWAY.
WHO IS IT?
WHERE'S MY HAT?
OF COURSE I'LL PICK UP THE DRY-CLEANING...
UH, DOCTOR QUBIT, THANK YOU FOR **SEEING** US. WE REALIZE HOW, UM, **BUSY** YOU ARE. WE NEED YOU TO ARBITRATE A **LABOR DISPUTE**--
YES, YES, THE DELEGATION FROM PRECINCT TEN. HOW CAN I HELP YOU?
HMM, VERY FINE PROSE...

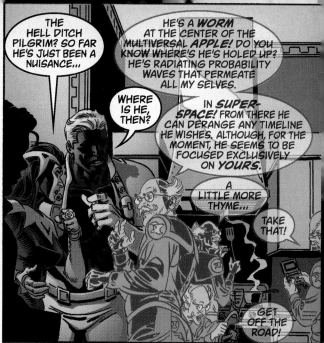

LABOR DISPUTE! WE DON'T HAVE TIME FOR SUCH TRIVIAL MATTERS NOW! CAN'T YOU SINGLETONS FOCUS ON WHAT'S IMPORTANT? WE'VE GOT TO STOP THIS MADMAN!

SUCH A WONDERFUL COMEDIAN!

WISH I COULD HELP...

THE HELL DITCH PILGRIM? SO FAR HE'S JUST BEEN A NUISANCE...

HE'S A WORM AT THE CENTER OF THE MULTIVERSAL APPLE! DO YOU KNOW WHERE'S HE'S HOLED UP? HE'S RADIATING PROBABILITY WAVES THAT PERMEATE ALL MY SELVES.

WHERE IS HE, THEN?

IN SUPER-SPACE! FROM THERE HE CAN DERANGE ANY TIMELINE HE WISHES. ALTHOUGH, FOR THE MOMENT, HE SEEMS TO BE FOCUSED EXCLUSIVELY ON YOURS.

A LITTLE MORE THYME...

TAKE THAT!

GET OFF THE ROAD!

YOU HAVE TO TAKE THIS MONSTER DOWN! AS SOON AS POSSIBLE! NOW, GET HOME AND DO YOUR DUTY!

SUCH A LITTLE INNOCENT...

OH, BABY!

DEAR GOD...

YOU WILL NEVER SUCCEED...

WELL, THAT JOKE OF AN INTERVIEW WAS PRETTY MUCH AS SATISFYING AS I FIGURED IT WOULD BE...

ALL RIGHT, PEOPLE, LISTEN UP!

WE'RE GOING IN THERE NOW, AND IT'S NOT GOING TO BE EASY. BUT I'M COUNTING ON ALL OF YOU TO BE PROFESSIONALS AND DO YOUR JOB, NO MATTER WHAT THE DISTRACTIONS.

IGNORE THE NOISE AND THE ANGER, KEEP A TIGHT REIN ON YOUR OWN EMOTIONS, DON'T GET SWEPT UP BY ANY UNEXPECTED OFFENSIVE OR DEFENSIVE MOVES, AND YOU'LL DO JUST FINE.

EVERYBODY READY? EXCELLENT!

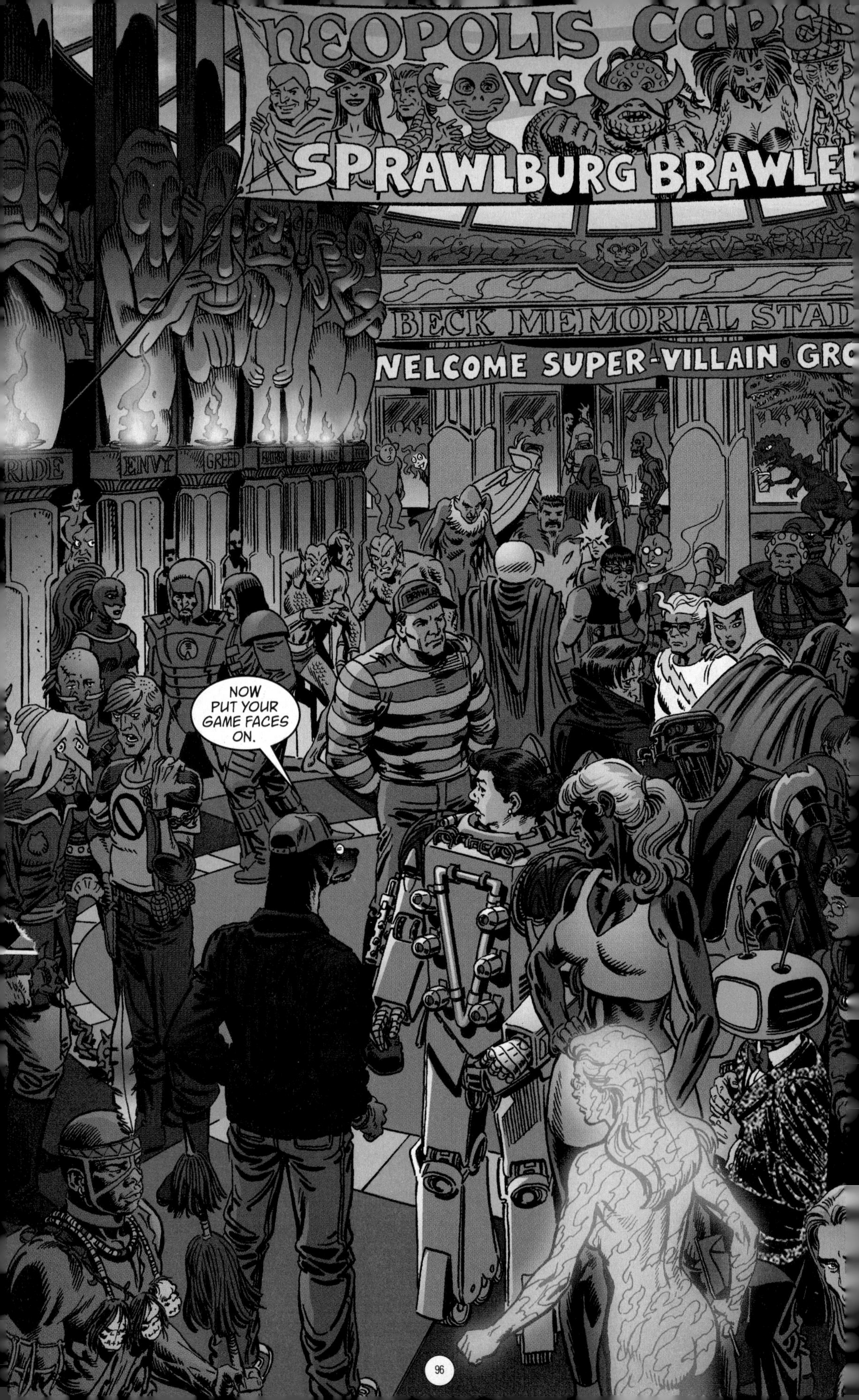
NEOPOLIS CAPES
VS
SPRAWLBURG BRAWLE
BECK MEMORIAL STAD
NELCOME SUPER-VILLAIN GRO
RIDE
ENVY
GREED
BRAWLE
NOW PUT YOUR GAME FACES ON.

OKAY, WE SPLIT UP NOW. EACH TEAM KNOW WHICH QUADRANT THEY NEED TO COVER?

GREAT. BY *SPREADING OUT*, WE SHOULD BE ABLE TO SPOT *ANYTHING* THE DERRIDADAISTS TRY TO *PULL*.

PLAY BALL!

BRAWLERS

MAN, I PURELY DETEST SPORTS.

THAT'S GOOD, THEN. YOU WON'T BE *DISTRACTED* BY THE GAME.

HOW ABOUT YOU?

I *LOVE* BASEBALL. BUT I'LL STAY *SHARP* AS AN ORANGE QUARTER-NOTE...

Cool Cola

WE MIGHT AS WELL *SETTLE DOWN*. NO TELLING WHEN THESE JERK-ASS *TERRORISTS* WILL MAKE AN APPEARANCE, IF AT ALL.

I NEED A *BEER*.

YOU KNOW THE SARGE SAID *NO BOOZE*...

I STILL *NEED* ONE.

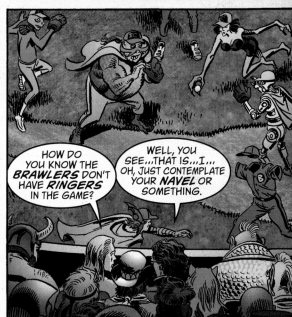

HOW DO YOU KNOW THE *BRAWLERS* DON'T HAVE *RINGERS* IN THE GAME?

WELL, YOU SEE...THAT IS...I... OH, JUST CONTEMPLATE YOUR *NAVEL* OR SOMETHING.

| CAPES | 0 | 0 | 1 |
| BRAWL | 3 | 4 | 3 |

DUFF BEER

CHARGE!

BRAW GO HOME!

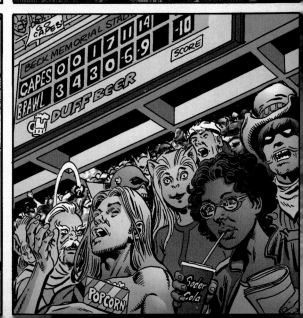

GO CAPES

BECK MEMORIAL STADIUM

	1	7	11	14	-10
CAPES	0	0	1	7	3 0	5 9	SCORE
BRAWL	3	4	3				

DUFF BEER

POPCORN

Soder Cola

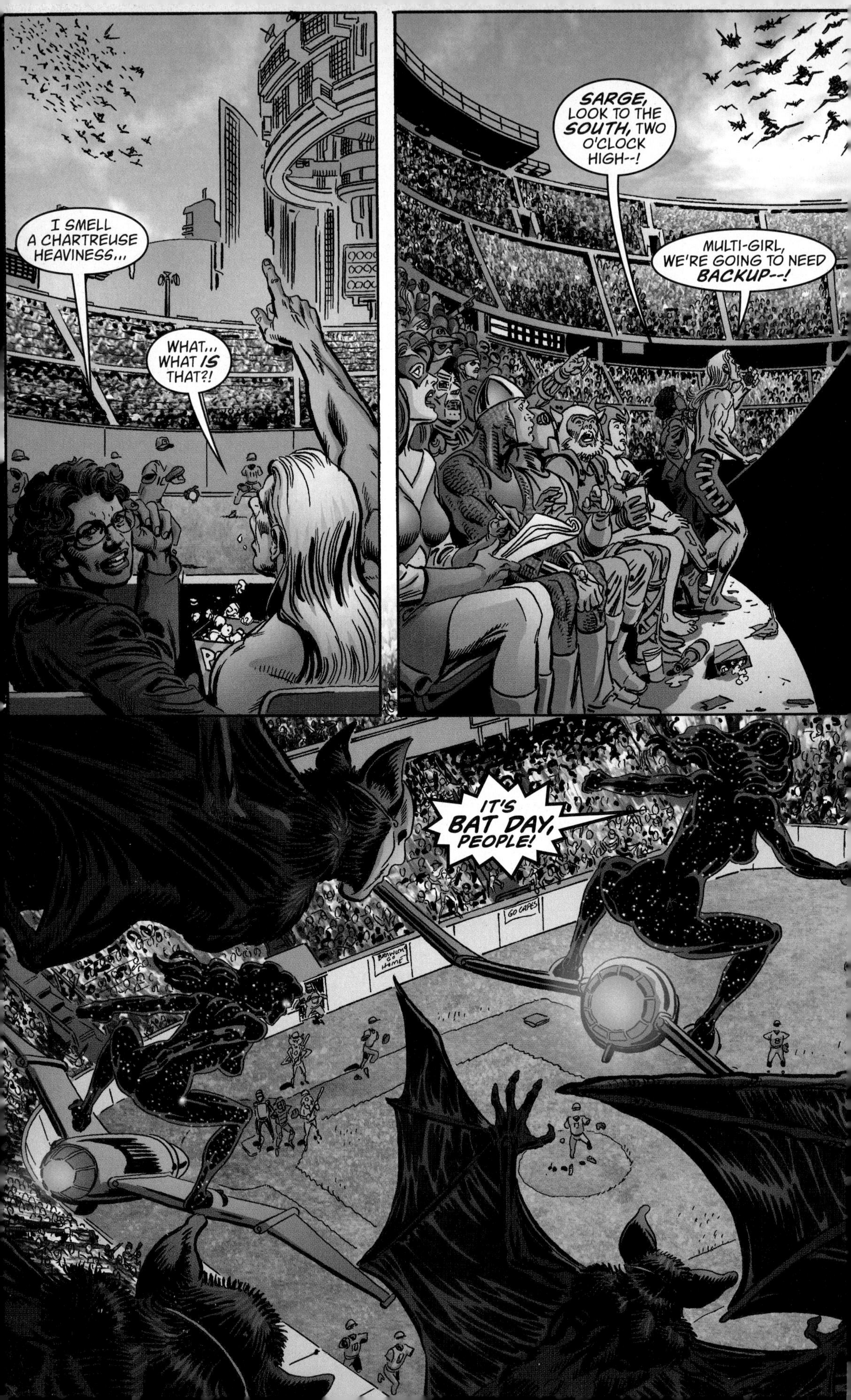
I SMELL A CHARTREUSE HEAVINESS...
WHAT... WHAT IS THAT?!
SARGE, LOOK TO THE SOUTH, TWO O'CLOCK HIGH--!
MULTI-GIRL, WE'RE GOING TO NEED BACKUP--!
IT'S BAT DAY, PEOPLE!
GO CAPES

CHAPTER #5

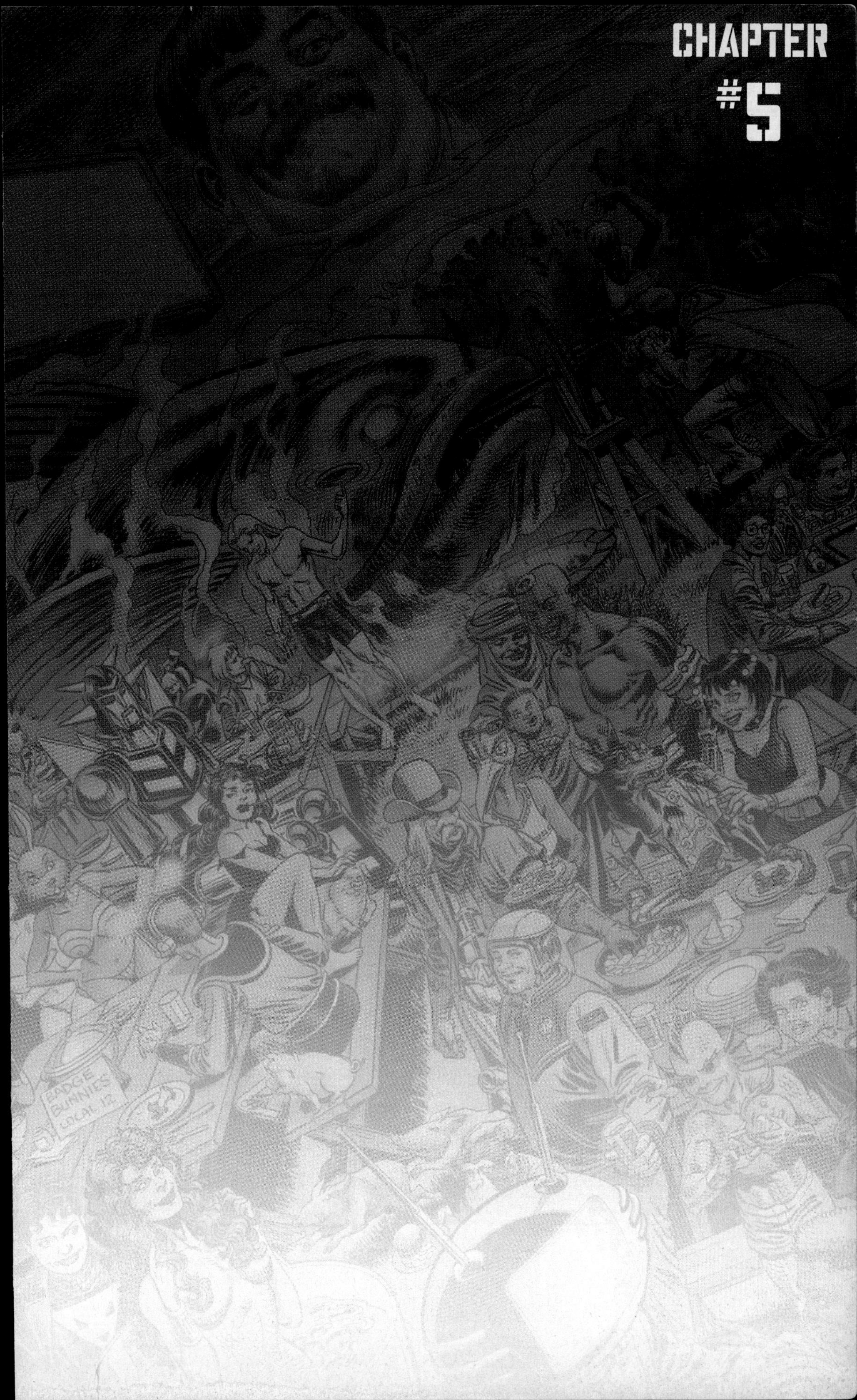
BADGE BUNNIES LOCAL 12

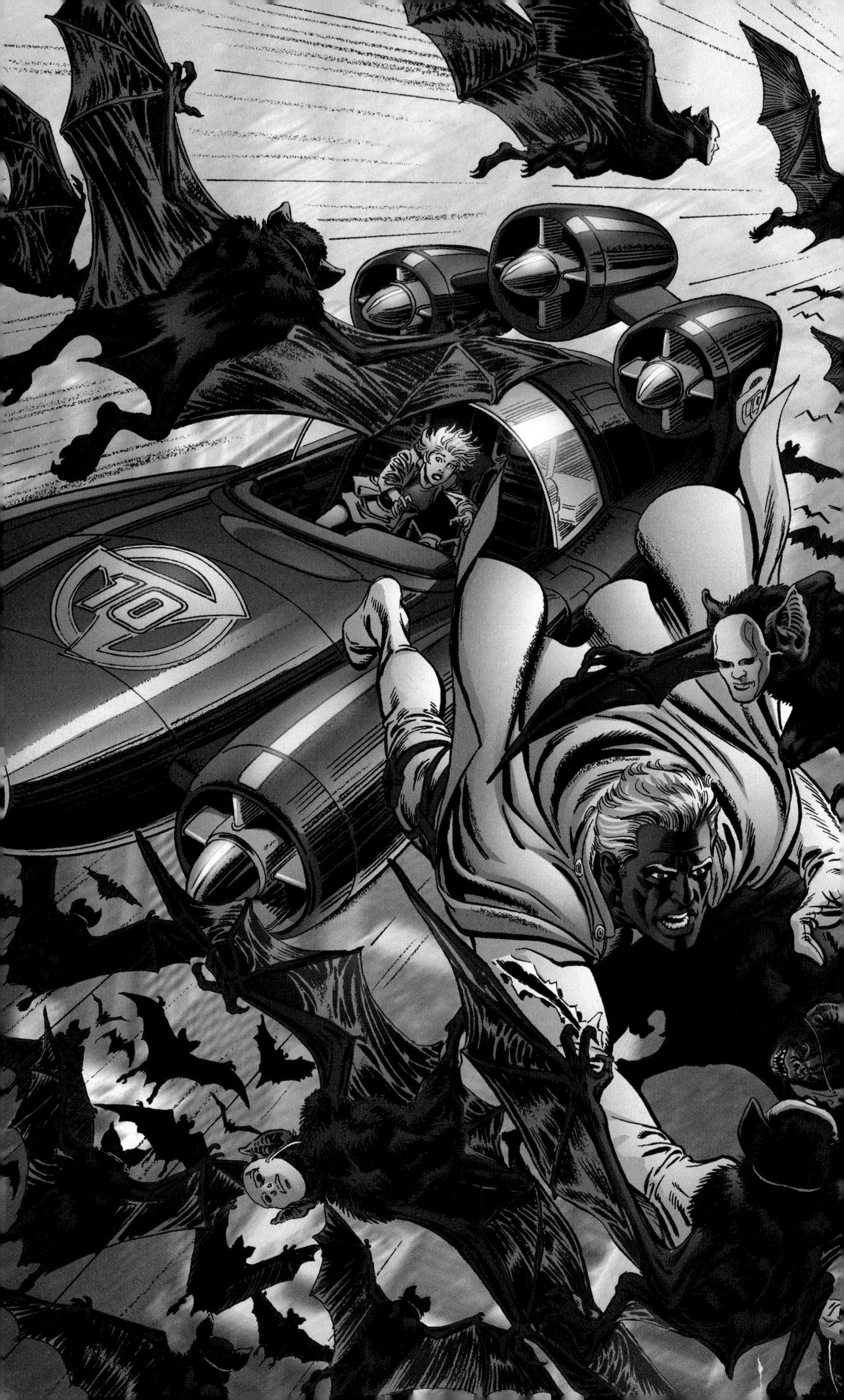

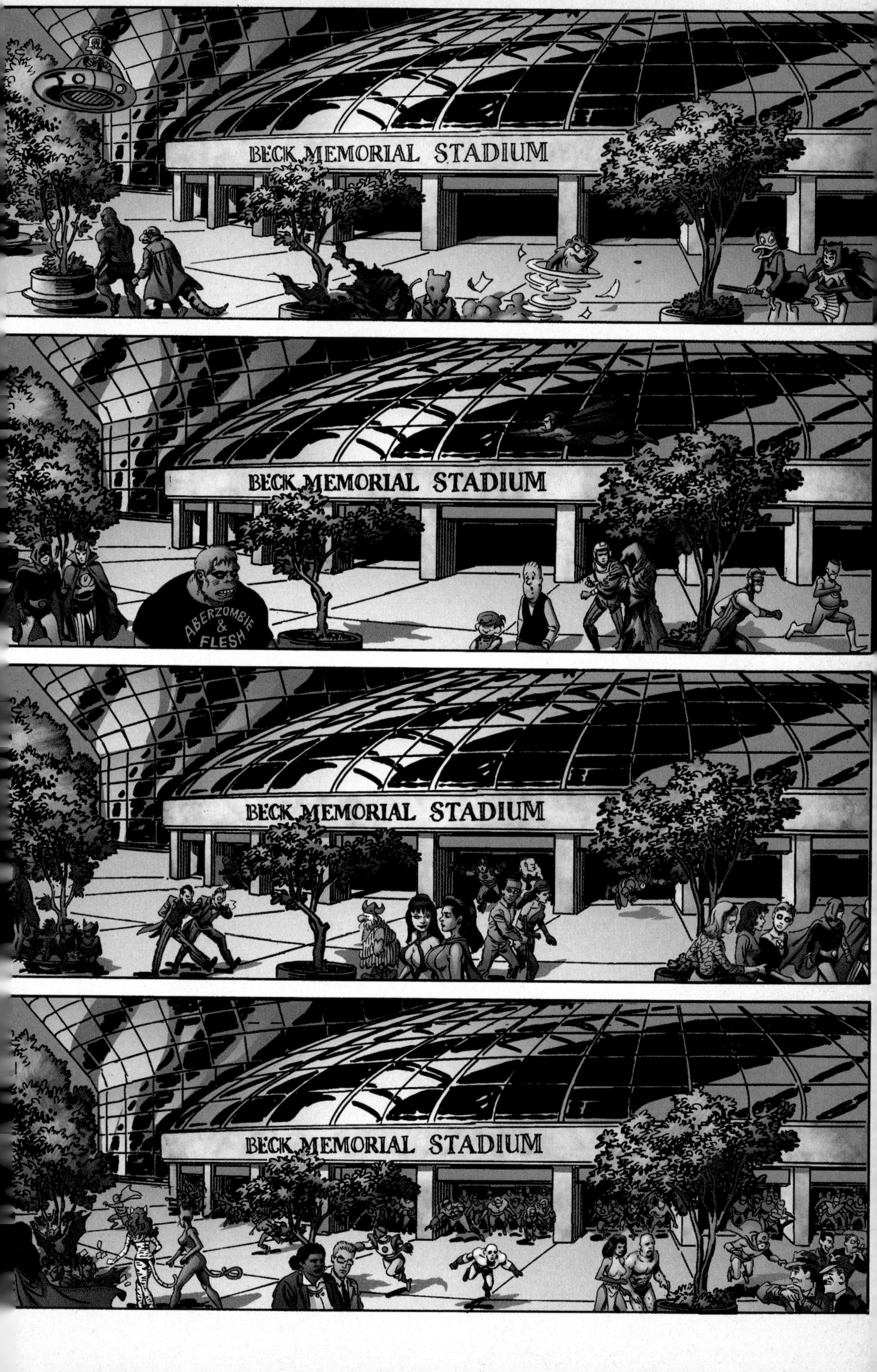
BECK MEMORIAL STADIUM
BECK MEMORIAL STADIUM
ABERZOMBIE & FLESH
BECK MEMORIAL STADIUM
BECK MEMORIAL STADIUM

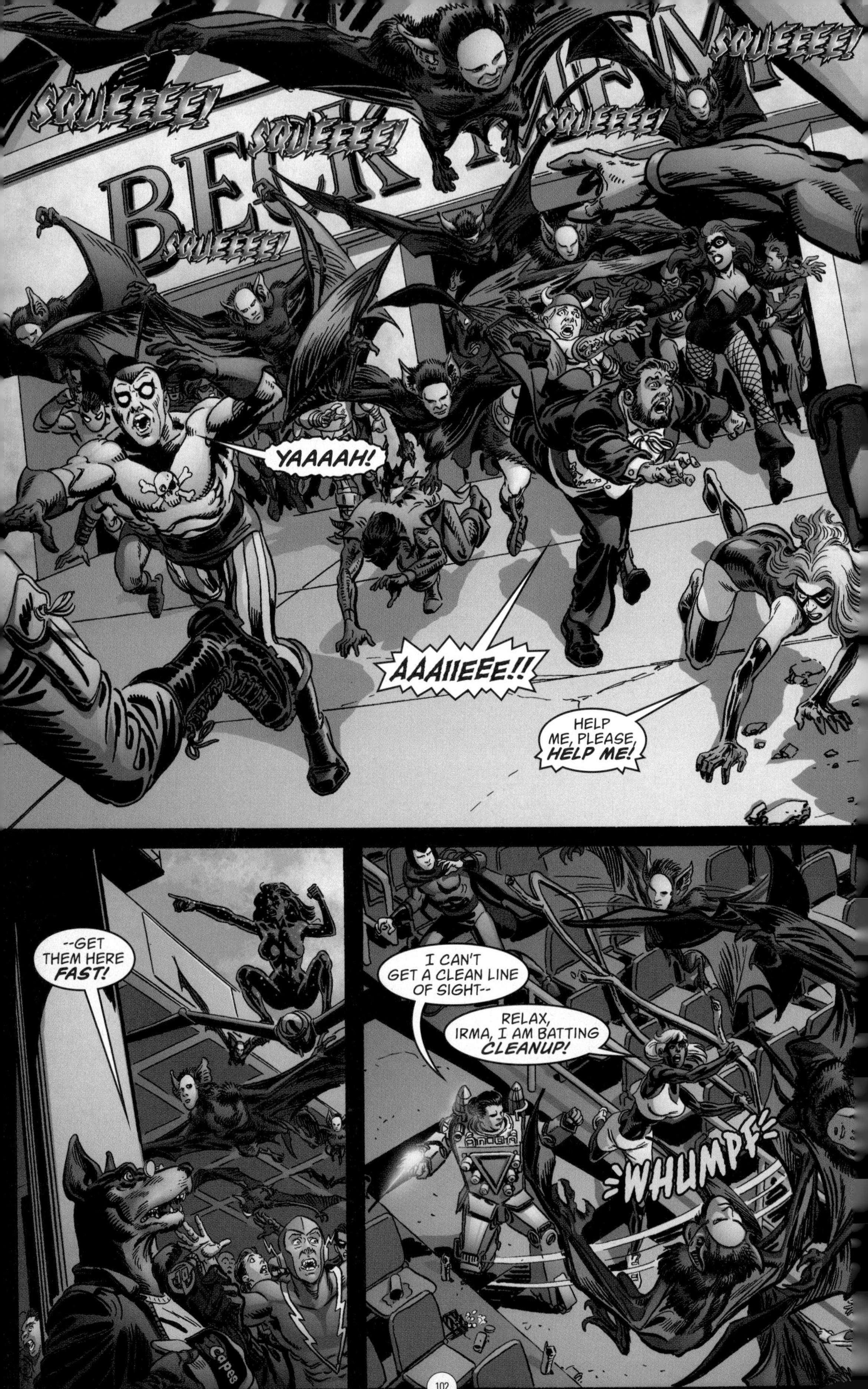
SQUEEEE!
SQUEEEE!
SQUEEEE!
SQUEEEE!
SQUEEEE!
YAAAAH!
AAAIIEEE!!
HELP ME, PLEASE, HELP ME!
--GET THEM HERE FAST!
I CAN'T GET A CLEAN LINE OF SIGHT--
RELAX, IRMA, I AM BATTING CLEANUP!
WHUMPF
Capes

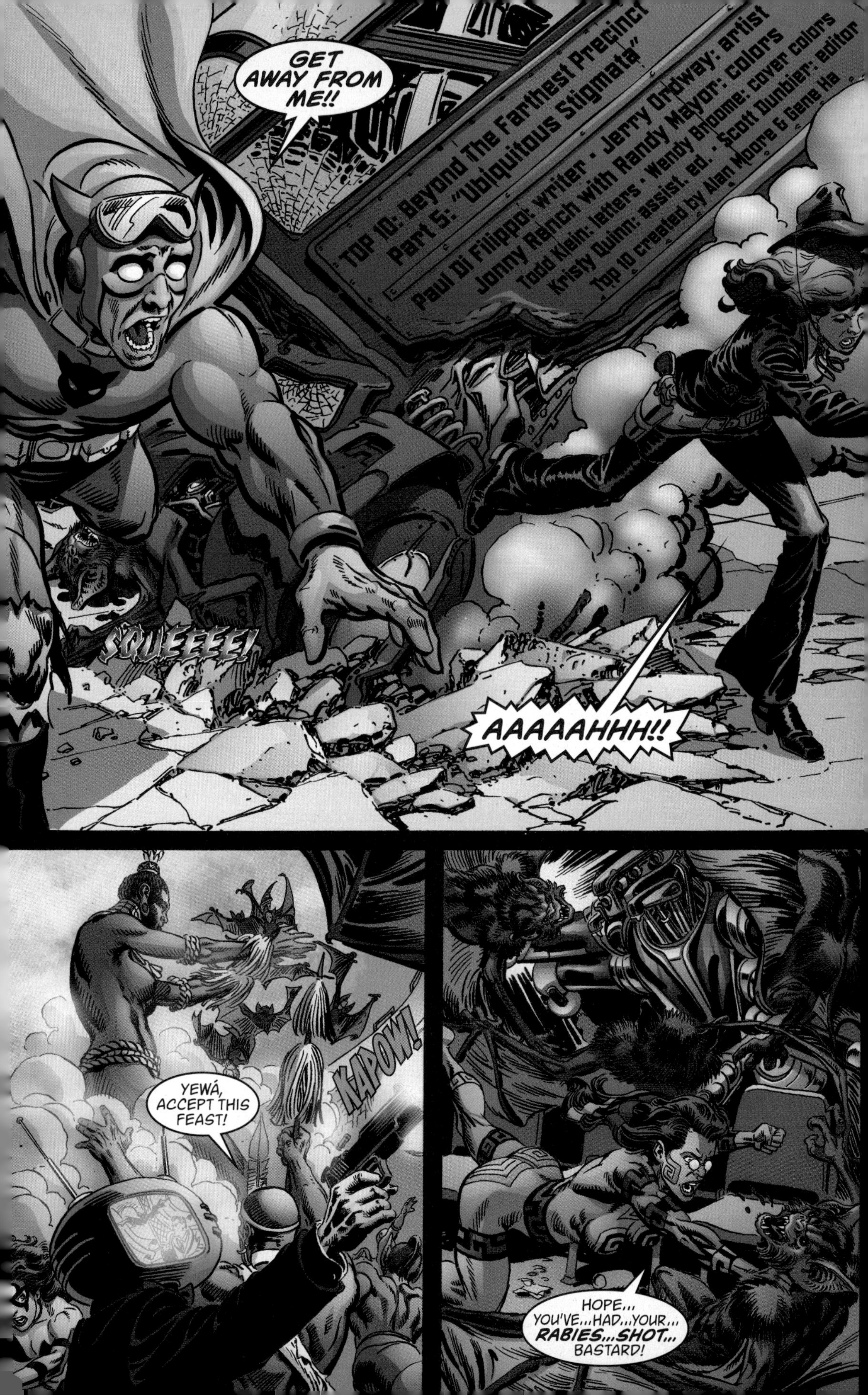
GET AWAY FROM ME!!
TOP 10: Beyond The Farthest Precinct
Part 5: "Ubiquitous Stigmata"
Paul Di Filippo: writer · Jerry Ordway: artist
Jonny Ranch with Randy Mayor: colors
Todd Klein: letters · Wendy Broome: cover colors
Kristy Quinn: assist. ed. · Scott Dunbier: editor
Top 10 created by Alan Moore & Gene Ha
SQUEEEEE!
AAAAAHHH!!
YEWÁ, ACCEPT THIS FEAST!
KAPOW!
HOPE... YOU'VE...HAD...YOUR... RABIES...SHOT... BASTARD!

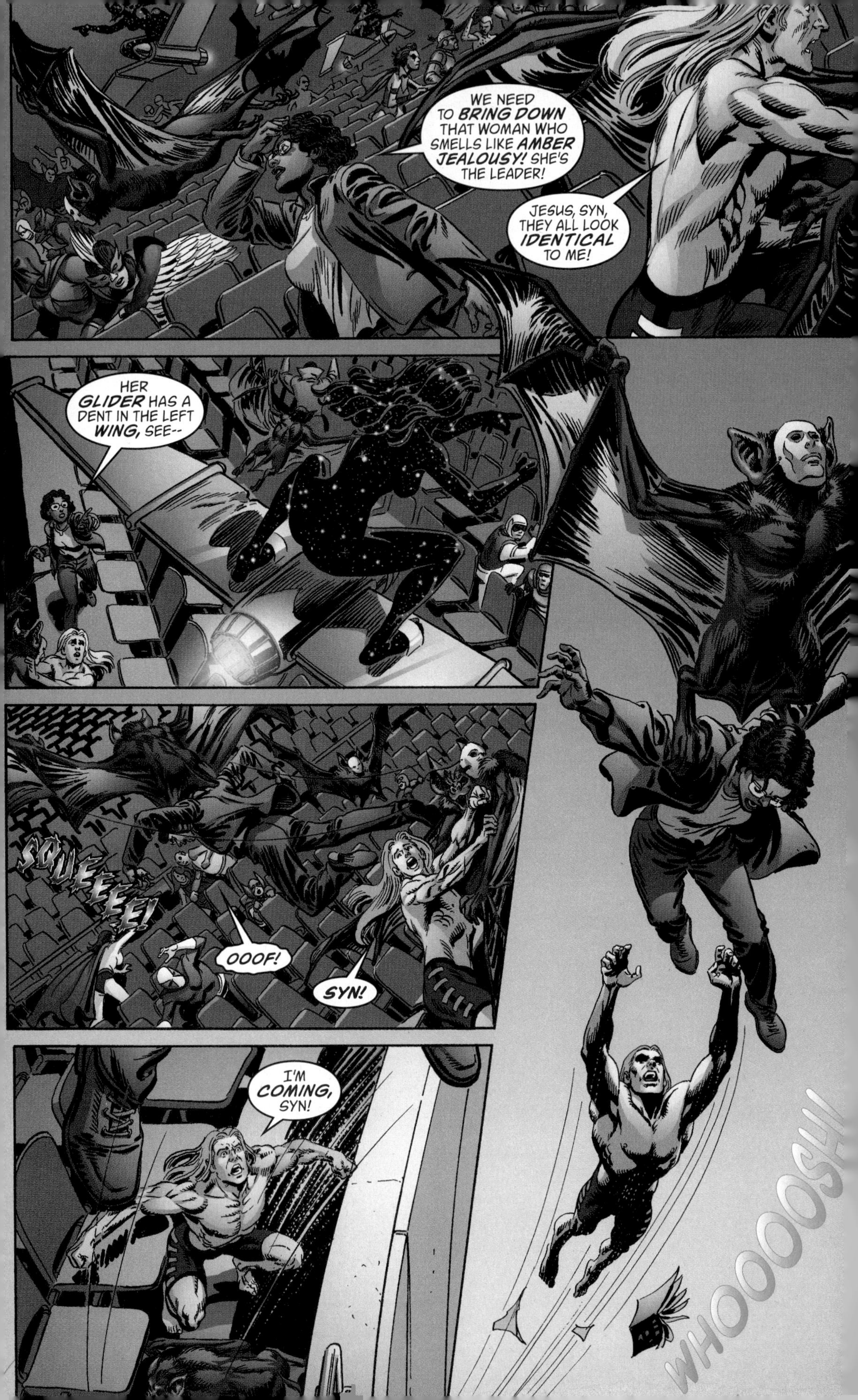
WE NEED TO BRING DOWN THAT WOMAN WHO SMELLS LIKE AMBER JEALOUSY! SHE'S THE LEADER!
JESUS, SYN, THEY ALL LOOK IDENTICAL TO ME!
HER GLIDER HAS A DENT IN THE LEFT WING, SEE--
SQUEEEEE!
OOOF!
SYN!
I'M COMING, SYN!
WHOOOOSH!

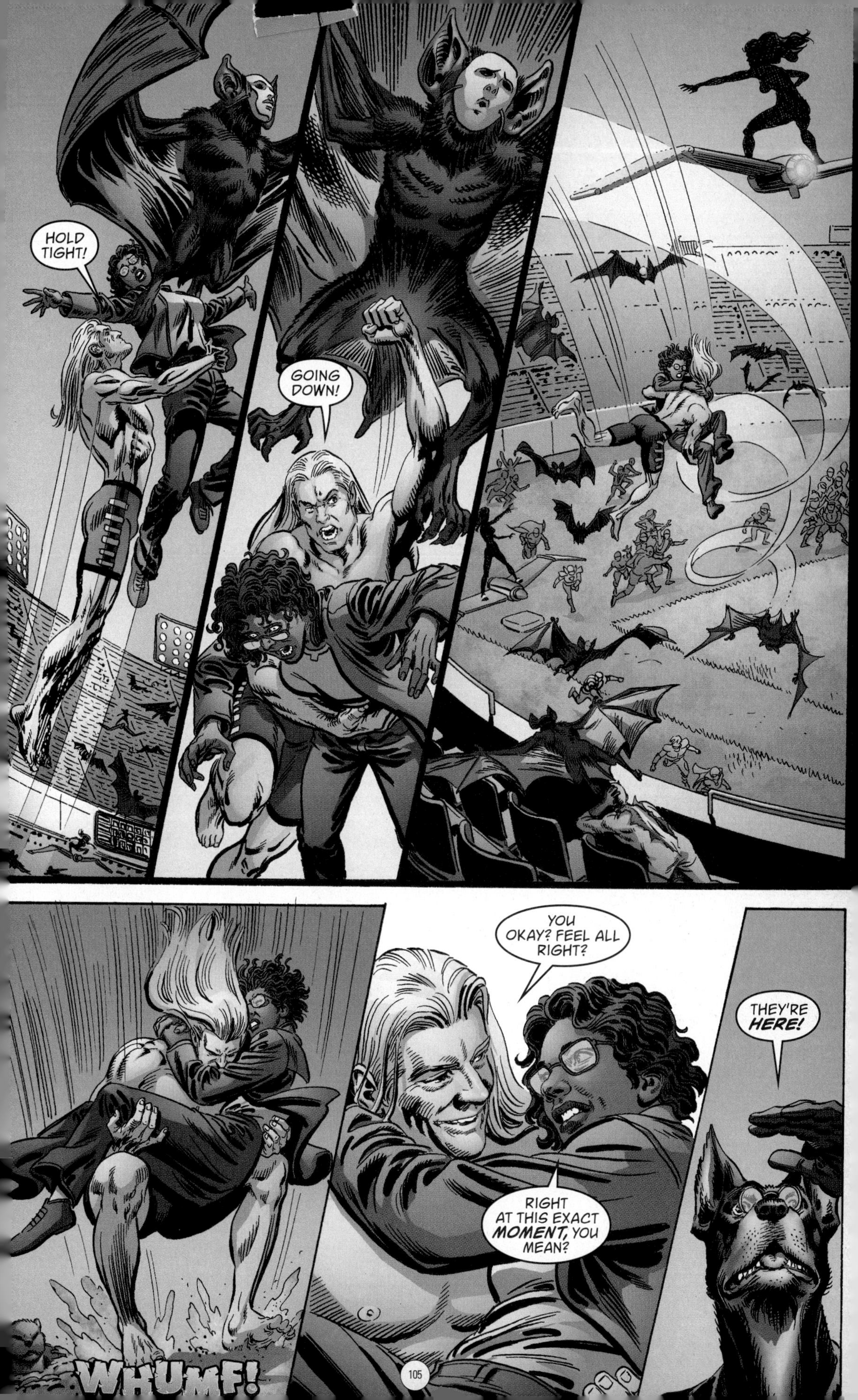
HOLD TIGHT!
GOING DOWN!
WHUMF!
YOU OKAY? FEEL ALL RIGHT?
RIGHT AT THIS EXACT *MOMENT,* YOU MEAN?
THEY'RE *HERE!*

GIVE 'EM *HELL*, CHELLE!

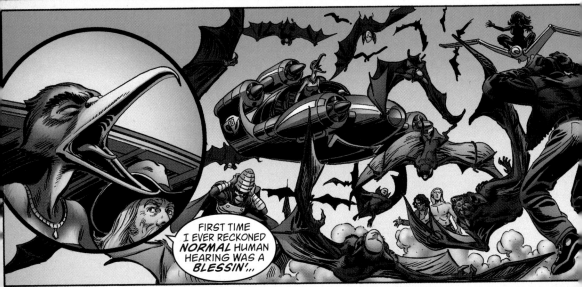

FIRST TIME I EVER RECKONED *NORMAL* HUMAN HEARING WAS A *BLESSIN'*...

THE *WOMEN* ARE GETTING AWAY!

NOT ALL OF THEM--

EVERYBODY OKAY?

FWNNNSH!

I'VE GOT *BAT-SNOT* IN MY SOLENOIDS...

SURE, SARGE.

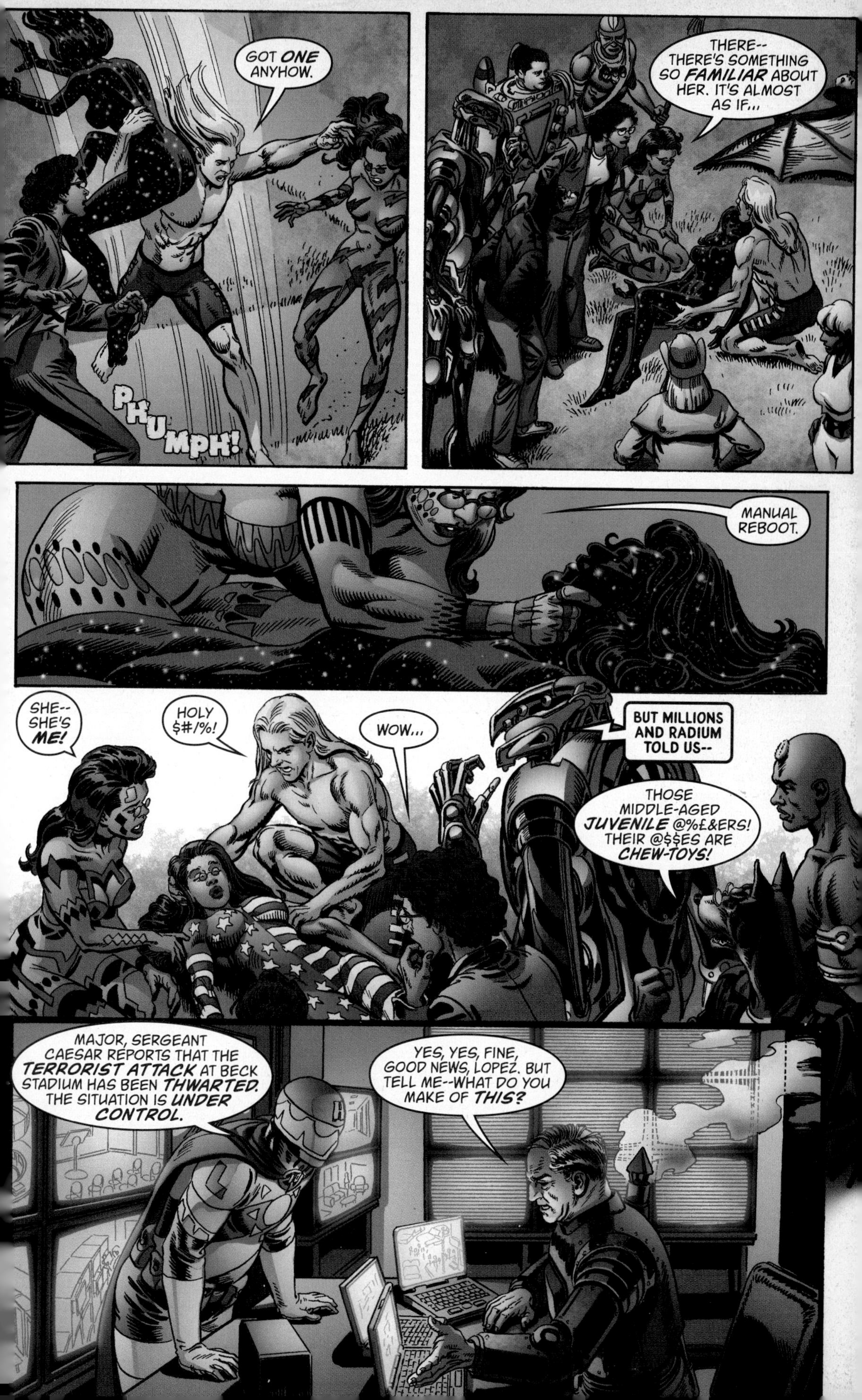
GOT ONE ANYHOW.
PHUMPH!
THERE-- THERE'S SOMETHING SO FAMILIAR ABOUT HER. IT'S ALMOST AS IF...
MANUAL REBOOT.
SHE-- SHE'S ME!
HOLY $#/%!
WOW...
BUT MILLIONS AND RADIUM TOLD US--
THOSE MIDDLE-AGED JUVENILE @%£&ERS! THEIR @$$ES ARE CHEW-TOYS!
MAJOR, SERGEANT CAESAR REPORTS THAT THE TERRORIST ATTACK AT BECK STADIUM HAS BEEN THWARTED. THE SITUATION IS UNDER CONTROL.
YES, YES, FINE, GOOD NEWS, LOPEZ. BUT TELL ME--WHAT DO YOU MAKE OF THIS?

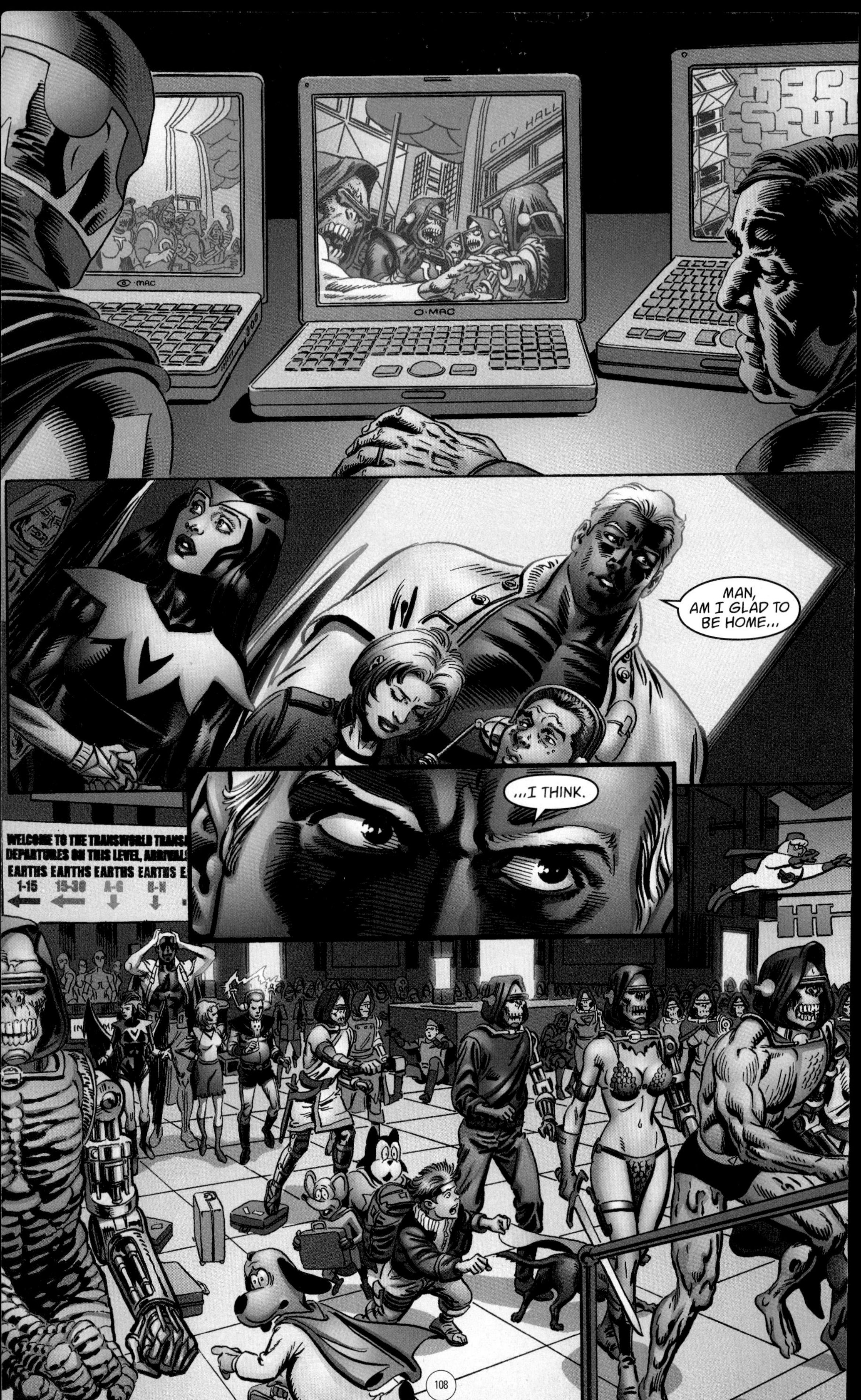
CITY HALL
O-MAC
O-MAC
MAN, AM I GLAD TO BE HOME...
...I THINK.
WELCOME TO THE TRANSWORLD TRANS
DEPARTURES ON THIS LEVEL, ARRIVALS
EARTHS 1-15
EARTHS 15-30
EARTHS A-G
EARTHS H-N

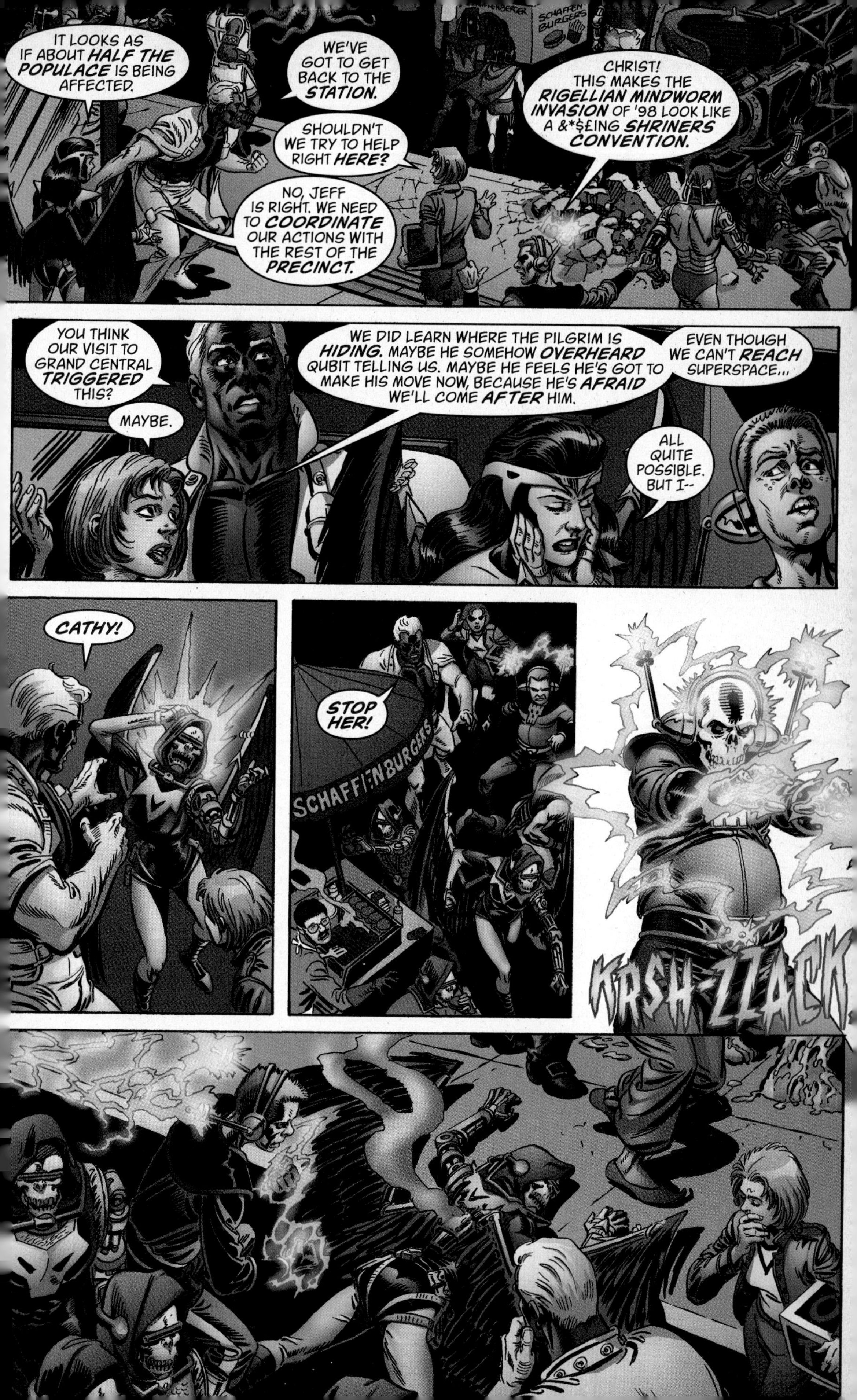
IT LOOKS AS IF ABOUT HALF THE POPULACE IS BEING AFFECTED.
WE'VE GOT TO GET BACK TO THE STATION.
SHOULDN'T WE TRY TO HELP RIGHT HERE?
NO, JEFF IS RIGHT. WE NEED TO COORDINATE OUR ACTIONS WITH THE REST OF THE PRECINCT.
CHRIST! THIS MAKES THE RIGELLIAN MINDWORM INVASION OF '98 LOOK LIKE A &*$£ING SHRINERS CONVENTION.
SCHAFFEN BURGERS
YOU THINK OUR VISIT TO GRAND CENTRAL TRIGGERED THIS?
MAYBE.
WE DID LEARN WHERE THE PILGRIM IS HIDING. MAYBE HE SOMEHOW OVERHEARD QUBIT TELLING US. MAYBE HE FEELS HE'S GOT TO MAKE HIS MOVE NOW, BECAUSE HE'S AFRAID WE'LL COME AFTER HIM.
EVEN THOUGH WE CAN'T REACH SUPERSPACE...
ALL QUITE POSSIBLE. BUT I--
CATHY!
STOP HER!
SCHAFFENBURGERS
KRSH-ZZACK

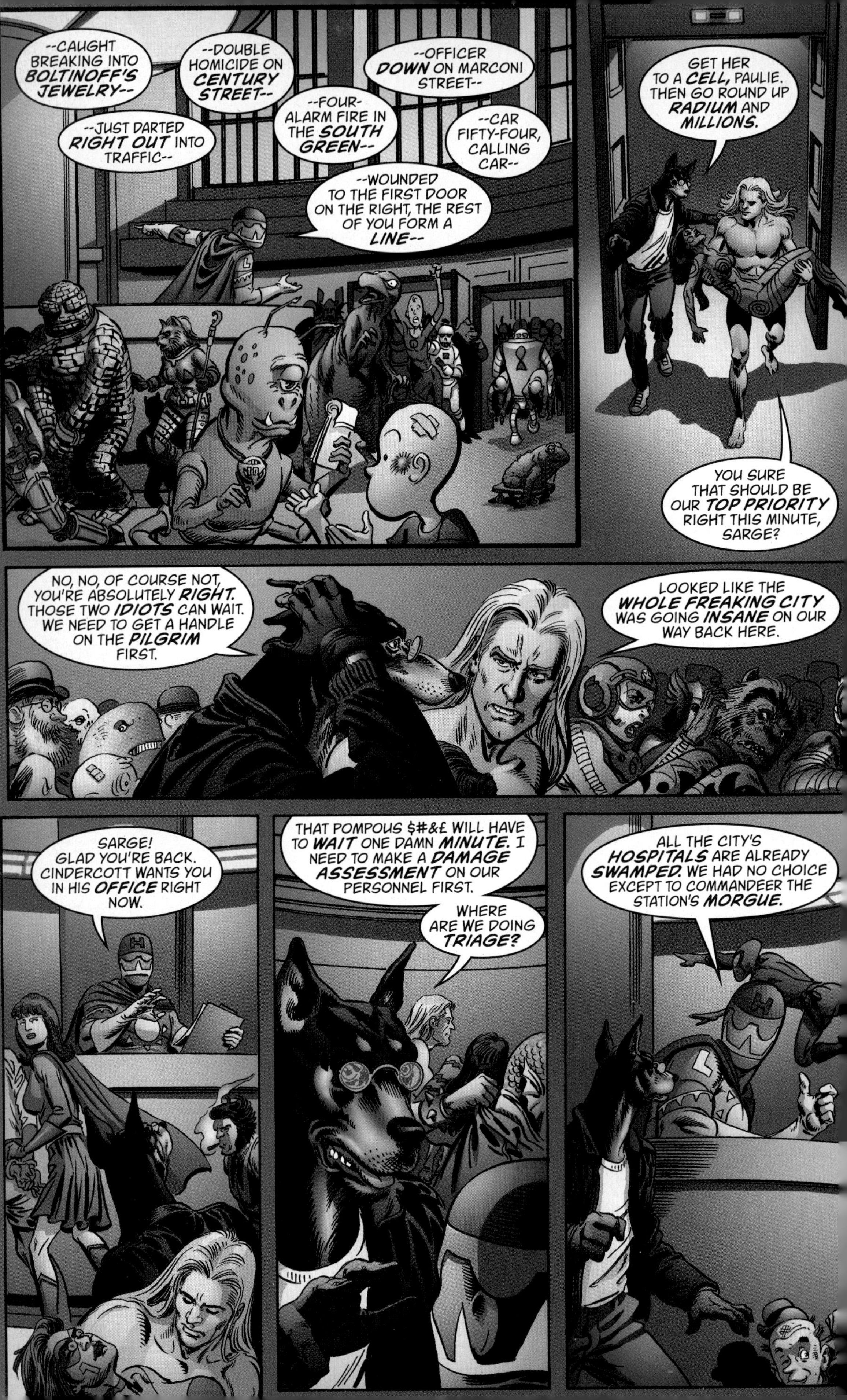
--CAUGHT BREAKING INTO BOLTINOFF'S JEWELRY--
--DOUBLE HOMICIDE ON CENTURY STREET--
--OFFICER DOWN ON MARCONI STREET--
--JUST DARTED RIGHT OUT INTO TRAFFIC--
--FOUR-ALARM FIRE IN THE SOUTH GREEN--
--CAR FIFTY-FOUR, CALLING CAR--
--WOUNDED TO THE FIRST DOOR ON THE RIGHT, THE REST OF YOU FORM A LINE--
GET HER TO A CELL, PAULIE. THEN GO ROUND UP RADIUM AND MILLIONS.
YOU SURE THAT SHOULD BE OUR TOP PRIORITY RIGHT THIS MINUTE, SARGE?
NO, NO, OF COURSE NOT, YOU'RE ABSOLUTELY RIGHT. THOSE TWO IDIOTS CAN WAIT. WE NEED TO GET A HANDLE ON THE PILGRIM FIRST.
LOOKED LIKE THE WHOLE FREAKING CITY WAS GOING INSANE ON OUR WAY BACK HERE.
SARGE! GLAD YOU'RE BACK. CINDERCOTT WANTS YOU IN HIS OFFICE RIGHT NOW.
THAT POMPOUS $#&£ WILL HAVE TO WAIT ONE DAMN MINUTE. I NEED TO MAKE A DAMAGE ASSESSMENT ON OUR PERSONNEL FIRST.
WHERE ARE WE DOING TRIAGE?
ALL THE CITY'S HOSPITALS ARE ALREADY SWAMPED. WE HAD NO CHOICE EXCEPT TO COMMANDEER THE STATION'S MORGUE.

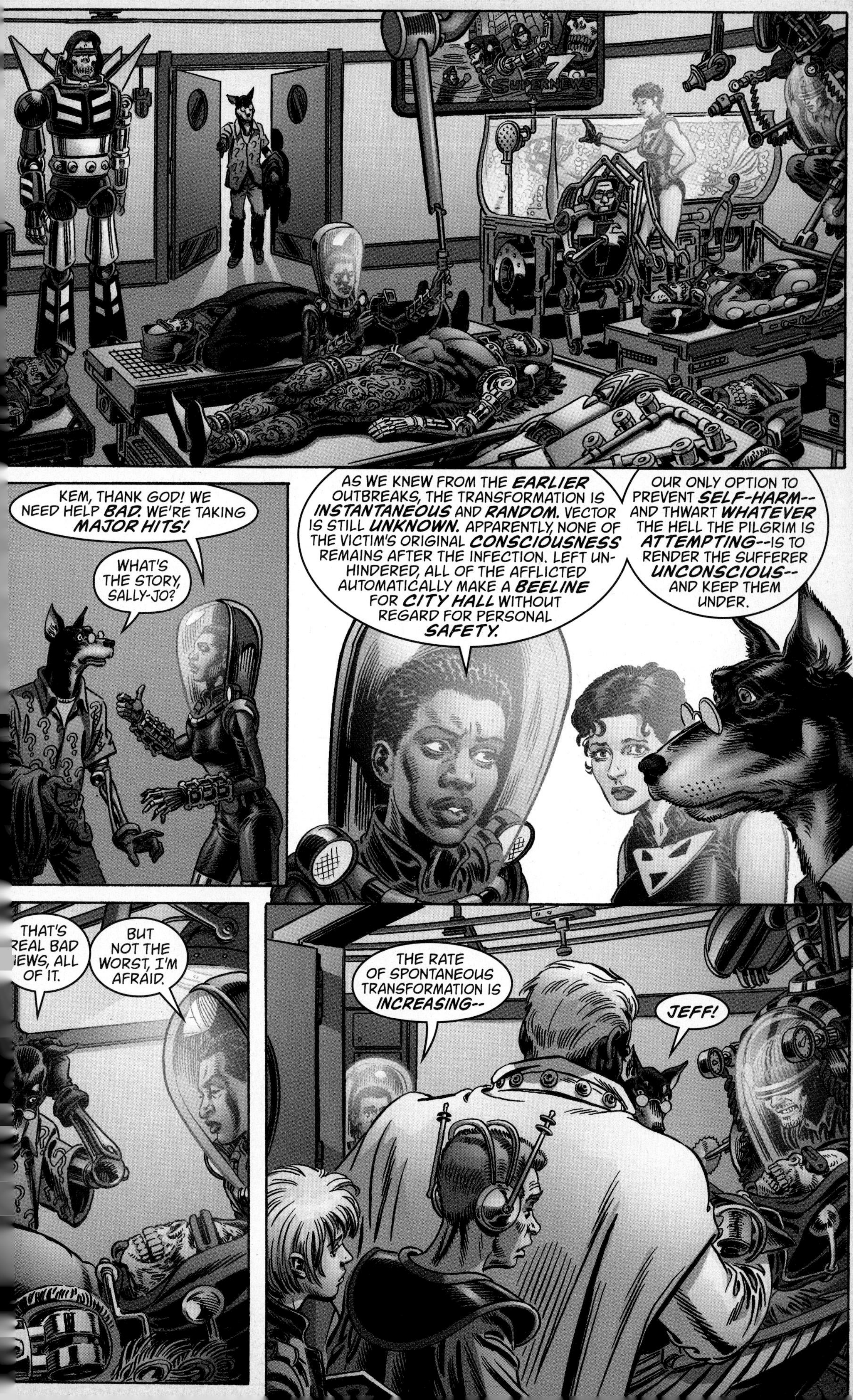
SUPERNEWS 7
KEM, THANK GOD! WE NEED HELP BAD. WE'RE TAKING MAJOR HITS!
WHAT'S THE STORY, SALLY-JO?
AS WE KNEW FROM THE EARLIER OUTBREAKS, THE TRANSFORMATION IS INSTANTANEOUS AND RANDOM. VECTOR IS STILL UNKNOWN. APPARENTLY, NONE OF THE VICTIM'S ORIGINAL CONSCIOUSNESS REMAINS AFTER THE INFECTION. LEFT UNHINDERED, ALL OF THE AFFLICTED AUTOMATICALLY MAKE A BEELINE FOR CITY HALL WITHOUT REGARD FOR PERSONAL SAFETY.
OUR ONLY OPTION TO PREVENT SELF-HARM-- AND THWART WHATEVER THE HELL THE PILGRIM IS ATTEMPTING--IS TO RENDER THE SUFFERER UNCONSCIOUS-- AND KEEP THEM UNDER.
THAT'S REAL BAD IEWS, ALL OF IT.
BUT NOT THE WORST, I'M AFRAID.
THE RATE OF SPONTANEOUS TRANSFORMATION IS INCREASING--
JEFF!

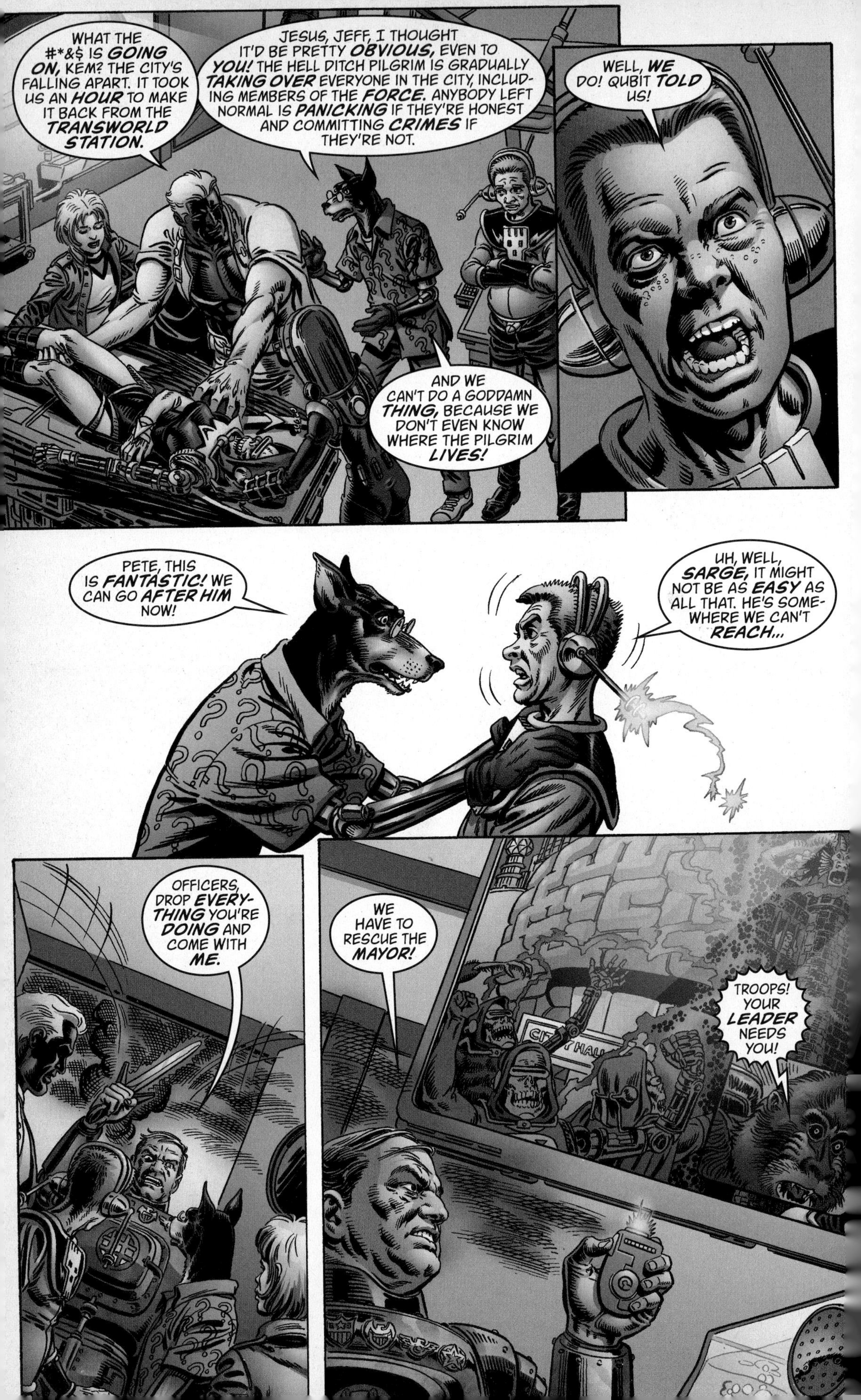

WHAT THE #*&$ IS GOING ON, KEM? THE CITY'S FALLING APART. IT TOOK US AN HOUR TO MAKE IT BACK FROM THE TRANSWORLD STATION.
JESUS, JEFF, I THOUGHT IT'D BE PRETTY OBVIOUS, EVEN TO YOU! THE HELL DITCH PILGRIM IS GRADUALLY TAKING OVER EVERYONE IN THE CITY, INCLUDING MEMBERS OF THE FORCE. ANYBODY LEFT NORMAL IS PANICKING IF THEY'RE HONEST AND COMMITTING CRIMES IF THEY'RE NOT.
AND WE CAN'T DO A GODDAMN THING, BECAUSE WE DON'T EVEN KNOW WHERE THE PILGRIM LIVES!
WELL, WE DO! QUBIT TOLD US!
PETE, THIS IS FANTASTIC! WE CAN GO AFTER HIM NOW!
UH, WELL, SARGE, IT MIGHT NOT BE AS EASY AS ALL THAT. HE'S SOMEWHERE WE CAN'T REACH...
OFFICERS, DROP EVERYTHING YOU'RE DOING AND COME WITH ME.
WE HAVE TO RESCUE THE MAYOR!
CITY HALL
TROOPS! YOUR LEADER NEEDS YOU!

BEGGING YOUR *PARDON*, MAJOR, BUT NONE OF MY PEOPLE ARE GOING *ANYWHERE* UNTIL WE ASSESS OUR *PRIORITIES* AND *STRENGTHS*. IN FACT, WE'VE JUST GOTTEN A *LEAD* ON THE *WHEREABOUTS* OF THE PILGRIM--

BUT THIS IS THE MAYOR'S PERSONAL *SAFETY* AT STAKE!

HE'S THE SUPREME FIGURE OF *AUTHORITY* FOR NEOPOLIS!

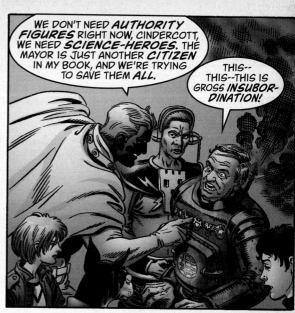

WE DON'T NEED *AUTHORITY FIGURES* RIGHT NOW, CINDERCOTT, WE NEED *SCIENCE-HEROES*. THE MAYOR IS JUST ANOTHER *CITIZEN* IN MY BOOK, AND WE'RE TRYING TO SAVE THEM *ALL*.

THIS-- THIS--THIS IS GROSS *INSUBORDINATION!*

LIKE IT OR LUMP IT, TINPOT.

SO. THAT'S HOW IT'S GOING TO BE, THEN? WELL, YOU'LL ALL *PAY* FOR THIS WHEN THINGS ARE BACK TO *NORMAL*.

THE HERO OF THE *BURMA FREEDOM CAMPAIGN* CAN RESCUE THE MAYOR *ALONE!*

WELL, KEM, LOOKS LIKE YOU'RE IN CHARGE.

WHAT'S NEXT, SARGE?

TELL ME *WHY* WE CAN'T REACH THE PILGRIM.

HE'S HOLED UP IN *SUPERSPACE*, SARGE. THE REALM *BEYOND* ALL PARALLELS.

THE PLACE THAT *JOE* AND *IRMA* TOLD US ABOUT, WHERE ALL THE *DARK ENERGY* COMES FROM?

YEAH. AND EVEN *PROJECT JOOTS* HASN'T BEEN ABLE TO SEND ANYONE THERE YET.

BUT I CAN.

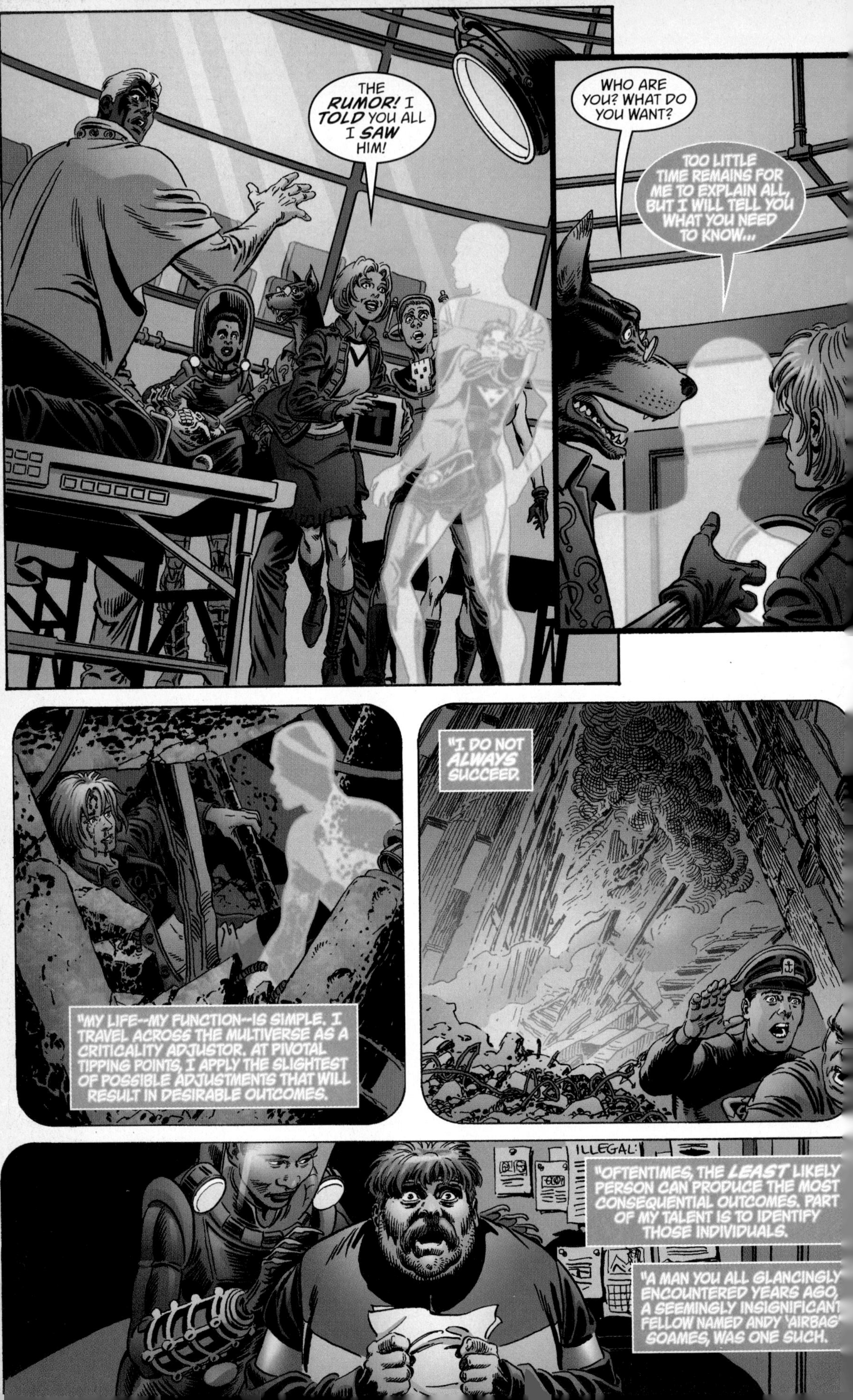
THE RUMOR! I TOLD YOU ALL I SAW HIM!
WHO ARE YOU? WHAT DO YOU WANT?
TOO LITTLE TIME REMAINS FOR ME TO EXPLAIN ALL, BUT I WILL TELL YOU WHAT YOU NEED TO KNOW...
"MY LIFE--MY FUNCTION--IS SIMPLE. I TRAVEL ACROSS THE MULTIVERSE AS A CRITICALITY ADJUSTOR. AT PIVOTAL TIPPING POINTS, I APPLY THE SLIGHTEST OF POSSIBLE ADJUSTMENTS THAT WILL RESULT IN DESIRABLE OUTCOMES.
"I DO NOT ALWAYS SUCCEED.
ILLEGAL
"OFTENTIMES, THE LEAST LIKELY PERSON CAN PRODUCE THE MOST CONSEQUENTIAL OUTCOMES. PART OF MY TALENT IS TO IDENTIFY THOSE INDIVIDUALS.
"A MAN YOU ALL GLANCINGLY ENCOUNTERED YEARS AGO, A SEEMINGLY INSIGNIFICANT FELLOW NAMED ANDY 'AIRBAG' SOAMES, WAS ONE SUCH.

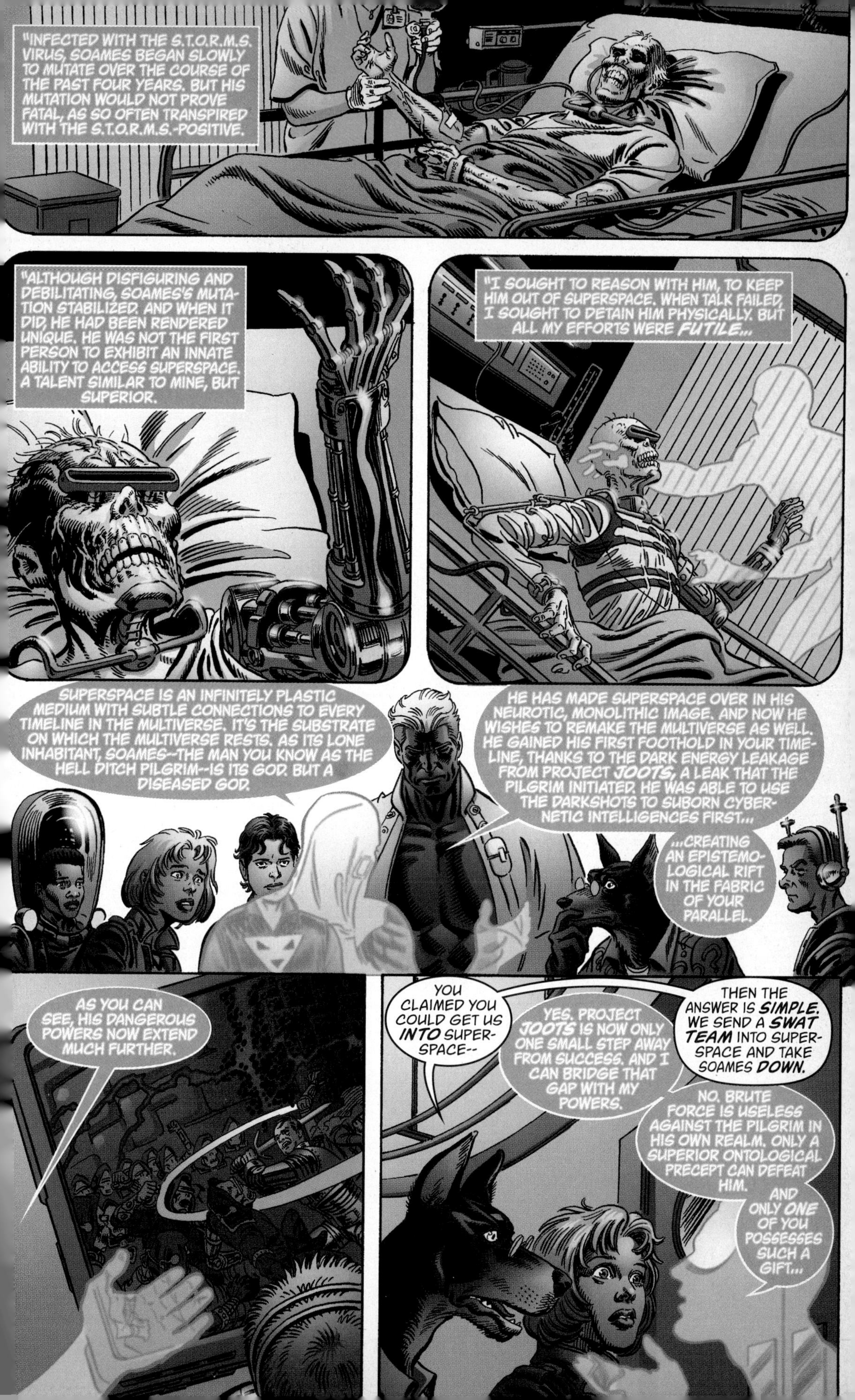
"INFECTED WITH THE S.T.O.R.M.S. VIRUS, SOAMES BEGAN SLOWLY TO MUTATE OVER THE COURSE OF THE PAST FOUR YEARS. BUT HIS MUTATION WOULD NOT PROVE FATAL, AS SO OFTEN TRANSPIRED WITH THE S.T.O.R.M.S.-POSITIVE.
"ALTHOUGH DISFIGURING AND DEBILITATING, SOAMES'S MUTATION STABILIZED. AND WHEN IT DID, HE HAD BEEN RENDERED UNIQUE. HE WAS NOT THE FIRST PERSON TO EXHIBIT AN INNATE ABILITY TO ACCESS SUPERSPACE. A TALENT SIMILAR TO MINE, BUT SUPERIOR.
"I SOUGHT TO REASON WITH HIM, TO KEEP HIM OUT OF SUPERSPACE. WHEN TALK FAILED, I SOUGHT TO DETAIN HIM PHYSICALLY. BUT ALL MY EFFORTS WERE FUTILE...
SUPERSPACE IS AN INFINITELY PLASTIC MEDIUM WITH SUBTLE CONNECTIONS TO EVERY TIMELINE IN THE MULTIVERSE. IT'S THE SUBSTRATE ON WHICH THE MULTIVERSE RESTS. AS ITS LONE INHABITANT, SOAMES--THE MAN YOU KNOW AS THE HELL DITCH PILGRIM--IS ITS GOD. BUT A DISEASED GOD.
HE HAS MADE SUPERSPACE OVER IN HIS NEUROTIC, MONOLITHIC IMAGE. AND NOW HE WISHES TO REMAKE THE MULTIVERSE AS WELL. HE GAINED HIS FIRST FOOTHOLD IN YOUR TIMELINE, THANKS TO THE DARK ENERGY LEAKAGE FROM PROJECT JOOTS, A LEAK THAT THE PILGRIM INITIATED. HE WAS ABLE TO USE THE DARKSHOTS TO SUBORN CYBERNETIC INTELLIGENCES FIRST...
...CREATING AN EPISTEMOLOGICAL RIFT IN THE FABRIC OF YOUR PARALLEL.
AS YOU CAN SEE, HIS DANGEROUS POWERS NOW EXTEND MUCH FURTHER.
YOU CLAIMED YOU COULD GET US INTO SUPERSPACE--
YES. PROJECT JOOTS IS NOW ONLY ONE SMALL STEP AWAY FROM SUCCESS. AND I CAN BRIDGE THAT GAP WITH MY POWERS.
THEN THE ANSWER IS SIMPLE. WE SEND A SWAT TEAM INTO SUPERSPACE AND TAKE SOAMES DOWN.
NO. BRUTE FORCE IS USELESS AGAINST THE PILGRIM IN HIS OWN REALM. ONLY A SUPERIOR ONTOLOGICAL PRECEPT CAN DEFEAT HIM.
AND ONLY ONE OF YOU POSSESSES SUCH A GIFT...

THAT ONE IS ROBYN SLINGER.

ME? WHY ME? WHAT'S SO SPECIAL ABOUT ME?

IT IS NOT SO MUCH YOU AS WHAT YOU POSSESS. YOUR MOTHER'S INHERITANCE.

MY MOTHER? BUT I NEVER KNEW MY MOTHER. AND SHE LEFT ME NOTHING.

THERE YOU ARE WRONG. I WAS PRESENT AT YOUR BIRTH. I KNOW YOUR LINEAGE OF OLD. YOUR MOTHER LEFT YOU SOMETHING BEYOND PRICE...

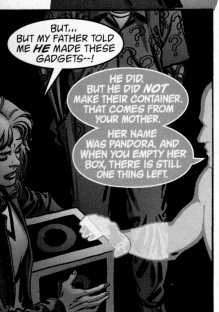

BUT... BUT MY FATHER TOLD ME HE MADE THESE GADGETS--!

HE DID. BUT HE DID NOT MAKE THEIR CONTAINER. THAT COMES FROM YOUR MOTHER.

HER NAME WAS PANDORA. AND WHEN YOU EMPTY HER BOX, THERE IS STILL ONE THING LEFT.

WAIT ONE GODDAMN MINUTE HERE!

ARE ANY OF YOU SERIOUSLY THINKING OF SENDING ROBYN IN AFTER THE PILGRIM ALONE, ALL ON THE WORD OF SOME GUY WHO CAN'T EVEN BE BOTHERED TO SHOW US HIS FACE?

DON'T PANIC! I'VE GOT THEM!

I DON'T LIKE IT EITHER, JEFF. BUT I DON'T THINK WE HAVE MUCH CHOICE...

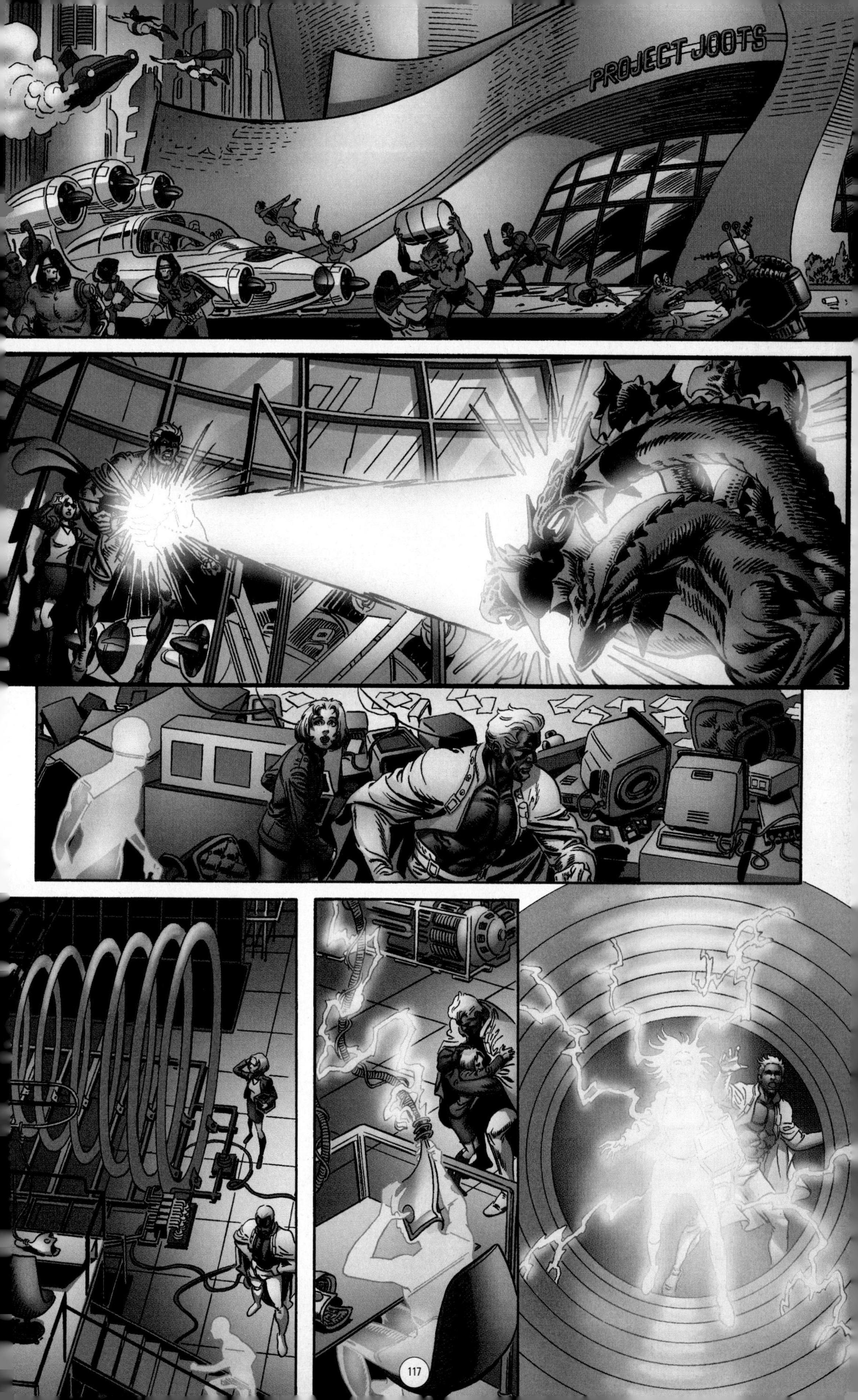
PROJECT JOOTS

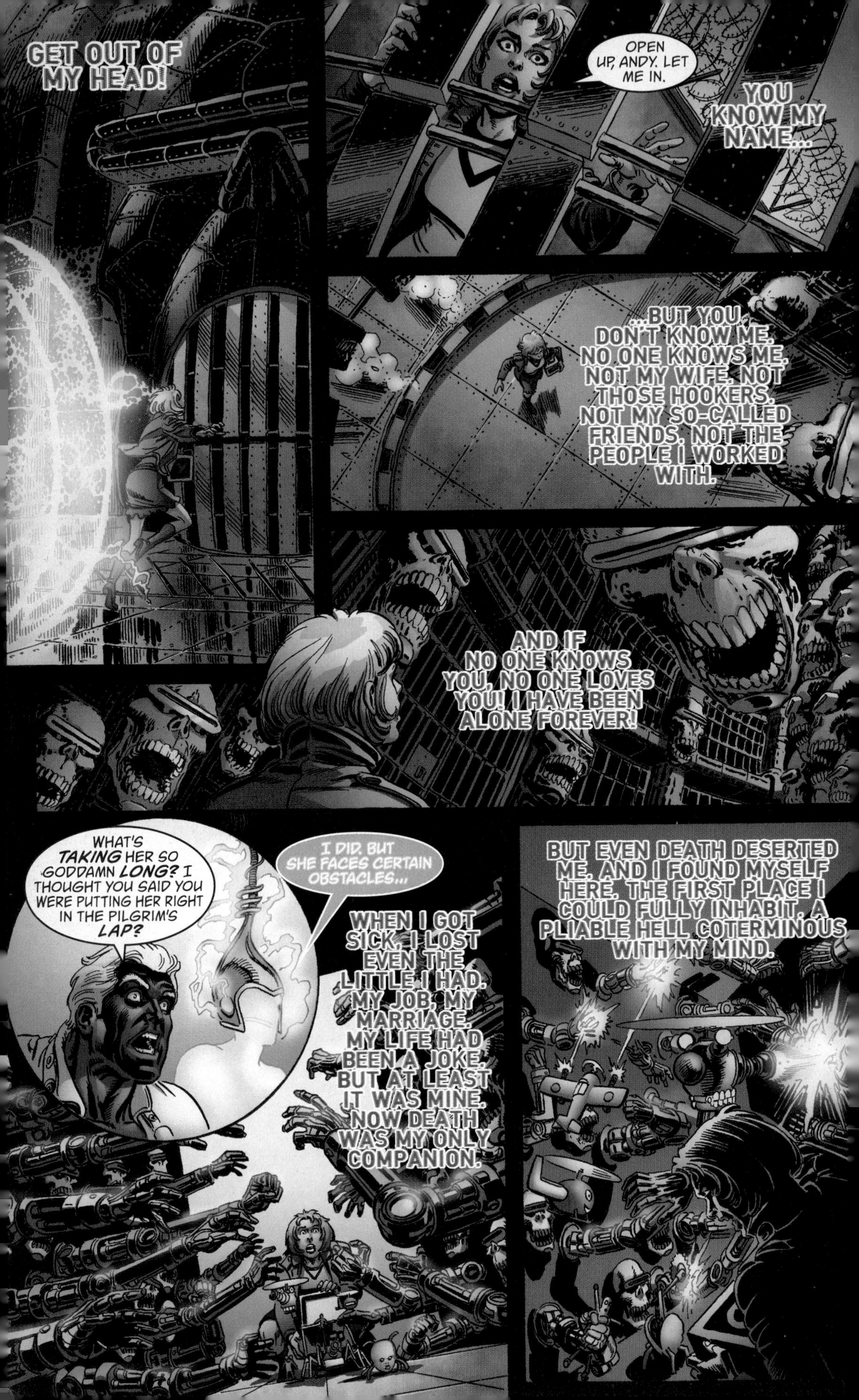
GET OUT OF MY HEAD!
OPEN UP, ANDY. LET ME IN.
YOU KNOW MY NAME...
...BUT YOU DON'T KNOW ME. NO ONE KNOWS ME. NOT MY WIFE. NOT THOSE HOOKERS. NOT MY SO-CALLED FRIENDS. NOT THE PEOPLE I WORKED WITH.
AND IF NO ONE KNOWS YOU, NO ONE LOVES YOU! I HAVE BEEN ALONE FOREVER!
WHAT'S TAKING HER SO GODDAMN LONG? I THOUGHT YOU SAID YOU WERE PUTTING HER RIGHT IN THE PILGRIM'S LAP?
I DID. BUT SHE FACES CERTAIN OBSTACLES...
WHEN I GOT SICK, I LOST EVEN THE LITTLE I HAD. MY JOB, MY MARRIAGE. MY LIFE HAD BEEN A JOKE, BUT AT LEAST IT WAS MINE. NOW DEATH WAS MY ONLY COMPANION.
BUT EVEN DEATH DESERTED ME, AND I FOUND MYSELF HERE. THE FIRST PLACE I COULD FULLY INHABIT. A PLIABLE HELL COTERMINOUS WITH MY MIND.

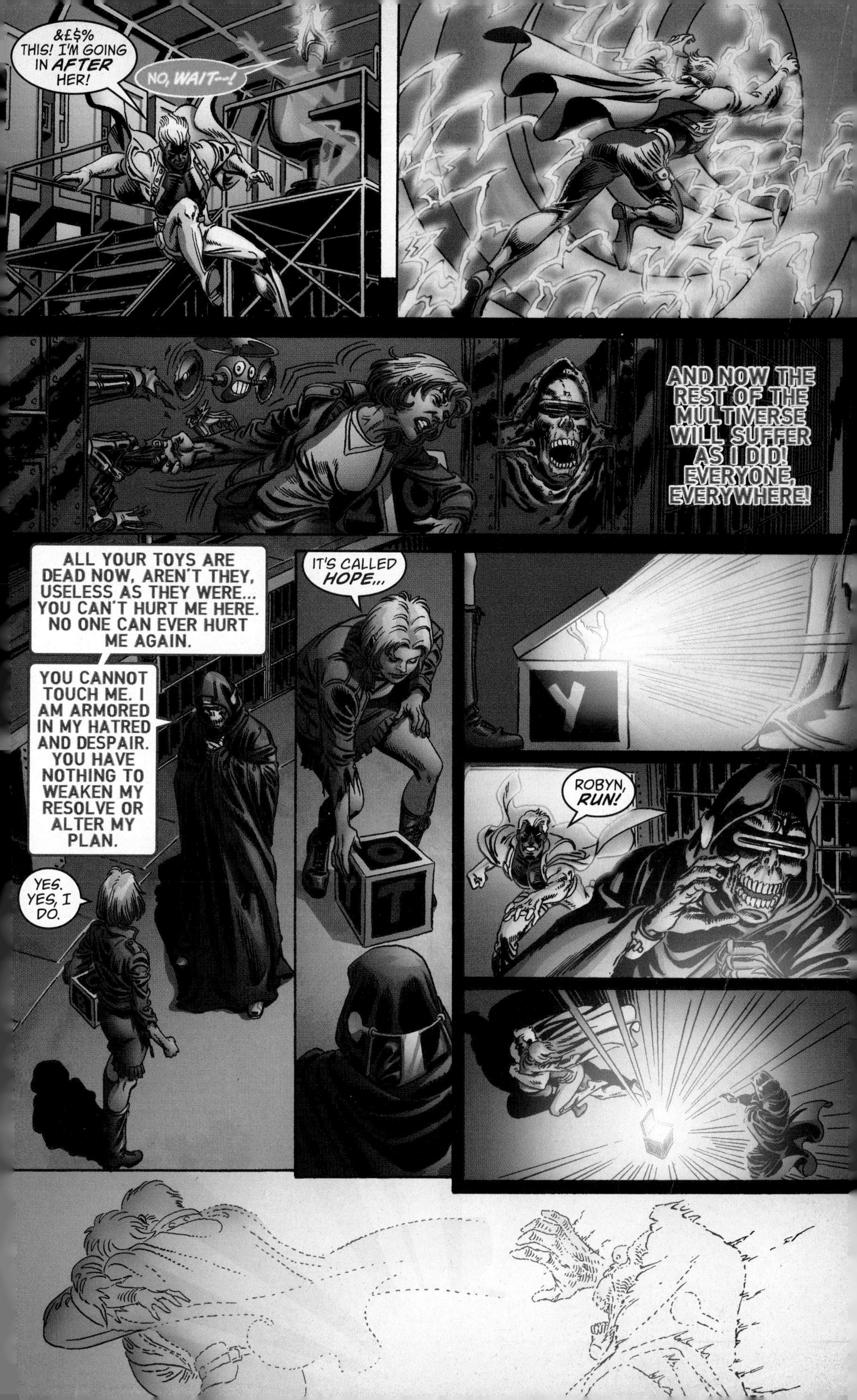
&£$% THIS! I'M GOING IN AFTER HER!
NO, WAIT--!
AND NOW THE REST OF THE MULTIVERSE WILL SUFFER AS I DID! EVERYONE, EVERYWHERE!
ALL YOUR TOYS ARE DEAD NOW, AREN'T THEY, USELESS AS THEY WERE... YOU CAN'T HURT ME HERE. NO ONE CAN EVER HURT ME AGAIN.
YOU CANNOT TOUCH ME. I AM ARMORED IN MY HATRED AND DESPAIR. YOU HAVE NOTHING TO WEAKEN MY RESOLVE OR ALTER MY PLAN.
YES. YES, I DO.
IT'S CALLED HOPE...
ROBYN, RUN!

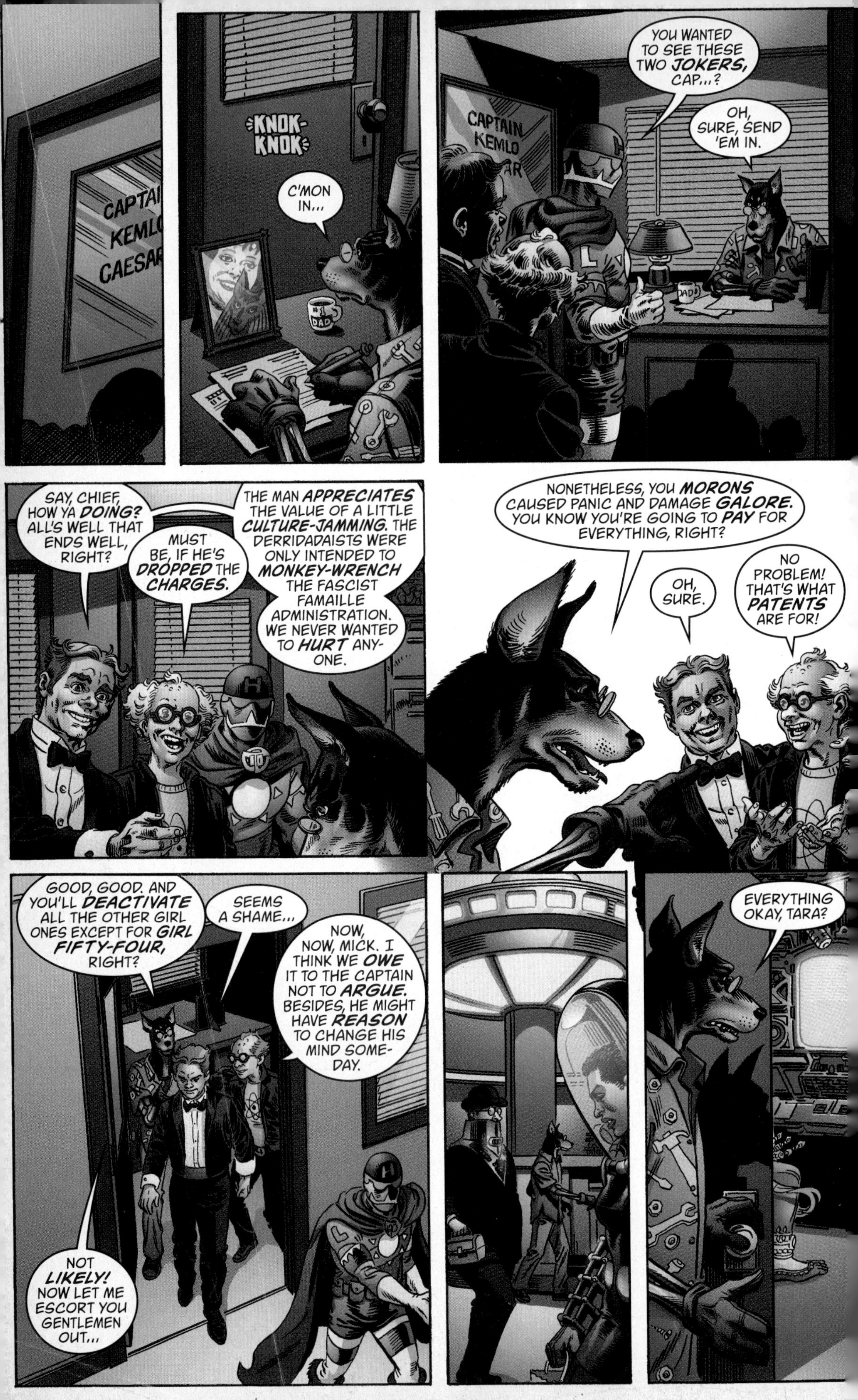
CAPTAIN KEMLO CAESAR
KNOK-KNOK
C'MON IN...
#1 DAD
CAPTAIN KEMLO CAESAR
YOU WANTED TO SEE THESE TWO JOKERS, CAP...?
OH, SURE, SEND 'EM IN.
SAY, CHIEF, HOW YA DOING? ALL'S WELL THAT ENDS WELL, RIGHT?
MUST BE, IF HE'S DROPPED THE CHARGES.
THE MAN APPRECIATES THE VALUE OF A LITTLE CULTURE-JAMMING. THE DERRIDADAISTS WERE ONLY INTENDED TO MONKEY-WRENCH THE FASCIST FAMAILLE ADMINISTRATION. WE NEVER WANTED TO HURT ANYONE.
NONETHELESS, YOU MORONS CAUSED PANIC AND DAMAGE GALORE. YOU KNOW YOU'RE GOING TO PAY FOR EVERYTHING, RIGHT?
OH, SURE.
NO PROBLEM! THAT'S WHAT PATENTS ARE FOR!
GOOD, GOOD. AND YOU'LL DEACTIVATE ALL THE OTHER GIRL ONES EXCEPT FOR GIRL FIFTY-FOUR, RIGHT?
SEEMS A SHAME...
NOW, NOW, MICK. I THINK WE OWE IT TO THE CAPTAIN NOT TO ARGUE. BESIDES, HE MIGHT HAVE REASON TO CHANGE HIS MIND SOMEDAY.
NOT LIKELY! NOW LET ME ESCORT YOU GENTLEMEN OUT...
EVERYTHING OKAY, TARA?

Panel 1:
IT'S A QUIET DAY OUT THERE, CAPTAIN.

WE SHOULD BE ABLE TO GET BY WITH A *SKELETON CREW* WHILE THE PICNIC'S ON.

YOU GO AND ENJOY YOURSELF.

I'LL TRY MY BEST...

Panel 2:
ANY LUCK, SALLY-JO?

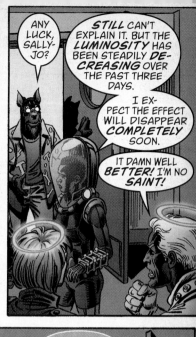

Panel 3:
STILL CAN'T EXPLAIN IT. BUT THE *LUMINOSITY* HAS BEEN STEADILY *DE-CREASING* OVER THE PAST THREE DAYS.

I EXPECT THE EFFECT WILL DISAPPEAR *COMPLETELY* SOON.

IT DAMN WELL *BETTER!* I'M NO *SAINT!*

Panel 4:
SO, ROBYN, HAVE YOU THOUGHT ABOUT A NEW *SCIENCE-HERO NAME* FOR YOURSELF YET?

IT'S TOO SOON, CAPTAIN. BUT I HAVE SOME OPTIONS.

WELL, ALL IN DUE TIME...LET'S GO NOW, THE *REST* OF THE PRECINCT IS ALREADY HAVING *FUN* WITH-OUT US.

Panel 5:
YOUR DESTINY IS NOT TOTALLY FULFILLED YET, YOU KNOW.

YES, I *DO* KNOW...

CITY HALL

FEININGER PARK

121

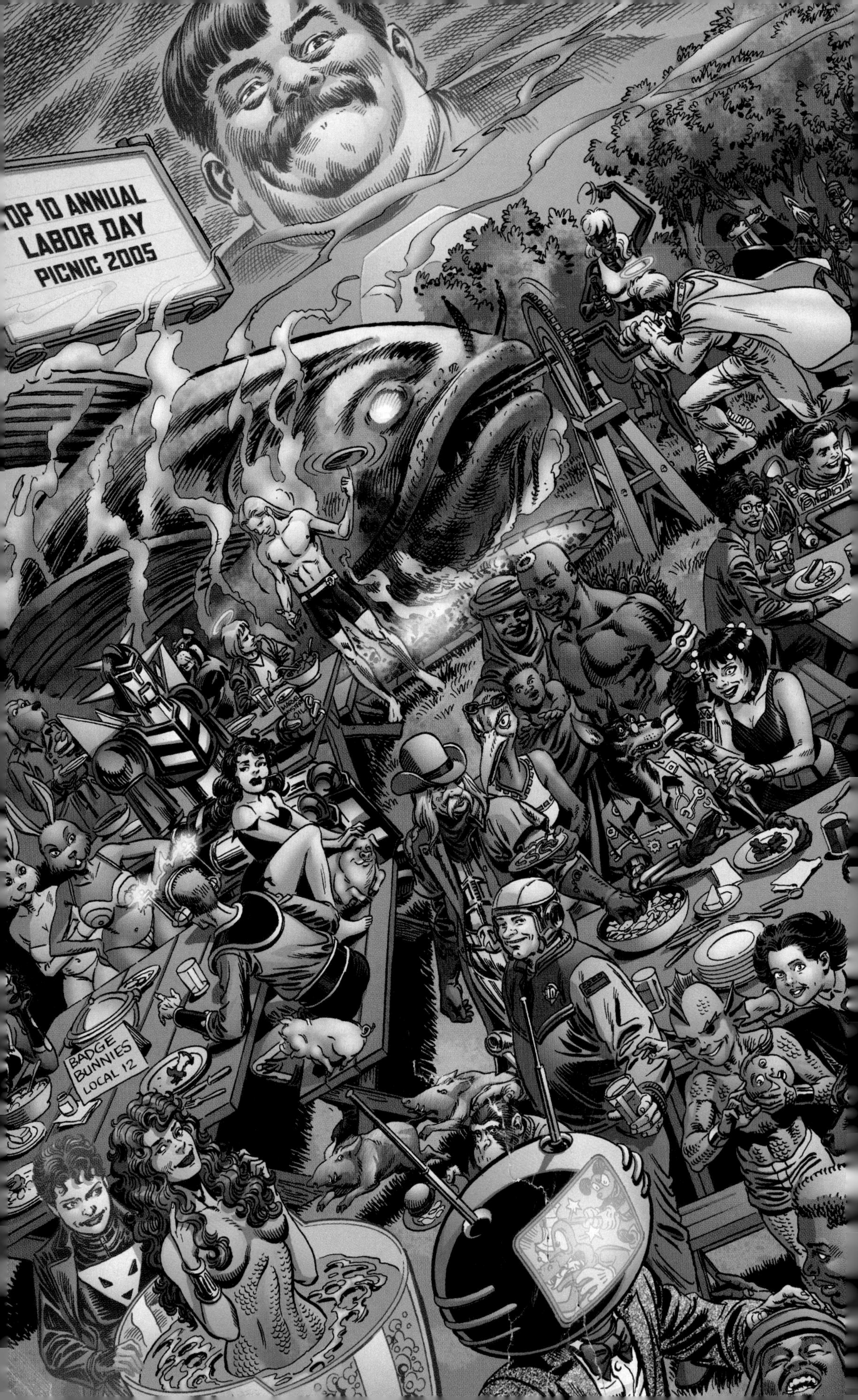
OP 10 ANNUAL
LABOR DAY
PICNIC 2005
BADGE
BUNNIES
LOCAL 12

This page and the following ones offer a rare glimpse at artist Jerry Ordway's cover sketches for

TOP10:BTFP

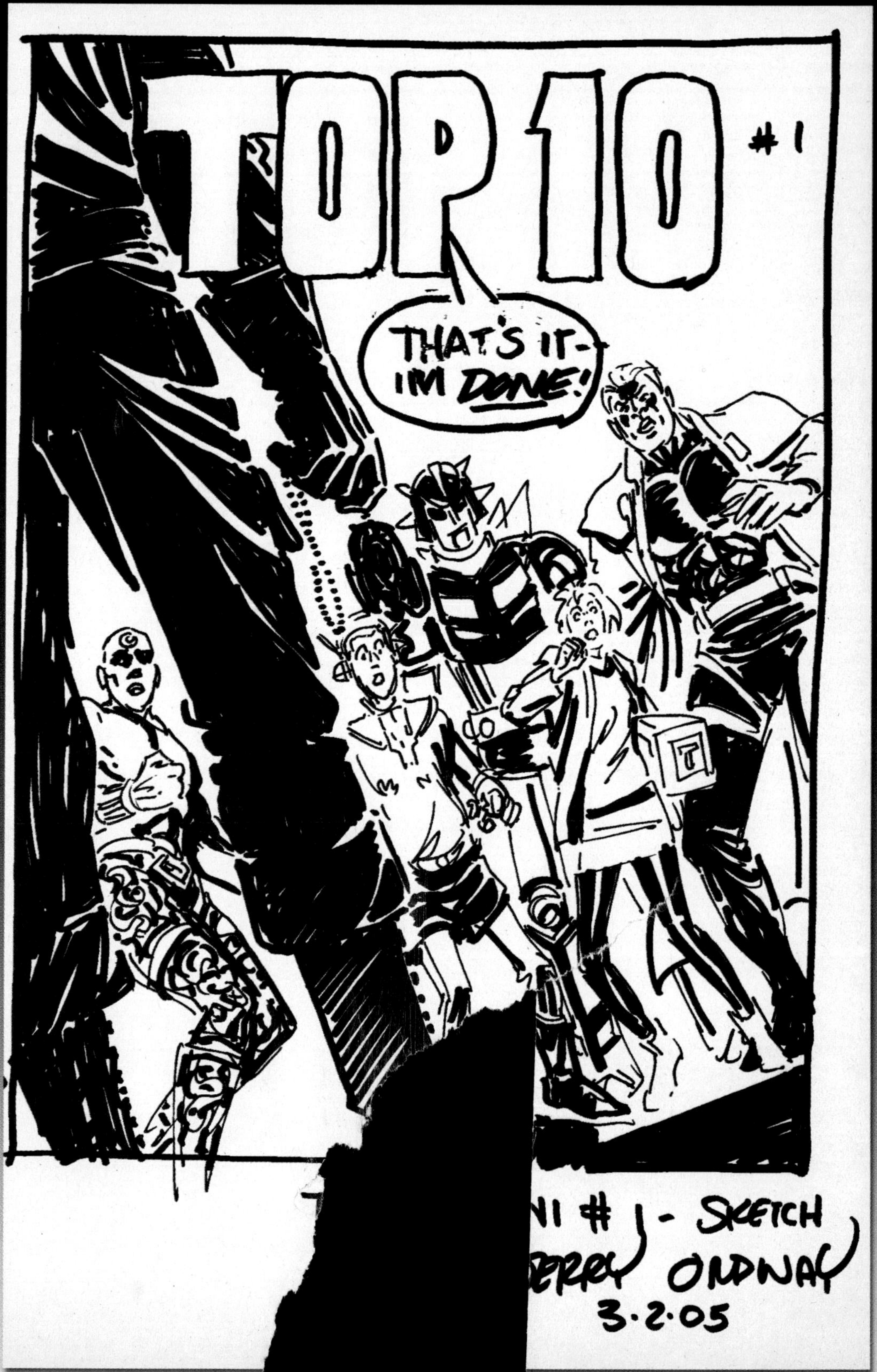
TOP 10
#1
THAT'S IT- I'M DONE!
NI # 1 - SKETCH
ERRY ORDWAY
3·2·05

TO SCOTT DUNBIER TOP TEN #4. SKETCH

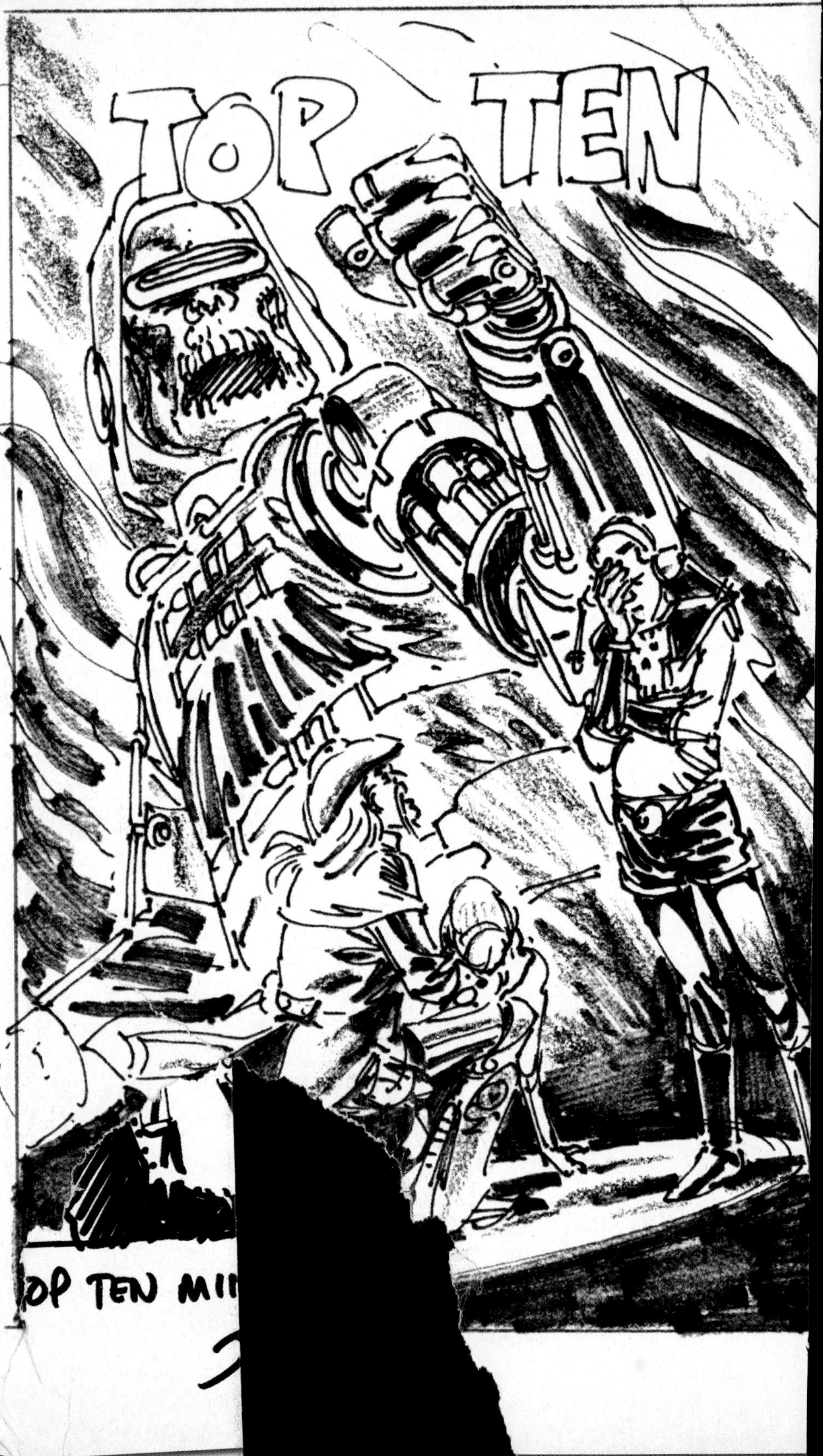
TOP TEN

BATGUYS ATTACK SMAX & TOYBOX
TOYBOX REACHES FOR STEERING AS SMAX LEAPS!

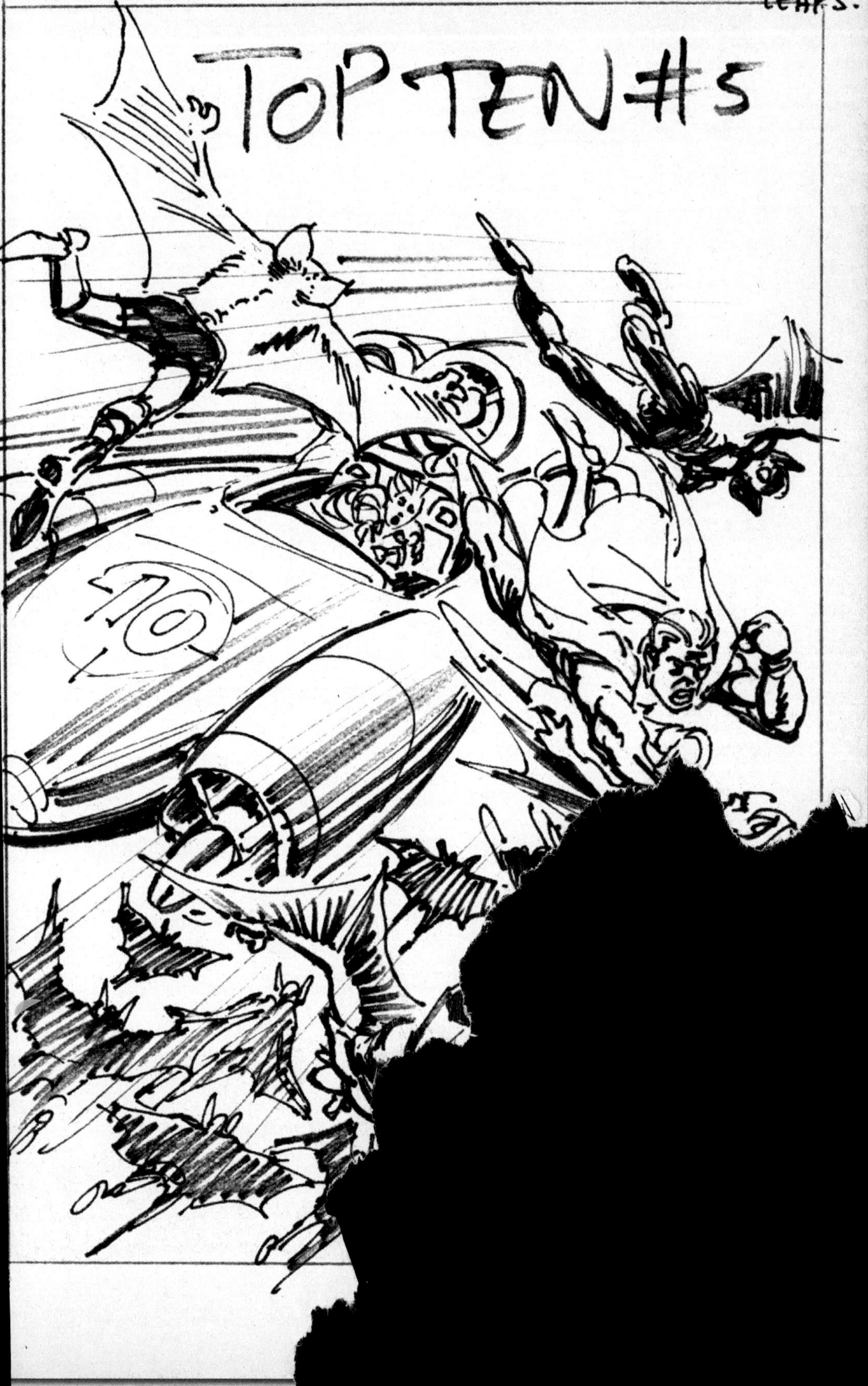
TOP TEN #5
10

#2 COVER IDEA

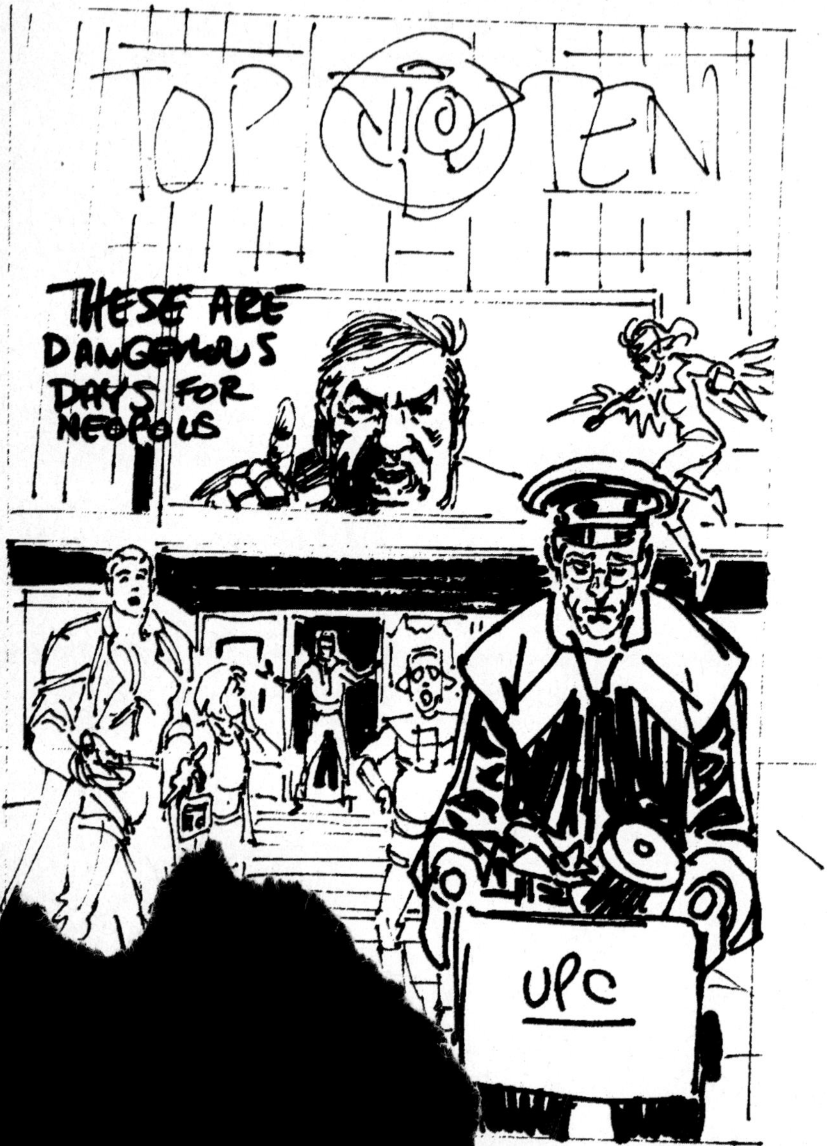
TOP TEN
THESE ARE DANGEROUS DAYS FOR NEOPOLIS
UPC

TRAYNOR HANGS HEAD

MAND A
EAD
E . . .
!

(JOKE BEING THAT CINDERCOTT IS HALF ROBOT!)

BEGIN YOUR TOUR OF NEOPOLIS IN

TOP 10

BOOK 1 BY ALAN MOORE, GENE HA AND ZANDER CANNON.

ALAN MOORE
GENE HA
ZANDER CANNON
TOP 10
Multi-Eisner Award Winner

Neopolis was created as a haven for returning allied super-beings in the days after World War II. In need of a special police force to keep the hyper-powered peace, Precinct 10 was formed. Now, the officers of Top10 walk, cruise--and sometimes hover--their beats, knowing they've got the power to keep their city safe.

And don't miss the further adventures of the officers of Precinct 10:

TOP10 BOOK 2

ALAN MOORE · GENE HA · ZANDER CANNON
TOP 10
BOOK TWO OF THE INNOVATIVE NEW SERIES

MOORE/HA/CANNON

SMAX

ALAN MOORE
FROM THE PAGES OF THE HIT SERIES TOP 10:
SMAX
ZANDER CANNON
ANDREW CURRIE

MOORE/CANNON/CURRIE

TOP10: THE FORTY-NINERS

TOP 10
THE FORTY-NINERS
From the writer of WATCHMEN and LEAGUE OF EXTRAORDINARY GENTLEMEN
ALAN MOORE
TODD KLEIN
GENE HA
ART LYON

MOORE/HA

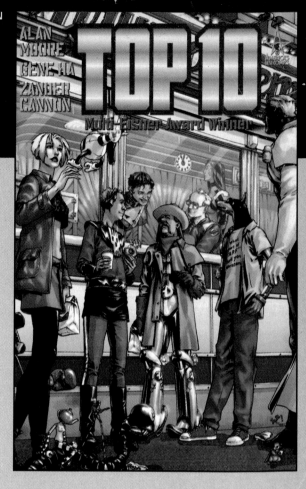

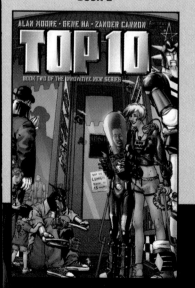

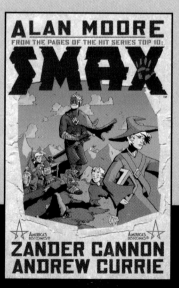

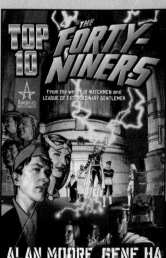

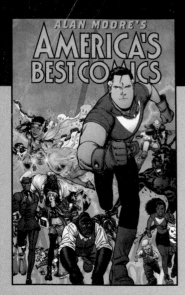
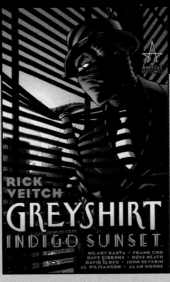

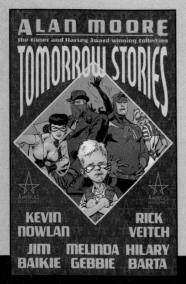

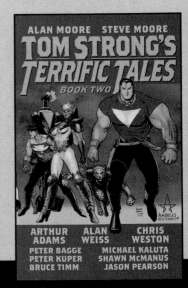